제5판

교원임용고시
일반영어 필독서

임용영어 수험생 대다수가 선택하는
전공영어의 보통명사

- 교원임용고시 전공영어 독보적 전국 1위
  (2025년 예스24 전공영어 부문 박문각 누적 판매량 1위)
- 1996년 이후 최근까지의 전공영어 기출 주요 어휘 수록
- 전공영어 학습에 최적화된 30일 완성 사이클

유희태 일반영어

⑤ 기출 VOCA 30days

LSI 영어연구소 편 [유희태 박사, 로렌 장]

박문각 임용

동영상강의 www.pmg.co.kr

CONTENTS

2026
Day 01 6
Day 02 20

2025
Day 03 32
Day 04 46
Day 05 60

2024
Day 06 74
Day 07 88
Day 08 102

2023
Day 09 114
Day 10 128
Day 11 142

2022
Day 12 156
Day 13 170

2021
Day 14 184
Day 15 198
Day 16 212

2020

Day 17 224

Day 18 236

2019

Day 19 248

Day 20 260

Day 21 272

2018

Day 22 284

Day 23 298

Day 24 312

2017

Day 25 326

Day 26 338

Day 27 350

2016
and
before

Day 28 362

Day 29 374

Day 30 386

Appendix 398

Index 420

2026

DAY

01

유희태 일반영어
⑤ 기출 VOCA 30days

flaunting	○○○	intimacy	○○○
stench	○○○	semantic contribution	○○○
manifestation	○○○	logic gate	○○○
pathetic	○○○	cellar	○○○
commemorate	○○○	indicate	○○○
ridicule	○○○	stroll	○○○
overhear	○○○	brace	○○○
savage	○○○	proposal	○○○
verify	○○○	causation	○○○
chalked	○○○	fabulous	○○○
degeneration of culture	○○○	convince	○○○
wretched	○○○	derivational suffix	○○○
dignity	○○○	preoccupation	○○○
damp	○○○	in-depth analysis	○○○
feign	○○○	permit	○○○
beyond doubt	○○○	quantum mechanics	○○○
court	○○○	assume	○○○
amuck / amok	○○○	deprivation	○○○
distaste	○○○	drag	○○○
observant	○○○	emission	○○○
unveiling	○○○	landscape	○○○
plaque	○○○	visual waveform	○○○
rifle	○○○	pragmatic skill	○○○
sipping on the flask	○○○	suprasegmental feature	○○○
owe	○○○	coronal	○○○
fling onto	○○○	atelic	○○○
decease	○○○	accurate	○○○
elaborate	○○○	artificialize	○○○
hornet	○○○	bare	○○○
vice-versa	○○○	bound	○○○

flaunting
과시하는, 드러내며 자랑하는

['flɔːntɪŋ]

showing off openly and provocatively
(syn) showing off, parading
(e.g.) Many saw the character as **flaunting** his success without regard for others.

stench
악취, 매우 고약한 냄새

[stɛntʃ]

a strong, unpleasant smell
(syn) reek, stink
(e.g.) A **stench** rose from the abandoned building as the door swung open.

manifestation
표현, 나타남, 감정 · 현상이 겉으로 드러남

[ˌmænəfɛ'steɪʃən]

an outward display or sign of an inner condition
(syn) expression, display
(e.g.) His anger was a **manifestation** of deeper frustration.

pathetic
불쌍한, 한심한, 동정 혹은 경멸을 자아내는

[pə'θɛtɪk]

arousing pity or contempt
(syn) pitiful, miserable
(e.g.) The narrator described the attempt as utterly **pathetic**.

commemorate
기념하다, 사람 · 사건을 기억하여 표하다

[kə'mɛmərˌeɪt]

to honor or remember someone or something
(syn) honor, memorialize
(e.g.) The ceremony was held to **commemorate** those who had died.

ridicule
조롱하다, 비웃으며 폄하하다

['rɪdɪˌkjuːl]

to mock or make someone seem foolish
(syn) mock, deride
(e.g.) He feared his views would be **ridiculed** by his peers.

overhear
엿듣다, 우연히 듣게 되다

[ˌoʊvərˈhɪr]

to hear something unintentionally
(syn) catch, eavesdrop (accidentally)
(e.g.) She **overheard** two students discussing the test answers.

savage
잔혹한, 포악한, 극도로 폭력적이거나 거친

[ˈsævɪdʒ]

extremely aggressive or brutal
(syn) brutal, fierce
(e.g.) The attack was described as a **savage** display of anger.

verify
확인하다, 사실임을 증명하다

[ˈvɛrəˌfaɪ]

to confirm something is true or accurate
(syn) confirm, validate
(e.g.) The teacher asked him to **verify** the source of the quote.

chalked
분필로 그리거나 기록된

[tʃɔːkt]

written or marked with chalk
(syn) marked, written
(e.g.) Directions were **chalked** on the sidewalk for participants.

degeneration of culture
문화의 타락, 문화적 가치의 쇠퇴

[dɪˌdʒɛnəˈreɪʃən əv ˈkʌltʃər]

the decline or deterioration of cultural standards
(syn) cultural decline, decay
(e.g.) Critics claimed the show symbolized the **degeneration of culture**.

wretched
비참한, 극도로 불행하고 초라한

[ˈrɛtʃɪd]

extremely unhappy or miserable
(syn) miserable, forlorn
(e.g.) The refugees were living in **wretched** conditions.

dignity
존엄성, 품위와 자기 존중

['dɪgnəti]
a sense of self-respect and worthiness
(syn) self-respect, honor
(e.g.) He tried to maintain his **dignity** despite the insults.

damp
(a) 축축한, (n) 약간 젖은 상태

[dæmp]
slightly wet or moist
(syn) moist, humid
(e.g.) The cellar floor was cold and **damp** in the early morning.

feign
꾸미다, 가장하다, 감정·행동을 거짓으로 보이다

[feɪn]
to pretend or fake a feeling or response
(syn) pretend, simulate
(e.g.) He **feigned** interest, though he barely listened.

beyond doubt
의심의 여지 없이, 확실하게

[bɪˈɑːnd daʊt]
certainly; without question
(syn) unquestionably, undeniably
(e.g.) The evidence showed **beyond doubt** that the event happened as described.

court
(n) 경기장, (v) 구애하다

[kɔːrt]
(n) an area for sports; (v) to seek someone's favor or approval
(syn) (n) arena; (v) woo, pursue
(e.g.) Loud cheering filled the entire **court** during the championship game.

amuck / amok
(a) 미친 듯 날뛰는, (n) 통제가 안 된 상태

[əˈmʌk] / [əˈmɒk]
behaving wildly and uncontrollably
(syn) wild, frenzied
(e.g.) Rumors ran **amuck** throughout the school.

distaste
혐오감, 싫어하거나 거부하는 감정

[dɪsˈteɪst]
a feeling of dislike or aversion
(syn) aversion, dislike
(e.g.) He spoke with obvious **distaste** about the proposal.

observant
잘 관찰하는, 세부를 잘 알아차리는

[əbˈzɜːrvənt]
quick to notice details
(syn) perceptive, attentive
(e.g.) The student was **observant** enough to detect the change in tone.

unveiling
공개, 발표, 새로운 것을 드러냄

[ʌnˈveɪlɪŋ]
the act of revealing something for the first time
(syn) revelation, presentation
(e.g.) The **unveiling** of the statue drew a large crowd.

plaque
명판, 기념 문구가 새겨진 판

[plæk]
a flat tablet commemorating a person or event
(syn) memorial plate, marker
(e.g.) A bronze **plaque** was mounted to honor the founder.

rifle
소총, 긴 총기류

[ˈraɪfəl]
a long-barreled firearm
(syn) long gun, firearm
(e.g.) The guard carried a **rifle** slung over his shoulder.

sipping on the flask
수통을 조금씩 마시기, 플라스크에서 조금씩 마시는 행동

[ˈsɪpɪŋ ɑːn ðə flæsk]
drinking slowly from a small container or flask
(syn) taking sips, drinking lightly
(e.g.) He stood by the door, **sipping on the flask** to stay warm.

owe
빚지다, 감사하다, 원인이나 책임을 돌리다

[oʊ]

to be indebted; to attribute something to a cause
(syn) be indebted, attribute
(e.g.) He **owed** his progress to constant practice.

fling onto
세게 던져 얹다, 힘 있게 던져 올리다

[flɪŋ ˈɑːntuː]

to throw forcefully onto something
(syn) hurl onto, toss onto
(e.g.) He **flung** the coat **onto** the chair without a glance.

decease
사망, 공식적 표현의 죽음

[dɪˈsiːs]

a formal term for death
(syn) death, passing
(e.g.) The document recorded the date of **decease**.

elaborate
상세히 설명하다, 더 자세히 말하다

[ɪˈlæbəˌreɪt]

to explain or expand in detail
(syn) expand, clarify
(e.g.) She asked him to **elaborate** on his earlier comment.

hornet
말벌

[ˈhɔːrnɪt]

a large stinging wasp
(syn) wasp
(e.g.) A **hornet** spun inside the rotten pear he held up to the speaker's eye.

vice-versa
반대로, 거꾸로

[ˌvaɪs ˈvɜːrsə]

the other way around
(syn) conversely
(e.g.) The computer's design ensures that outputs do not affect inputs, not **vice-versa**.

intimacy
친밀감

[ˈɪntəməsi]

emotional closeness
(syn) closeness
(e.g.) Writing his name would have assumed an **intimacy** they had not yet reached.

semantic contribution
의미적 기여

[sɪˈmæntɪk ˌkɑːntrəˈbjuːʃən]

the meaning a morpheme adds to a base
(syn) meaning contribution
(e.g.) The **semantic contribution** of a plural suffix is predictable, unlike many derivational forms.

logic gate
논리 게이트

[ˈlɑːdʒɪk ɡeɪt]

a basic digital circuit performing logical operations
(syn) digital gate
(e.g.) **Logic gates** are constructed so that inputs determine outputs in one direction only.

cellar
지하 저장고

[ˈsɛlər]

a storage room below ground
(syn) basement
(e.g.) He drank from the icy spigot by the **cellar** door.

indicate
나타내다

[ˈɪndɪˌkeɪt]

to show or signal
(syn) signal
(e.g.) Adding a plural suffix **indicates** "more than one."

stroll
산책하다

[stroʊl]

to walk slowly in a relaxed manner
(syn) wander
(e.g.) They may have **strolled** in silence among the windfall pears.

brace
버티다, 몸을 지탱하다

[breɪs]

to support oneself physically
(syn) steady
(e.g.) His father **braced** his left hand on his knee to lift the pear.

proposal
제안서

[prə'poʊzəl]

a written plan or suggestion
(syn) plan
(e.g.) Both teachers submitted a **proposal** for purchasing speaking-related technology.

causation
인과 관계

[kɔ'zeɪʃən]

the act of causing something
(syn) cause-effect relation
(e.g.) Models of **causation** help explain how machines convert inputs into outputs.

fabulous
굉장히 좋은, 멋진

['fæbjələs]

extremely good or impressive
(syn) remarkable
(e.g.) Modern computers are built on **fabulous** chains of cause and effect.

convince
설득하다

[kən'vɪns]

to persuade someone
(syn) persuade
(e.g.) Sam wanted Pam to try to **convince** Jim to hire the narrator.

derivational suffix
파생 접미사

[ˌderə'veɪʃənəl 'sʌfɪks]

a suffix forming a new word or category
(syn) word-forming suffix
(e.g.) -*less* turns *heart* into *heartless*, showing how a **derivational suffix** changes word class.

preoccupation
집착, 몰두

[pri,ɑːkjəˈpeɪʃən]

something one is deeply concerned with
(syn) fixation
(e.g.) His **preoccupation** with arranging cause-and-effect stories shapes how he interprets nature.

in-depth analysis
심층 분석

[ɪn dɛpθ əˈnæləsɪs]

thorough or detailed examination
(syn) detailed analysis
(e.g.) Teachers conducted an **in-depth analysis** of the textbook before using it.

permit
(v) 허락하다, (n) 허가증

[pərˈmɪt] (v) /
[ˈpɜːrmɪt] (n)

(v) to allow something to happen, especially by authority or rule;
(n) an official document that gives permission to do something
(syn) (v) allow, authorize, license; (n) license, authorization
(e.g.) The task design **permits** learners to interact freely during the activity.
A building **permit** is required before construction can begin.

quantum mechanics
양자역학

[ˈkwɑːntəm məˈkænɪks]

the physics of subatomic particles
(syn) quantum theory
(e.g.) In **quantum mechanics**, observing one particle can influence another far away.

assume
가정하다

[əˈsuːm]

to take something as true without proof
(syn) presume
(e.g.) People **assume** that force "causes" acceleration, though the equation itself doesn't say so.

deprivation
결핍

[ˌdɛprəˈveɪʃən]

a condition of lacking something important
(syn) shortage
(e.g.) His loneliness felt like a **deprivation** he hadn't anticipated.

drag
질질 끌다

[dræg]

to pull something across the ground
(syn) trail
(e.g.) The sari's free end was **dragging** on the footpath when the dog seized it.

emission
배출, 방출

[ɪˈmɪʃən]

release of sound, gas, or radiation
(syn) discharge
(e.g.) Noise **emission** from stadium crowds strains the surrounding areas.

landscape
경관

[ˈlændskeɪp]

the visible features of land
(syn) scenery
(e.g.) Golf courses alter the natural **landscape** as they expand into green belts.

visual waveform
시각 음파, 소리를 파형으로 시각화한 것

[ˈvɪʒuəl ˈweɪvˌfɔːrm]

a graphic representation of sound amplitude over time
(syn) speech wave graph, spectrogram
(e.g.) The app displayed learners' stress and intonation patterns on **visual waveforms**.

pragmatic skill

화용 능력, 상황·사회적 맥락에 맞게 언어를 사용하는 능력

[præg'mætɪk skɪl]

the ability to use language appropriately according to context and social norms

(syn) sociolinguistic skill, contextual competence

(e.g.) The speaking activity was designed to help students practice **pragmatic skills** such as polite requests.

suprasegmental feature

초분절적 요소, 음성에서 강세·억양·리듬 등을 포함하는 요소

[ˌsuːprəseg'mɛntl 'fiːtʃər]

a prosodic feature like stress, rhythm, and intonation beyond individual sounds

(syn) intonational feature

(e.g.) Mr. Park realized his students struggled with **suprasegmental features** despite accurate segmental sounds.

coronal

치조·치경음, 혀끝이나 앞부분으로 만드는 자음

['kɔːrənl]

a consonant articulated with the front part of the tongue

(syn) anterior consonant, apical consonant

(e.g.) /t, d, s, z/ are classified as **coronal** consonants.

atelic

비종결적인, 자연스러운 끝점이 없는

[eɪ'tɛlɪk]

describing an action without an inherent endpoint

(syn) unbounded, non-terminating

(e.g.) "Run" is an **atelic** verb because the activity can continue indefinitely.

accurate

(오류 없이) 정확한

['ækjərət]

free from error; correct in all details

(syn) precise, exact

(e.g.) The program provides **accurate** feedback on learners' pronunciation.

artificialize

인공화하다, 자연을 인공적으로 바꾸다

[ˌɑːrtɪˈfɪʃəˌlaɪz]

to make something artificial or to modify nature mechanically
(syn) mechanize, industrialize
(e.g.) Expanding golf courses **artificializes** the surrounding environment.

bare

(a) 텅 빈, 드러난, (n) 아무것도 없는 상태

[bɛər]

uncovered, empty, or lacking vegetation/items
(syn) exposed, empty
(e.g.) The ground was **bare** after the last onions were pulled.

bound

묶인, 연결된, 서로 결속된

[baʊnd]

tied or held together by obligation or connection
(syn) connected, linked
(e.g.) They were **bound** together by marriage despite barely knowing each other.

2026

DAY

02

유희태 일반영어

5 기출 VOCA 30days

braised	○○○	vermilion	○○○
concession	○○○	sea swine	○○○
conjure	○○○	close-up shot	○○○
dorsal	○○○	noise pollution	○○○
reconfiguration	○○○	strain	○○○
intonation	○○○	labial	○○○
irritation	○○○	side effect	○○○
isolated	○○○	mute play	○○○
delicacy	○○○	trace	○○○
landmark	○○○	windfall	○○○
leash	○○○	overtly	○○○
manicured	○○○	convey	○○○
rate of speech	○○○	recursive	○○○
mishap	○○○	extension activity	○○○
mixed-ability	○○○	telegram	○○○
mountain mold	○○○	intimate	○○○
peer feedback	○○○	fronted	○○○
recreational	○○○	part	○○○
end-weight principle	○○○	critic	○○○
salutation	○○○	stem	○○○
scolded	○○○	hypocritical	○○○
seize	○○○	worksheet	○○○
signify	○○○	specification	○○○
soliloquy	○○○	whereabouts	○○○
spigot	○○○	worthwhile	○○○
spectator sports	○○○	wavelength	○○○
startle	○○○	vertical	○○○
process loss	○○○	uninhibited	○○○
sustainable	○○○	underlie	○○○
proactive	○○○	vehicle	○○○

braised
복아 익힌, 약한 불에서 천천히 익힌

[breɪzd]

cooked slowly in liquid after browning
(syn) stewed, simmered
(e.g.) He described his dinner: shrimp **braised** in sesame oil and garlic.

concession
매점, 행사장에서 음식을 파는 곳

[kən'sɛʃən]

a stand selling food or goods at events
(syn) kiosk, booth
(e.g.) Plastic waste from **concession** stands accumulates after large sports events.

conjure
떠올리다, 마음속에 이미지를 불러오다

['kʌndʒər]

to bring a memory or image vividly to mind
(syn) evoke, summon
(e.g.) He could not **conjure** her full face, only fragments.

dorsal
후설음의, 혀 뒤쪽으로 조음되는

['dɔːrsəl]

articulated with the back of the tongue
(syn) velar, post-palatal
(e.g.) /k/ and /g/ are typical **dorsal** consonants.

reconfiguration
재구성

[riːkɒn.fig.jə'reɪ.ʃən]

a new arrangement or structural change
(syn) restructuring, rearrangement
(e.g.) The **reconfiguration** of classrooms improved learning flow.

intonation
억양, 말의 높낮이 변화

[ˌɪntə'neɪʃən]

the rise and fall of pitch in speech
(syn) pitch contour, melody
(e.g.) Students practiced **intonation** to detect differences in emotional nuance.

irritation

짜증, 불쾌하거나 신경 쓰이는 감정

[ˌɪrɪ'teɪʃən]

a feeling of annoyance or discomfort

(syn) annoyance, exasperation

(e.g.) He remembered with **irritation** how Mala had cried over a short distance from home.

isolated

고립된, 혼자 떨어진

['aɪsəˌleɪtɪd]

separated from others; alone

(syn) solitary, remote

(e.g.) The learner felt **isolated** despite being surrounded by peers.

delicacy

섬세함, 미묘함

['delɪkəsi]

the quality of being subtle or fine

(syn) fineness

(e.g.) The **delicacy** of the colors amazed viewers.

landmark

이정표, 상징물, 눈에 띄는 장소

['lændmɑːrk]

a notable feature used for recognition

(syn) milestone, marker

(e.g.) The maple tree glowing at sunset became a personal **landmark** in his memory.

leash

목줄, 동물을 통제하기 위해 목에 매는 줄

[liːʃ]

a strap or cord used to control and guide an animal, especially a dog

(syn) lead, tether, line

(e.g.) The little black dog on the **leash** suddenly started barking at the woman in a sari.

manicured

정교하게 다듬어진, 손질이 잘 된

['mænɪˌkjʊrd]

neatly maintained or trimmed

(syn) groomed, polished

(e.g.) Many hikers admire **manicured** golf courses despite their ecological impact.

rate of speech
말하는 속도

[reɪt əv spiːtʃ]
the speed at which a person speaks
(syn) speech tempo, fluency rate
(e.g.) The assessment tool measured pauses and **rate of speech** for fluency.

mishap
불운한 일, 작은 사고

[ˈmɪsˌhæp]
a minor and unexpected accident
(syn) misfortune, accident
(e.g.) He realized that such a **mishap** would become his responsibility once Mala arrived.

mixed-ability
다양한 수준의, 능력 차가 나는

[mɪkst əˈbɪləti]
containing learners at different proficiency levels
(syn) multi-level, heterogeneous
(e.g.) Ms. Choi differentiated tasks for her **mixed-ability** class.

mountain mold
산 모형, 화산 실험용 점토 구조

[ˈmaʊntən moʊld]
a clay structure shaped like a mountain
(syn) clay volcano, model mount
(e.g.) Students built a **mountain mold** around a bottle before adding vinegar.

peer feedback
동료 피드백, 서로의 작업에 대한 평가

[pɪr ˈfiːdbæk]
feedback exchanged among learners
(syn) peer review, collaborative feedback
(e.g.) Ms. Song wanted more opportunities for **peer feedback** online.

recreational
오락의, 즐거움 목적으로 하는

[ˌrɛkriˈeɪʃənəl]
relating to leisure activities
(syn) leisure-related, non-professional
(e.g.) Sports offer **recreational** value but also environmental harm.

end-weight principle
종말가중 원리, 무거운 요소가 뒤로 가는 경향

[ɛnd weɪt 'prɪnsəpəl]

the preference for placing heavier constituents later in a sentence
(syn) heavy shift, rightward placement
(e.g.) Native speakers follow the **end-weight principle** by placing long NPs at the end.

salutation
인사말, 편지의 첫 인사

[ˌsæljə'teɪʃən]

the greeting at the beginning of a letter
(syn) greeting
(e.g.) Mala's letter had no **salutation** because using his name felt too intimate.

scolded
야단맞은, 꾸중을 들은

['skoʊldɪd]

reprimanded sharply
(syn) rebuked, reprimanded
(e.g.) The American woman **scolded** the barking dog before walking away.

seize
붙잡다, 갑자기 움켜잡다

[siːz]

to grasp suddenly and forcefully
(syn) grab, snatch
(e.g.) The dog **seized** the free end of the sari with its teeth.

signify
의미하다, 상징하거나 표시하다

['sɪgnəˌfaɪ]

to represent or indicate meaning
(syn) symbolize, denote
(e.g.) Vermilion in a woman's hair **signifies** marriage in many Indian traditions.

soliloquy
독백, 혼자 있을 때의 고백적 말

[sə'lɪləkwi]

a character's inner speech spoken aloud
(syn) monologue, inner speech
(e.g.) The film uses silent **soliloquies** rather than spoken monologues.

spigot	수도꼭지, 물이 나오는 장치
['spɪgət]	a faucet or valve for drawing liquid (syn) tap, valve (e.g.) He drank from the icy metal **spigot** beside the cellar.

spectator sports	관중 스포츠, 많은 사람들이 관람하는 스포츠
['spɛkteɪtər spɔːrts]	sports watched by large crowds (syn) viewing sports, arena sports (e.g.) **Spectator sports** generate large amounts of plastic waste and noise.

startle	깜짝 놀라게 하다, 갑작스레 놀라게 하다
['stɑːrtəl]	to surprise suddenly (syn) alarm, shock (e.g.) The sudden barking **startled** the woman pushing her child.

process loss	과정 손실, 그룹 활동에서 조정·동기 저하로 발생하는 생산성 감소
['prɑːses lɔːs]	a reduction in group productivity due to coordination or motivation problems (syn) inefficiency, decline (e.g.) Large teams often suffer **process loss** when members fail to coordinate.

sustainable	지속 가능한, 환경을 해치지 않는
[sə'steɪnəbəl]	environmentally responsible and long-lasting (syn) eco-friendly, renewable (e.g.) Reducing waste is essential for creating **sustainable** sports environments.

proactive	선제적으로 행동하는, 문제가 생기기 전에 미리 대응하는
[proʊ'æktɪv]	taking action in advance to deal with an expected difficulty or opportunity (syn) preventive, anticipatory, preemptive (e.g.) The passage argues that sport organizations must be **proactive** in reducing environmental damage.

vermilion
주홍색, 선명한 붉은색 안료나 색채

[vərˈmɪljən]

a bright red pigment or color, often used symbolically in cultural or artistic contexts
(syn) scarlet, crimson, bright red
(e.g.) Mala wore **vermilion** in the parting of her hair to show, or signify, that she was a newly married bride.

sea swine
바다 돼지, 중세 지도에 등장한 괴물형 바다 생물

[siː swaɪn]

a legendary sea creature depicted in medieval maps
(syn) sea monster
(e.g.) Sailors feared **sea swine** appearing in unexplored waters.

close-up shot
클로즈업 장면, 얼굴이나 작은 부분을 크게 잡는 촬영

[ˈkloʊsʌp ʃɑːt]

a camera shot that tightly frames a person's face or detail
(syn) tight shot, zoom-in
(e.g.) In the film, the **close-up shot** revealed emotions hidden from other characters.

noise pollution
소음 공해, 과도한 소음으로 인한 환경 피해

[ˈnɔɪz pəˌluːʃən]

harmful or disruptive environmental noise
(syn) sound pollution, acoustic disturbance
(e.g.) Stadium crowds often create severe **noise pollution** around public spaces.

strain
압박, 부담, 긴장이나 압력을 주는 힘

[streɪn]

pressure or stress put on a system or person
(syn) tension, burden
(e.g.) The arrival and departure of spectators put **strain** on the neighborhood.

labial
순음, 입술로 조음되는 자음

[ˈleɪbiəl]

a consonant produced with the lips
(syn) bilabial sound, lip consonant
(e.g.) /p, b, m/ are categorized as **labial** sounds in phonetics.

side effect
부작용, 의도하지 않은 추가 효과

['saɪd ˌɪfɛkt]

an unintended secondary effect
(syn) unintended effect, consequence
(e.g.) Environmental **side effects** appear when sport facilities are developed too quickly.

mute play
무언 연기, 말 없이 표정이나 움직임으로 드러나는 연기

[mjuːt pleɪ]

facial or bodily expression shown without spoken words
(syn) silent expression, nonverbal acting
(e.g.) The film uses the **mute play** of features to reveal a character's inner thoughts.

trace
자취, 흔적, 남아 있는 작은 표시

[treɪs]

a small sign showing that something existed
(syn) mark, sign
(e.g.) The that-**trace** effect explains why subjects cannot move across an overt complementizer.

windfall
바람에 떨어진 과일, 뜻밖의 횡재, 자연스럽게 떨어진 것 또는 갑작스러운 이익

['wɪndˌfɔːl]

fruit blown down by wind; unexpected gain
(syn) dropfruit; bonus, gain
(e.g.) He remembered walking among the **windfall** pears with his father.

overtly
공공연하게, 숨기지 않고 드러내어

[oʊˈvɜːrtli]

done openly without concealment
(syn) openly, explicitly
(e.g.) Subjects cannot be moved **overtly** across an overt complementizer.

convey
전달하다, 의미나 감정을 전하다

[kənˈveɪ]

to communicate meaning or emotion
(syn) communicate, express
(e.g.) Intonation helps **convey** attitude that words alone cannot show.

recursive

재귀적인, 구조가 반복적으로 안에 포함되는

[rɪˈkɜːrsɪv]

characterized by repeated embedding of structure
(syn) self-embedded, repeated
(e.g.) Human language is **recursive**, allowing clauses inside other clauses.

extension activity

확장 활동, 기본 과제를 마친 후의 추가 활동

[ɪkˈstɛnʃən ækˈtɪvɪti]

a supplemental task for students who finish early
(syn) enrichment task, follow-up activity
(e.g.) Providing an **extension activity** helps advanced learners stay engaged.

telegram

전보, 짧은 메시지를 급히 보내는 통신

[ˈtɛləˌgræm]

a message sent by telegraph
(syn) wire message, cable
(e.g.) He received a **telegram** with Mala's flight information.

intimate

친밀한, 가까운 관계를 나타내는

[ˈɪntəmət]

showing close personal connection
(syn) close, personal
(e.g.) Using his name would have sounded too **intimate** for their early relationship.

fronted

전위된, 문장 앞쪽으로 이동된

[ˈfrʌntɪd]

moved to the beginning of a clause
(syn) preposed, initial-positioned
(e.g.) In wh-questions the wh-phrase is **fronted**, leaving a gap.

part

헤어지다, 갈라지다, 서로 떨어지게 되다

[pɑːrt]

to separate or move apart
(syn) separate, divide
(e.g.) They **parted** after only a few days together as newlyweds.

critic
비평가, 분석하거나 평가하는 사람

['krɪtɪk]
a person who judges or evaluates works or actions
(syn) commentator, reviewer
(e.g.) **Critics** said the legal system appeared troubled by arrogance.

stem
(언어학) 어간, 단어의 핵심 의미를 담는 형태

[stɛm]
the base form to which affixes attach
(syn) base form, root
(e.g.) Inflectional suffixes do not change the grammatical category of the **stem**.

hypocritical
위선적인, 말과 행동이 불일치하는

[ˌhɪpəˈkrɪtɪkəl]
pretending to have virtues one does not possess
(syn) insincere, two-faced
(e.g.) The passage notes that even a practisedly **hypocritical** face reveals hidden feelings.

worksheet
학습지, 학생 활동을 위해 준비된 과제지

['wɜːrkʃiːt]
a sheet of exercises or tasks for learners
(syn) activity sheet, task sheet
(e.g.) Students wrote the meanings of proverbs on **Worksheet** 1.

specification
명세, 요구 기준, 평가·활동을 위한 구체 기준

[ˌspɛsɪfɪˈkeɪʃən]
a detailed requirement or guideline
(syn) criterion, requirement
(e.g.) Test items were created based on the test **specifications**.

whereabouts
소재, 행방

['wɛərəˌbaʊts]
the place where someone or something is
(syn) location, position
(e.g.) The police tried to discover the suspect's **whereabouts**.

worthwhile | 가치 있는

[ˌwɜːrθ'waɪl]

worth the time, effort, or attention
(syn) valuable, rewarding
(e.g.) It was a **worthwhile** experience that taught us a lot.

wavelength | 파장, (은유) 사고 방식

['weɪvˌlɛŋkθ]

the distance between two waves; also a metaphor for shared understanding
(syn) frequency, rhythm
(e.g.) The two researchers were on the same **wavelength** during the project.

vertical | 수직의

['vɜːrtɪkəl]

positioned upright or perpendicular to the horizon
(syn) upright, perpendicular
(opp) horizontal
(e.g.) The chart shows a **vertical** line separating two categories.

uninhibited | 억압되지 않은, 거리낌 없는

[ˌʌnɪn'hɪbɪtɪd]

free and natural in behavior; not held back
(syn) unrestrained, free, spontaneous
(e.g.) Children often speak in an **uninhibited** manner.
(n) inhibition(억제), (v) inhibit(억누르다)

underlie | 기초가 되다

[ˌʌndər'laɪ]

to be the basic cause or foundation of something
(syn) support, ground, form the basis of
(e.g.) Several psychological principles **underlie** this language-learning theory.

vehicle | 차량, (비유) 매개체, 전달 장치, (문학) 알레고리·은유에서 전달하는 형상, (언어학) 의미·기능을 운반하는 형식적 요소를 가리킬 때 사용

['viːɪkəl]

a means of transport; also something used to express or convey ideas
(syn) medium, carrier
(e.g.) In the metaphor "Time is a thief," *thief* is the **vehicle** that carries the meaning.

유희태 일반영어
⑤ 기출 VOCA 30days

vantage	○○○	obligation	○○○
testament	○○○	implement	○○○
violation	○○○	feedback	○○○
theta-criterion	○○○	schemata	○○○
collaboratively	○○○	contraction	○○○
neurological	○○○	phylogenetically	○○○
recalibration	○○○	abundance	○○○
navigate	○○○	biome	○○○
haggling	○○○	denizen	○○○
temper tantrum	○○○	conceptualized	○○○
excessive	○○○	diversity	○○○
disregard	○○○	drifting	○○○
fervently	○○○	transparency	○○○
scornful	○○○	manufacture	○○○
failing	○○○	outlive	○○○
guarantee	○○○	engrave	○○○
falsity	○○○	unmoved	○○○
logically	○○○	pierce	○○○
equivalent	○○○	persuade	○○○
truth-value	○○○	scanning	○○○
contradiction	○○○	tolerate	○○○
attribute	○○○	imprint	○○○
particularity	○○○	process	○○○
reside	○○○	transform	○○○
dispute	○○○	peruse	○○○
condition	○○○	avoid	○○○
maxim of quantity	○○○	compulsive	○○○
restriction	○○○	shun	○○○
topical	○○○	foster	○○○
structure	○○○	unattested	○○○

vantage 우월, 유리함, 좋은 위치

['væntɪdʒ]

a place or position affording a good view or any other advantage
(syn) advantage, perspective
(e.g.) From their strategic **vantage** point on the hill, they could see the approaching storm.

testament 증거, 유언

['testəmənt]

something that serves as a sign or evidence of a specified fact or quality
(syn) proof, evidence
(e.g.) Her long and successful career is a **testament** to her unwavering commitment.

violation 위반, (언어학에서) 규칙 · 격률을 어기는 행위

[ˌvaɪəˈleɪʃən]

breaking a rule or maxim
(syn) breach, infringement
(e.g.) A conversational **violation** would occur.

theta-criterion 세타 기준 (언어학 용어)

[ˈθeɪtə kraɪˈtɪəriən]

the principle that each argument bears one and only one theta role, and each theta role is assigned to one and only one argument
(syn) semantic role principle (전문 용어)
(e.g.) The **theta-criterion** helps linguists analyze the thematic roles of participants in a sentence structure.

collaboratively 공동으로, 협력하여

[kəˌlæbəˈreɪtɪvli]

in a way that involves working jointly with others
(syn) jointly, together
(e.g.) To finish the proposal on time, the departments had to work **collaboratively**.

neurological

신경(학)의

[ˌnʊrəlɑːdʒɪkl]

relating to the anatomy, functions, and organic diseases of the nerves and nervous system

(syn) neural, cerebral

(e.g.) Scientists are studying the **neurological** effects of chronic stress on memory.

recalibration

재조정, 재측정

[ˌriːkælɪˈbreɪʃn]

the action or process of adjusting something to work accurately again, or adjusting a mental or emotional framework

(syn) readjustment, fine-tuning

(e.g.) After the market shift, a complete **recalibration** of our business strategy was necessary.

navigate

(길을) 찾다, 항해하다

[ˈnævɪɡeɪt]

to plan and direct the route or course of a journey; to find one's way

(syn) direct, steer

(e.g.) Students need strong study skills to succeed at **navigating** the demands of college life.

haggling

(값을) 흥정, 실랑이

[ˈhæɡlɪŋ]

disputing or bargaining persistently, especially over the cost of something

(syn) bargaining, negotiating

(e.g.) The tourist enjoyed the cultural experience of **haggling** for souvenirs at the local market.

temper tantrum

(아이의) 짜증, 분통

[ˈtempər ˈtæntrəm]

an uncontrolled outburst of anger and frustration, typically in a young child

(syn) fit of rage, outburst

(e.g.) She realized she had to forgo the luxury of her own emotional **temper tantrums** to support her mother.

excessive
과도한, 지나친

[ɪkˈsesɪv]

more than is necessary, normal, or desirable; immoderate
(syn) undue, extreme
(e.g.) The regulation was intended to prevent the **excessive** use of harmful chemicals in food production.

disregard
무시, 경시

[ˌdɪsrɪˈɡɑːrd]

the fact of paying no attention to something; lack of attention
(syn) ignore, overlook (as a verb)
(e.g.) The supervisor expressed his disappointment at the team's casual **disregard** for the deadlines.

fervently
열렬히, 강렬하게

[ˈfɜːrvəntli]

very enthusiastically or passionately
(syn) passionately, zealously
(e.g.) The members **fervently** debated the motion until late in the evening.

scornful
경멸하는, 비웃는

[ˈskɔːrnfl]

feeling or expressing contempt or derision
(syn) contemptuous, disdainful
(e.g.) He gave a **scornful** dismissal of the new theory as utterly nonsensical.

failing
실패, 결함

[ˈfeɪlɪŋ]

the condition of not achieving success
(syn) failure, shortcoming
(e.g.) The most important stories we tell about ourselves ⋯ are primarily tales of **failing**.

guarantee
보장하다, 확신하다

[ˌgærənˈtiː]

to assure or promise that a specified condition will be fulfilled
(syn) ensure, promise
(e.g.) The truth of P **guarantees** the truth of Q.

falsity
거짓, 허위, 틀림

[ˈfɔːlsəti]

the state of being untrue or erroneous
(syn) untruth, deception
(e.g.) The lawyer attempted to prove the **falsity** of the witness's statement.

logically
논리적으로, 이치에 맞게

[ˈlɑːdʒɪkli]

in a way that is reasonable and makes sense; according to the rules of logic
(syn) reasonably, rationally
(e.g.) If P is true, then Q must **logically** follow.

equivalent
동등한, 상당하는

[ɪˈkwɪvələnt]

equal in value, amount, function, meaning, or measure
(syn) equal, comparable
(e.g.) The two phrases are **equivalent** in meaning.

truth-value
진리값

[truːθ ˈvæljuː]

the status of a proposition as true or false
(syn) logical status
(e.g.) In logic, every statement has a single **truth-value** of either true or false.

contradiction
모순, 반박

[ˌkɑːntrəˈdɪkʃn]

a combination of statements, ideas, or features which are opposed to one another
(syn) inconsistency, paradox
(e.g.) The statement that a square circle exists is a **contradiction**.

attribute

속성, 특성

['ætrɪbjuːt]

a quality or feature regarded as a characteristic or inherent part of someone or something

(syn) trait, characteristic

(e.g.) Critical thinking is a valuable **attribute** for students.

particularity

특수성, 특이성, 까다로움

[pə,tɪrkjə'lærəti]

the quality of being individual or specific; specific details

(syn) specificity, distinctiveness

(e.g.) The document focuses on the **particularity** of the local dialect.

reside

거주하다, (속성 등이) 존재하다, 있다

[rɪ'zaɪd]

to be situated, found, or fixed in a particular place or position

(syn) dwell, lie

(e.g.) The problem often **resides** in the lack of communication.

dispute

논쟁, 분쟁

[dɪ'spjuːt]

a disagreement, argument, or controversy

(syn) argument, controversy

(e.g.) The two parties are in **dispute** over the contract terms.

condition

조건, 상태

[kən'dɪʃn]

a stipulation or requirement that must be met; the state of something

(syn) requirement, prerequisite

(e.g.) A prerequisite **condition** must be met before approval.

maxim of quantity

양의 격률

['mæksɪm əv 'kwɒntɪti]

Grice's rule requiring appropriate informational amount

(e.g.) Tom broke the **maxim of quantity** by giving far more details than the listener needed.

restriction
제한, 규제

[rɪ'strɪkʃn]

a limiting condition or measure, especially a legal one
(syn) limitation, constraint
(e.g.) There are severe **restrictions** on the use of water during the drought.

topical
주제의, 시사적인

['tɑːpɪkl]

relating to or dealing with current subject matter; relating to a theme
(syn) relevant, current, pertinent
(e.g.) The conference covered a range of **topical** and pressing global issues.

structure
구조, 조직

['strʌktʃər]

the arrangement of and relations between the parts or elements of something complex
(syn) framework, composition
(e.g.) The grammatical **structure** of the sentence is complex.

obligation
의무

[ˌɒblɪ'geɪʃən]

a duty or responsibility
(syn) duty, responsibility
(e.g.) Teachers have an **obligation** to provide fair and consistent assessment.

implement
실행하다, 이행하다

['ɪmpləment]

to put a decision, plan, agreement, etc., into effect
(syn) execute, apply
(e.g.) The team is responsible for **implementing** the new policy.

feedback
피드백, 반응

['fiːdbæk]

information about reactions to a product, a person's performance of a task, etc., used as a basis for improvement
(syn) response, comment
(e.g.) Constructive **feedback** is essential for improvement.

schemata
스키마 (도식, 인지 틀)

[skiːˈmɑːtə]

plural of schema; a representation of a plan or theory in the form of an outline or model
(syn) mental frameworks, blueprints
(e.g.) Readers use existing **schemata** to process new information.

contraction
수축, 축소, (언어) 축약형

[kənˈtrækʃn]

the process of becoming smaller; a shortened form of a word or group of words
(syn) shrinkage, abbreviation
(e.g.) English uses many common **contractions** like 'don't' and 'it's'.

phylogenetically
계통 발생적으로

[ˌfaɪloʊdʒəˈnetɪkli]

in a manner relating to the evolutionary development and history of a species or larger taxonomic group
(syn) evolutionarily
(e.g.) The species are related **phylogenetically**.

abundance
풍부, 다수

[əˈbʌndəns]

a very large quantity of something
(syn) plenty, profusion
(e.g.) The ocean is home to an **abundance** of marine life.

biome
생물군계

[ˈbaɪoʊm]

a large naturally occurring community of flora and fauna occupying a major habitat, e.g., forest or tundra
(syn) habitat, environment, ecological region
(e.g.) The Amazon rainforest is a vast and complex **biome** with unparalleled biodiversity.

denizen
(특정 장소의) 주민, 서식 동물

[ˈdenɪzn]

an inhabitant or occupant of a particular place
(syn) inhabitant, resident
(e.g.) The deep sea has strange and mysterious **denizens**.

conceptualized

개념화하다

[kənˈseptʃuəlaɪzd]

formed a concept or idea of (something)
(syn) theorized, formulated
(e.g.) The idea was first **conceptualized** in the 1980s.

diversity

다양성, 차이

[daɪˈvɜːrsəti]

the state of being diverse; variety
(syn) variety, range
(e.g.) Cultural **diversity** enriches the community.

drifting

표류하는, 떠다니는

[ˈdrɪftɪŋ]

moving slowly without a clear direction or purpose
(syn) wandering, floating
(e.g.) She stared out the window with a **drifting** gaze.

transparency

투명성, 정직함

[trænsˈpærənsi]

(in linguistics) clarity of structural relationship, especially between active/passive
(syn) clarity, openness
(e.g.) Voice **transparency** between active and passive forms.

manufacture

제조하다, 생산하다

[ˌmænjuˈfæktʃər]

to make (something) on a large scale using machinery
(syn) produce, make
(e.g.) The company **manufactures** electronic components.

outlive

~보다 오래 살다, ~을 견뎌내다

[ˌaʊtˈlɪv]

to live or last longer than
(syn) survive, remain
(e.g.) She feared her husband would not **outlive** the winter.

engrave
새기다, 조각하다

[ɪnˈɡreɪv]

to cut or carve a text or design on the surface of a hard object
(syn) carve, inscribe
(e.g.) His words were **engraved** in my memory forever.

unmoved
감동하지 않은, 미동도 않는

[ˌʌnˈmuːvd]

not affected by emotion or excitement; impassive
(syn) unaffected, indifferent
(e.g.) He remained **unmoved** by her tearful apology.

pierce
꿰뚫다, 구멍을 뚫다

[pɪrs]

to make a hole in something using a sharp object
(syn) puncture, penetrate
(e.g.) A sharp object **pierced** the thick fabric.

persuade
설득하다, 납득시키다

[pərˈsweɪd]

to induce someone to do something through reasoning or argument
(syn) convince, influence
(e.g.) It took a long time to **persuade** him to join the team.

scanning
훑어보기, 정밀 검사

[ˈskænɪŋ]

looking over all parts of (something) carefully in order to detect some feature
(syn) browsing, scrutinizing
(e.g.) **Scanning** the text quickly helps find key information.

tolerate
참다, 견디다, 용인하다

[ˈtɑːləreɪt]

to allow the existence, occurrence, or practice of (something that one does not necessarily like or agree with) without interference
(syn) endure, put up with
(e.g.) The school will not **tolerate** any form of bullying.

imprint

찍다, 감명시키다, (심리) 각인하다

[ɪmˈprɪnt]

to fix (an idea or feeling) firmly in someone's mind
(syn) stamp, mark
(e.g.) Early experiences are critical in **imprinting** behavior patterns.

process

처리하다, 가공하다

[ˈprɑːses]

to perform a series of mechanical or chemical operations on (something) in order to change or preserve it
(syn) handle, deal with
(e.g.) The computer is slow at **processing** large files.

transform

변형시키다, 완전히 바꾸다

[trænsˈfɔːrm]

to make a dramatic change in the form, appearance, or character of
(syn) convert, alter
(e.g.) The internet has **transformed** the way we communicate.

peruse

정독하다, 주의 깊게 읽다

[pəˈruːz]

to read or examine something carefully and thoroughly
(syn) examine, scrutinize, read carefully
(e.g.) Students were asked to **peruse** the passage before answering the inference questions.

avoid

피하다, 모면하다

[əˈvɔɪd]

to keep away from or prevent (something) from happening
(syn) evade, dodge
(e.g.) She kept **avoiding** eye contact during the interview.

compulsive

강박적인, 억제할 수 없는

[kəmˈpʌlsɪv]

resulting from or relating to an irresistible urge
(syn) obsessive, irresistible
(e.g.) He is a **compulsive** gambler and needs help.

shun
피하다, 멀리하다, 따돌리다

[ʃʌn]
to persistently avoid, ignore, or reject
(syn) avoid, ostracize
(e.g.) After the scandal, she was **shunned** by her former friends.

foster
조성하다, 발전시키다, 기르다

['fɔːstər]
to encourage or promote the development of (something, typically
something desirable)
(syn) encourage, nurture
(e.g.) The school **fostered** a love of reading in its students.

unattested
입증되지 않은, 실제 사용되지 않는

[ˌʌnə'tɛstɪd]
not found in actual language use; not attested in real data
(syn) unverified, non-occurring
(e.g.) The passage shows that forms like *afraider** or *activer** are
marked with an asterisk because they are **unattested**
comparatives in English.

2025

DAY

04

유희태 일반영어

⑤ 기출 VOCA 30days

forgo	○○○	calamity	○○○
distinguish	○○○	threshold	○○○
brainstorm	○○○	addiction	○○○
arms	○○○	parasite	○○○
reflect	○○○	purveyor	○○○
conceive	○○○	turpitude	○○○
enhance	○○○	selflessness	○○○
encourage	○○○	gait	○○○
promote	○○○	pathos	○○○
visualize	○○○	ordeal	○○○
shipwreck	○○○	auxiliary	○○○
trace	○○○	comparative	○○○
castaway	○○○	disyllabic	○○○
marine avian	○○○	dummy	○○○
cuttlefish	○○○	interlanguage	○○○
quill	○○○	deviation	○○○
terrace	○○○	scatter	○○○
subscription	○○○	practicality	○○○
evangelist	○○○	analogy	○○○
convert	○○○	abyss	○○○
agony	○○○	redemption	○○○
sloth	○○○	revelation	○○○
pursuit	○○○	prohibition	○○○
conditional	○○○	chatbot	○○○
acceptable behavior	○○○	theft	○○○
ditransitive	○○○	metacognitive	○○○
rubric	○○○	awareness	○○○
inquiry	○○○	omnipresent	○○○
pseudonym	○○○	endorsement	○○○
stipulation	○○○	problem-solving	○○○

forgo
포기하다, 없이 지내다

[fɔːrˈɡoʊ]

to go without (something desirable)
(syn) renounce, abstain from
(e.g.) I decided to **forgo** dessert to stick to my diet.

distinguish
구별하다, 식별하다

[dɪˈstɪŋɡwɪʃ]

to recognize or treat (someone or something) as different
(syn) differentiate, discern
(e.g.) It is hard to **distinguish** between the two dialects.

brainstorm
아이디어를 떠올리다, 브레인스토밍하다

[ˈbreɪnstɔːrm]

to produce an idea or way of solving a problem by holding a spontaneous group discussion
(syn) think up, ideate
(e.g.) Let's **brainstorm** some solutions to the problem.

arms
품, 팔(사람의 신체 일부), 무기, 병기

[ɑːrmz]

a person's upper limbs, especially used metaphorically as a place of affection, safety, or emotional refuge; weapons used for defense or attack
(syn) embrace, hold; weapons, armaments
(e.g.) After years of feeling lost in America, she seemed ready to fall into my **arms**, trusting that I could guide her through the patternless paths of our new life.

reflect
반영하다, 심사숙고하다

[rɪˈflekt]

to embody or represent (something) in a faithful or appropriate way; to think deeply or carefully about
(syn) mirror, contemplate
(e.g.) The art **reflects** the turbulent history of the period.

conceive
상상하다, 생각하다, 임신하다

[kənˈsiːv]

to form a plan or idea in the mind
(syn) imagine, formulate
(e.g.) He **conceived** a brilliant idea for a new business.

enhance
향상시키다, 높이다

[ɪnˈhæns]

to intensify, increase, or further improve the quality, value, or extent of
(syn) improve, boost
(e.g.) The new software will **enhance** productivity.

encourage
격려하다, 장려하다

[ɪnˈkɜːrɪdʒ]

to give support, confidence, or hope to (someone)
(syn) motivate, stimulate
(e.g.) Parents should **encourage** their children to read.

DAY
04

promote
촉진하다, 홍보하다, 승진시키다

[prəˈmoʊt]

to further the progress of (something, especially a cause, venture, or aim); to publicly support or recommend
(syn) advance, support
(e.g.) The campaign aims to **promote** healthy eating habits.

visualize
시각화하다, 마음속으로 그리다

[ˈvɪʒuəlaɪz]

to form a mental image of
(syn) imagine, picture
(e.g.) Try to **visualize** the setting of the story as you read.

shipwreck
난파, 난파선

[ˈʃɪprɛk]

the destruction of a ship at sea; a ship that has been destroyed in this way
(syn) disaster, wreck
(e.g.) Explorers found the remains of an ancient **shipwreck** near the coast.

trace
자취, 흔적

[treɪs]

a mark, sign, or amount of something that has existed or occurred
(syn) remnant, mark
(e.g.) Scientists found **traces** of ancient life in the rock.

castaway
조난자, 표류자

['kæstəweɪ]
a person who has been shipwrecked and marooned in an isolated place
(syn) survivor, derelict
(e.g.) The novel tells the story of a group of **castaways** on a deserted island.

marine avian
바다새 (해양 조류)

[mə'riːn 'eɪviən]
a bird adapted to life in a marine environment
(syn) oceanic bird, pelagic bird
(e.g.) **Marine avians** play a crucial role in coastal ecosystems.

cuttlefish
갑오징어

['kʌtəlˌfɪʃ]
a marine mollusk of the order Sepioidea, related to the squid, having a broad, flattened body and ten arms
(syn) cephalopod
(e.g.) The **cuttlefish** is famous for its ability to camouflage.

quill
깃펜, (고슴도치 등의) 가시

[kwɪl]
a pen made from a feather; a main flight feather of a bird; a stiff, hollow, horny spine on a porcupine or hedgehog
(syn) feather, spine
(e.g.) In the 18th century, letters were often written with **quills**.

terrace
계단식 논·밭, 테라스

['terəs]
a piece of sloped plane that has been cut into a series of successively receding flat surfaces or platforms
(syn) patio, balcony
(e.g.) The ancient farmers built irrigation systems to water the rice **terraces**.

subscription
구독(료), 기부

[səb'skrɪpʃn]
an amount of money regularly paid to receive a product or service
(syn) membership, fee
(e.g.) I renewed my annual **subscription** to the academic journal.

evangelist

전도사, 열렬한 지지자

[ɪˈvændʒəlɪst]

a zealous advocate of a particular cause
(syn) promoter, advocate
(e.g.) She is an enthusiastic **evangelist** for the new technology.

convert

(n) 개종자, 전향자, (v) 개종하다, 전환하다

[ˈkɑːnvɜːrt]

a person who has adopted a new religion, belief, or opinion
(syn) new devotee, proselyte
(e.g.) The former skeptics became the new technology's most vocal **converts**.

DAY

04

agony

극심한 고통, 괴로움

[ˈægəni]

extreme physical or mental suffering
(syn) pain, suffering
(e.g.) The patient was in **agony** until the doctor administered medication.

sloth

나무늘보, 나태, 게으름

[sloʊθ]

reluctance to work or exert oneself; laziness
(syn) laziness, idleness
(e.g.) The virtue of diligence is the opposite of the vice of **sloth**.

pursuit

추구, 뒤쫓음, 일

[pərˈsuːt]

the action of following or pursuing someone or something; an activity or task
(syn) quest, endeavor
(e.g.) The **pursuit** of happiness is a universal human goal.

conditional

조건문(조건절), 어떤 사건이나 상황이 특정 조건 충족 여부에 따라 달라지는 문장 구조

[kənˈdɪʃənəl]

a clause or sentence expressing that one situation depends on another, typically introduced by 'if' or equivalent forms
(syn) if-clause, conditional clause
(e.g.) In the sentence 'If it rains, we'll cancel,' the **conditional** shows how the outcome depends on the condition.

acceptable behavior
용인되거나 허용 가능한 행동

[ək'septəbl bɪ'heɪvjər]

behavior that is appropriate or allowed within a given social context
(syn) proper conduct, appropriate behavior
(e.g.) When we stepped into the exterior world, I was the one who told my mother what was **acceptable behavior** in our new suburban life.

ditransitive
(목적어를 2개 가지는) 이중 타동사

[daɪ'trænzɪtɪv]

(of a verb) taking two objects (a direct and an indirect object)
(syn) double-object (특수 용어)
(e.g.) The verb 'give' is a typical **ditransitive** verb, as in 'She gave him a gift.'

rubric
(시험 등의) 지침, 규정, 표제

['ruːbrɪk]

a set of instructions or an explanatory heading or title
(syn) instruction, guide
(e.g.) Please read the scoring **rubric** carefully before you begin.

inquiry
문의, 질문, 조사

[ɪn'kwaɪəri]

an act of asking for information; an official investigation
(syn) investigation, question
(e.g.) We have received several **inquiries** about the job opening.

pseudonym
필명, 가명

['suːdənɪm]

a fictitious name, especially one used by an author
(syn) alias, pen name
(e.g.) The author published his first novel under a **pseudonym**.

stipulation
규정, 조건, 조항

[ˌstɪpjuˈleɪʃn]

a condition or requirement that is specified or demanded as part of an agreement
(syn) prerequisite, mandate, provision
(e.g.) The contract included a strict **stipulation** regarding confidentiality.

calamity
재앙, 불행

[kəˈlæməti]

a disaster; an event causing great and often sudden damage or distress
(syn) disaster, catastrophe
(e.g.) The drought was a major **calamity** for the region.

DAY
04

threshold
문지방, 기준점, 시발점

[ˈθreʃhoʊld]

a point of entry or beginning; the magnitude or intensity that must be exceeded for a certain reaction to occur
(syn) verge, boundary
(e.g.) She has a high **threshold** for pain.

addiction
중독

[əˈdɪkʃn]

the fact or condition of being physically or mentally dependent on a particular substance or activity
(syn) dependency, craving
(e.g.) Technology **addiction** is a growing problem among youth.

parasite
기생충, 기생충 같은 사람

[ˈpærəsaɪt]

an organism that lives, in or on another organism (its host) and benefits by deriving nutrients at the host's expense
(syn) hanger-on, pest
(e.g.) Ticks and fleas are common external **parasites**.

purveyor
(식료품 등을) 공급하는 사람, 조달업자

[pər'veɪər]

a person or group who sells or deals in particular goods, often food; a promulgator of ideas
(syn) supplier, vendor
(e.g.) The restaurant uses local **purveyors** for its fresh ingredients.

turpitude
비열, 타락

['tɜːrpɪtuːd]

depraved or wicked behavior or character
(syn) depravity, wickedness
(e.g.) He was fired for moral **turpitude**.

selflessness
이타심, 무사함

[ˌselfləsnəs]

the quality of being more concerned with the needs and wishes of others than with one's own
(syn) altruism, generosity
(e.g.) Her **selflessness** in helping others was remarkable.

gait
걸음걸이, 태도

[geɪt]

a person's manner of walking
(syn) stride, bearing
(e.g.) The horse's smooth **gait** made the ride comfortable.

pathos
연민의 정, 비애, (수사학) 감성

['peɪθɑːs]

a quality that evokes pity or sadness
(syn) pity, compassion
(e.g.) The film evoked a great sense of **pathos**.

ordeal
시련, 고난

[ɔːr'diːəl]

a very unpleasant and prolonged experience; a severe trial
(syn) hardship, trial
(e.g.) The family went through many **ordeals** during the war.

auxiliary
조동사, 보조적인 요소

[ɔːgˈzɪliəri]

a verb or element that adds functional or grammatical meaning to a clause
(syn) helping verb, supportive element
(e.g.) In analyzing the sentence, students must consider how the **auxiliary** interacts with the negative to yield a different truth condition.

comparative
비교의, 상대적인

[kəmˈpærətɪv]

relating to or based on comparison; relative
(syn) relative, proportional
(e.g.) We need a **comparative** analysis of the two systems.

DAY 04

disyllabic
이음절의

[ˌdaɪsɪˈlæbɪk]

having two syllables
(syn) two-syllable
(e.g.) The word 'apple' is a **disyllabic** word.

dummy
모형, 마네킹, 가짜

[ˈdʌmi]

a model or replica of a human being; a thing designed to look like a real thing but lacking the full functions
(syn) substitute, model
(e.g.) In the sentence "It is raining," 'it' is a **dummy** subject with no semantic content.

interlanguage
중간언어

[ˌɪntərˈlæŋgwɪdʒ]

the linguistic system created by a second-language learner, which may not be the target language or the learner's native language
(syn) learner language (특수 용어)
(e.g.) Errors in an ESL student's speech can be analyzed as part of their **interlanguage** development.

deviation
일탈, 편차, 벗어남

[ˌdiːviˈeɪʃn]

the action of departing from an established course or accepted standard
(syn) divergence, abnormality
(e.g.) Any significant **deviation** from the safety protocol will result in a penalty.

scatter
(n) 무질서하게 흩어진 무리, (v) 흩어지다

[ˈskætər]

a number of things lying dispersed, to disperse
(syn) (n) dispersion; (v) spread
(e.g.) Go drifting away.
Behind a **scatter** of boys.

practicality
실용성, 현실성

[ˌpræktɪˈkæləti]

the quality or state of being useful or sensible
(syn) feasibility, usefulness
(e.g.) We need to consider the **practicality** of the proposed changes.

analogy
비유, 유추

[əˈnælədʒi]

a comparison between two things, typically for the purpose of explanation or clarification
(syn) comparison, parallel
(e.g.) He explained the concept using a simple **analogy**.

abyss
심연, 깊은 구렁

[əˈbɪs]

a deep or seemingly bottomless chasm
(syn) chasm, gulf
(e.g.) He felt like he was staring into an **abyss** of despair.

redemption
구원, 속죄, 회복

[rɪˈdempʃn]

the action of saving or being saved from sin, error, or evil; the act of gaining possession of something in exchange for payment
(syn) salvation, retrieval
(e.g.) The character's journey was one of **redemption**.

revelation
폭로, 계시

[ˌrevəˈleɪʃn]

the action of making known something that was previously secret or unknown
(syn) disclosure, realization
(e.g.) The document contained a shocking **revelation**.

prohibition
금지, 금지령

[ˌproʊˈbɪʃn]

the action of forbidding something, especially by law
(syn) ban, veto
(e.g.) There is a strict **prohibition** on smoking indoors.

chatbot
챗봇

[ˈtʃætbɑːt]

a computer program designed to simulate conversation with human users, especially over the Internet
(syn) AI assistant
(e.g.) I used a **chatbot** to get customer support online.

theft
절도, 도둑질

[θeft]

the action or crime of stealing
(syn) stealing, larceny
(e.g.) The security camera recorded the entire incident of **theft**.

metacognitive
메타인지의

[ˌmetəkɑːˈgnɪtɪv]

relating to or dependent on an awareness and understanding of one's own thought processes
(syn) self-aware, reflective
(e.g.) **Metacognitive** strategies help students plan their learning.

awareness
인식, 자각

[əˈwernəs]

knowledge or perception of a situation or fact
(syn) consciousness, knowledge
(e.g.) Public **awareness** of environmental issues is increasing.

DAY
04

omnipresent
세계적인, 전반적인

[ˌɑːmnɪˈpreznt]

relating to the whole world; comprehensive
(syn) worldwide, comprehensive
(e.g.) smartphones are **omnipresent** in our daily lives

endorsement
지지, 승인, 보증

[ɪnˈdɔːrsmənt]

the act of giving one's public approval or support to someone or something
(syn) affirmation, advocacy, sanction
(e.g.) The product received a strong **endorsement** from a well-known celebrity.

problem-solving
문제 해결

[ˈprɑːbləm ˈsɑːlvɪŋ]

the process of finding solutions to difficult or complex issues
(syn) resolution, troubleshooting
(e.g.) She has excellent **problem-solving** skills.

2025

DAY

05

유희태 일반영어

⑤ 기출 VOCA 30days

translate	○○○	scrutiny	○○○
suburban	○○○	sanctuary	○○○
inevitably	○○○	adolescent	○○○
tawny	○○○	skip over	○○○
sinewy	○○○	selectively	○○○
toil-hardened	○○○	efficient	○○○
literary	○○○	improvisation	○○○
persistent	○○○	malleable	○○○
wicked	○○○	visceral	○○○
aristocratic	○○○	lucid	○○○
disenfranchised	○○○	succinct	○○○
phonetic	○○○	bounded	○○○
wilderness	○○○	resilient	○○○
diagnostic test	○○○	maxim of relation	○○○
subsidiary	○○○	feasible	○○○
intensive	○○○	maxim	○○○
pleasurable	○○○	clash	○○○
sedentary	○○○	result state	○○○
grumpy	○○○	smallpox	○○○
prioritize	○○○	obsolete	○○○
indulgence	○○○	base adjective	○○○
ultimately	○○○	passive counterpart	○○○
interrelated	○○○	astute	○○○
narrative	○○○	prosaic	○○○
implicature	○○○	tenacious	○○○
vendor	○○○	foreground	○○○
primordial	○○○	incongruous	○○○
messiness	○○○	transient	○○○
fishmonger	○○○	vindicate	○○○
aroma-free	○○○	placate	○○○

translate
번역하다, 해석하다

[trænz'leɪt]
to express the sense of words or text in another language
(syn) render, convert
(e.g.) We hired an expert to **translate** the ancient documents.

suburban
교외의

[sə'bɜːrbən]
relating to residential areas outside a city
(syn) residential, out-of-city
(e.g.) It would help my mother through the ordinary **suburban** life.

inevitably
필연적으로, 불가피하게

[ɪn'evɪtəbli]
as is certain to happen; unavoidably
(syn) necessarily, unavoidably, certainly
(e.g.) Changes are **inevitably** coming to every part of life.

tawny
황갈색의, 누런

['tɔːni]
of an orange-brown or yellowish-brown color
(syn) brownish-yellow, beige
(e.g.) The lion's mane was a rich **tawny** color.

sinewy
힘줄이 많은, 강인한

['sɪnjuːi]
consisting of or resembling sinews; lean and muscular
(syn) muscular, wiry
(e.g.) The climber had **sinewy** arms and great strength.

toil-hardened
고된 노동으로 단련된

[tɔɪl 'hɑːrdənd]
made tough or calloused by hard work
(syn) tough, calloused
(e.g.) His **toil-hardened** hands showed years of manual labor.

literary
문학의, 문예의

['lɪtəreri]

relating to or concerned with the writing, study, or content of literature
(syn) artistic, written
(e.g.) He is known for his complex **literary** style.

persistent
끈기 있는, 집요한, 지속적인

[pər'sɪstənt]

continuing firmly or obstinately in a course of action in spite of difficulty or opposition
(syn) determined, continuous
(e.g.) Her **persistent** effort eventually led to success.

wicked
사악한, 못된

['wɪkɪd]

evil or morally wrong
(syn) evil, malicious
(e.g.) The fairy tale featured a **wicked** stepmother.

DAY
05

aristocratic
귀족적인, 귀족의

[ˌærɪstə'krætɪk]

belonging to, or typical of, the aristocracy (nobility)
(syn) noble, upper-class
(e.g.) She spoke with an **aristocratic** accent and carried herself with great poise.

disenfranchised
권리(특히 투표권)가 박탈된

[ˌdɪsɪn'fræntʃaɪzd]

deprived of a right or privilege, especially the right to vote
(syn) marginalized, deprived
(e.g.) The law affected the most **disenfranchised** members of society.

phonetic
음성(학)의, 표음식의

[fə'netɪk]

relating to speech sounds
(syn) vocal, acoustic
(e.g.) The dictionary uses **phonetic** symbols to show pronunciation.

wilderness

황야, 미지의 공간

['wɪldərnəs]

an uncultivated or uncontrolled region

(syn) wilds, wasteland

(e.g.) Into a **wilderness**, the gait of one who finds no path where the path should be.

diagnostic test

진단 검사, 언어학에서는 문장의 구조적 의미적 속성을 판별하는 테스트

[ˌdaɪəɡ'nɒstɪk tɛst]

a test used to determine structural or semantic properties

(e.g.) There are **diagnostic tests** to distinguish one from the other, which include using meaningless dummy pronouns and voice transparency.

subsidiary

보조의, 부차적인

[səb'sɪdiəri]

less important than but related to something else

(syn) supplementary, secondary

(e.g.) The topic of grammar is often **subsidiary** to communication.

intensive

집중적인, 집약적인

[ɪn'tensɪv]

concentrated on a single area or subject or into a short time; thorough

(syn) thorough, exhaustive

(e.g.) The course requires an **intensive** period of study.

pleasurable

즐거운, 기쁜

['pleʒərəbl]

giving a feeling of satisfaction or enjoyment; enjoyable

(syn) enjoyable, delightful

(e.g.) Reading a good book is a **pleasurable** experience.

sedentary

주로 앉아서 지내는, 정주성의

['sednteri]

characterized by much sitting and little physical exercise; not migratory

(syn) inactive, stationary

(e.g.) A **sedentary** lifestyle can lead to health problems.

grumpy
성격이 나쁜, 심술궂은

['grʌmpi]

bad-tempered and irritable
(syn) irritable, bad-tempered
(e.g.) He is always **grumpy** before he has his morning coffee.

prioritize
우선순위를 정하다

[praɪˈɔːrətaɪz]

to determine the order for dealing with (a series of items or tasks) according to their relative importance
(syn) rank, focus on
(e.g.) You must **prioritize** your most important tasks.

indulgence
탐닉, 사치, 관용

[ɪnˈdʌldʒəns]

the practice of allowing oneself to enjoy the pleasure of something; a luxury
(syn) luxury, gratification
(e.g.) Chocolate is my little **indulgence**.

DAY
05

ultimately
궁극적으로, 결국

['ʌltɪmətli]

finally; in the end
(syn) eventually, finally
(e.g.) **Ultimately**, the success of the project depends on the dedication of the entire team.

interrelated
상호 관련된

[ˌɪntərɪˈleɪtɪd]

relating to each other or mutually dependent
(syn) connected, interdependent
(e.g.) The concepts of language and culture are deeply **interrelated**.

narrative
이야기, 서사

['nærətɪv]

a spoken or written account of events
(syn) story, tale
(e.g.) Such are the **narratives** that fascinate us.

implicature
함축, 암시적 의미

[ɪmˈplɪkətʃər]

meaning implied rather than explicitly stated
(syn) implied meaning
(e.g.) "Are you using the ketchup?" yields the non-literal meaning "Please pass me the ketchup," which is an example of **implicature**.

vendor
노점 상인, 판매자

[ˈvendɔːr]

a person or company offering something for sale, especially a street seller
(syn) seller, purveyor
(e.g.) The market was filled with various **vendors** selling fresh produce.

primordial
원시의, 태고의, 근본적인

[praɪˈmɔːrdiəl]

existing at or from the beginning of time; fundamental
(syn) ancient, fundamental
(e.g.) The deep sea is often described as a **primordial** environment.

messiness
혼란, 뒤죽박죽

[ˈmesinəs]

a state of untidiness or disorder
(syn) disorder, clutter
(e.g.) She preferred the open-air market's inherent **messiness** to the sterile order of the supermarket.

fishmonger
생선 장수, 어물전 주인

[ˈfɪʃmʌŋɡər]

a person who sells a fish and a seafood
(syn) seafood vendor
(e.g.) The **fishmongers** at the market shouted out the prices of their fresh catch.

aroma-free
향이 없는, 냄새가 없는

[əˈroʊmə friː]

lacking a distinctive, typically pleasant smell
(syn) odorless, scentless
(e.g.) The modern store offered the **aroma-free** order of individually wrapped fillets.

scrutiny
정밀 조사, 세밀한 관찰

[ˈskruːtəni]

critical observation or examination
(syn) inspection, surveillance
(e.g.) Every detail of the new design will be subject to intense **scrutiny**.

sanctuary
피난처, 안식처, 신성한 장소

[ˈsæŋktʃuəri]

a place of refuge or safety
(syn) refuge, haven
(e.g.) The forest reserve serves as a **sanctuary** for many endangered species.

adolescent
(a) 청소년기의, 사춘기의, (n) 청소년

[ˌædəˈlesnt]

relating to the period between childhood and adulthood
(syn) teenage, youthful
(e.g.) She decided to forgo the luxury of **adolescent** experiments and temper tantrums.

skip over
건너뛰다, 생략하다

[ˈskɪp ˈoʊvər]

to omit or pass over (something) without attention
(syn) overlook, bypass
(e.g.) When I don't understand a word, I tend to **skip over** it, which harms comprehension.

selectively
선택적으로, 가려서

[sɪˈlektɪvli]

in a way that involves careful selection
(syn) carefully, partially
(e.g.) Reading **selectively** may help me become a more efficient reader by focusing on key ideas.

efficient
효율적인, 능률적인

[ɪˈfɪʃnt]

achieving maximum productivity with minimum wasted effort or expense
(syn) productive, streamlined
(e.g.) Using a digital tool makes the process much more **efficient**.

DAY
05

improvisation | 즉흥성

[ɪmˌprɒvɪˈzeɪʃən]

spontaneous action without preparation

(syn) spontaneity

(e.g.) She preferred the **improvisation** of haggling to the conventional certainty of discount coupons.

malleable | (성격 등이) 유연한, 잘 변하는, 가단성의

[ˈmæliəbl]

easily influenced; able to be shaped or bent easily

(syn) flexible, adaptable

(e.g.) Children's brains are highly **malleable** and capable of rapid learning.

visceral | 감정적인, 본능적인

[ˈvɪsərəl]

felt in the internal organs; deeply emotional

(syn) deep, instinctive

(e.g.) She felt a **visceral** sense of fear as the noise suddenly erupted.

lucid | 명료한, 이해하기 쉬운

[lúːsɪd]

expressing ideas in a way that is easy to follow; clear and easy to understand

(syn) clear, transparent, coherent, intelligible

(opp) obscure, confusing, vague

(e.g.) The professor gave a **lucid** explanation of the complex theory.

succinct | 간결한, 명료한

[səksíŋkt]

expressed clearly and briefly without unnecessary words

(syn) concise, terse, compact, brief

(opp) verbose, lengthy, wordy

(e.g.) Write a **succinct** summary of the main ideas.

bounded
경계가 있는, 한정된

['baʊndɪd]

having fixed limits or boundaries; confined within edges or borders
(syn) limited, delimited, confined
(e.g.) In *Monkey Bridge*, the narrator contrasts the lively chaos of the open-air market with the neatly **bounded** aisles of American supermarkets.

resilient
회복력 있는, 탄력적인

[rɪzɪljənt]

able to recover quickly from difficulties or adapt to change
(syn) tough, flexible, hardy, buoyant
(opp) fragile, weak, vulnerable
(e.g.) Students must be **resilient** to adapt to new challenges.

DAY

05

maxim of relation
관련성의 격률

['mæksɪm əv rɪ'leɪʃən]

Grice's principle requiring relevance
(e.g.) Mary violated the **maxim of relation** when she suddenly changed the topic during their conversation.

feasible
실현 가능한, 실행할 수 있는

[fiːzəbl]

possible and practical to achieve or carry out
(syn) practicable, workable, viable, achievable
(opp) impractical, impossible, unworkable
(e.g.) Online assessment is a **feasible** alternative to paper tests.

maxim
규범, 격률(담화 격률)

['mæksɪm]

a conversational principle that guides effective communication, such as being truthful, relevant, clear, and sufficiently informative
(syn) conversational rule, pragmatic principle
(e.g.) The student violated the **maxim** of quantity by giving far more information than necessary.

clash
두 강세가 충돌하는 현상

[klæʃ]
the meeting of two adjacent stressed syllables causing rhythmic conflict in speech
(syn) stress clash
(e.g.) In *fourteen men*, a **clash** is avoided by weakening the stress on *teen*.

result state
결과 상태

[rɪˈzʌlt steɪt]
the state that necessarily follows from a lexical meaning
(syn) consequent state
(e.g.) The sentence John has killed a mosquito has the **result state** of a mosquito being dead as part of its literal meaning.

smallpox
천연두

[ˈsmɔːlˌpɒks]
a severe infectious disease eradicated worldwide
(syn) variola (medical term)
(e.g.) Historians noted that **smallpox** dramatically reduced the population.

obsolete
쓸모없는, 구식의

[ˌɑbsəˈliːt]
[ˈɔbsəˌliːt]
no longer in use; outdated or replaced by something newer
(syn) outdated, archaic, old-fashioned, antiquated
(opp) current, modern, up-to-date
(e.g.) **Obsolete** methods should be replaced with modern approaches.

base adjective
기본 형용사

[beɪs ˈædʒɪktɪv]
an adjective to which an affix attaches
(syn) original adjective
(e.g.) In the passage, the comparative affix *-er* attaches only to certain **base adjectives**, such as *happy → happier*.

passive counterpart
수동태 형태 대응물

['pæsɪv 'kɑʊntərpɑːrt]

the passive form corresponding to an active sentence
(syn) passive equivalent
(e.g.) Only a raised subject allows its sentence to share the same meaning with its **passive counterpart**.

astute
기민한, 영리한

[əstjúːt]

having or showing an ability to accurately assess situations or people and turn this to one's advantage
(syn) shrewd, perceptive, clever, insightful
(opp) naive, dull, foolish
(e.g.) Her **astute** observations improved the project's strategy.

prosaic
평범한, 상상력이 없는

[prouzéɪɪk]

ordinary and dull; lacking imagination or originality
(syn) mundane, banal, unimaginative, pedestrian
(opp) poetic, imaginative, creative
(e.g.) The report was accurate but rather **prosaic** in tone.

tenacious
끈질긴, 집요한

[tənéɪʃəs]

holding firmly to ideas, goals, or beliefs; persistent in maintaining or seeking something
(syn) persistent, determined, resolute, dogged
(opp) yielding, weak, irresolute
(e.g.) Her **tenacious** pursuit of justice earned her wide respect.

foreground
(n) 전경, (v) ~을 강조하여 부각시키다

['fɔːrgraʊnd]

(n) the part of a view that is nearest; (v) to make something prominent
(syn) highlight, emphasize
(e.g.) Failure and storytelling are intimate friends, always working in cahoots, constantly appearing in the **foreground** of human narratives.

DAY
05

incongruous
조화되지 않는, 부적절한

[ɪnkáŋgruəs]

not in harmony with surroundings or other elements; out of place
(syn) inconsistent, incompatible, discordant, absurd
(opp) harmonious, fitting, appropriate
(e.g.) His cheerful tone was **incongruous** with the tragic news.

transient
임시적인, 덧없는

[trǽnʃənt]

lasting for a short time; temporary or fleeting
(syn) temporary, momentary, brief, ephemeral
(opp) permanent, enduring, lasting
(e.g.) Fame is often **transient**, but integrity endures.

vindicate
정당함을 입증하다, 무죄를 입증하다

[víndɪkeɪt]

to clear someone of blame or suspicion; to justify or prove right
(syn) justify, exonerate, defend, uphold
(opp) condemn, blame, incriminate
(e.g.) The evidence served to **vindicate** her claims.

placate
달래다, 진정시키다

[pléɪkeɪt]

to make someone less angry or hostile
(syn) appease, pacify, soothe, conciliate
(opp) provoke, irritate, enrage
(e.g.) The manager tried to **placate** the upset customer with a refund.

유희태 일반영어

⑤ 기출 VOCA 30days

acquisition	○○○	semantically	○○○
pragmatic	○○○	surface structure	○○○
utterance	○○○	reverse	○○○
retain	○○○	modal	○○○
symptom	○○○	variant forms	○○○
comprehension	○○○	proposition	○○○
receptive	○○○	transitive	○○○
productive	○○○	Case-less	○○○
pedagogy	○○○	anomalous	○○○
prospectus	○○○	expletive	○○○
inductive	○○○	placeholder	○○○
communicative	○○○	unmarked	○○○
infiniteness	○○○	conjunction	○○○
multimodal	○○○	coordinating	○○○
embed	○○○	subordinating	○○○
reorder	○○○	coordinative	○○○
staged authenticity	○○○	assessment	○○○
cadence	○○○	principle	○○○
contiguous	○○○	efficacy	○○○
consonant	○○○	cater to	○○○
syllable	○○○	consistency	○○○
foot	○○○	extent	○○○
dissimilation	○○○	validated	○○○
segment	○○○	facility	○○○
morpheme	○○○	proportion	○○○
suffix	○○○	discrimination	○○○
repetition	○○○	commendable	○○○
seclusion	○○○	miskeying	○○○
ambiguity	○○○	anthropology	○○○
scope	○○○	pilot testing	○○○

acquisition
습득, 획득

[ˌækwɪˈzɪʃən]

the learning or developing of a skill, habit, or quality
(syn) attainment, gaining
(e.g.) The book discussed the role of input in second language **acquisition**.

pragmatic
화용론적인, 실용적인

[præɡˈmætɪk]

relating to the practical consequences or implications of something
(syn) practical, contextual
(e.g.) Speech acts are an important aspect of the **pragmatic** knowledge L2 learners need.

utterance
발화, 말

[ˈʌtərəns]

a spoken word, statement, or vocal sound
(syn) speech, expression
(e.g.) My students did not recognize the fact that an **utterance** may have some hidden intended effects.

retain
보유하다, 유지하다

[rɪˈteɪn]

to keep or continue to possess something
(syn) preserve, maintain, keep
(e.g.) Some English varieties do not *retain* /ɹ/ in the coda position.

symptom
증상, 어떤 현상을 드러내는 징후

[ˈsɪmptəm]

a sign indicating an underlying physical or situational condition
(syn) sign, indicator
(e.g.) Rising student anxiety is a **symptom** of deeper problems in the school environment.

comprehension
이해

[ˌkɒmprɪˈhenʃn]

the ability to understand something
(syn) understanding, grasp
(e.g.) Research suggests that L2 learners employ various strategies to increase **comprehension**.

receptive

수용적인, (언어) 수동적인

[rɪ'septɪv]

willing to consider or accept new suggestions and ideas; (in language) relating to listening or reading
(syn) open-minded, responsive
(e.g.) We have to make sure that both **receptive** and productive skills are included.

productive

생산적인, (언어) 발화 능동적인

[prə'dʌktɪv]

relating to the production of something; (in language) relating to speaking or writing
(syn) constructive, generative
(e.g.) We have to make sure that both receptive and **productive** skills are included.

pedagogy

교수법, 교육학

['pedəgɔʊdʒi]

the method and practice of teaching, especially as an academic subject or theoretical concept
(syn) teaching, education, instruction
(e.g.) Effective **pedagogy** is essential for student success in any curriculum.

prospectus

안내서, 요강

[prə'spektəs]

a printed document that advertises or describes a school, commercial enterprise, or other institution in order to attract or inform clients, members, or investors
(syn) brochure, catalog, outline
(e.g.) The university's **prospectus** provided detailed information about all available courses.

inductive

귀납적인

[ɪn'dʌktɪv]

characterized by the inference of general laws from particular instances
(syn) reasoning, inferential
(e.g.) Crucially, I prefer **inductive** activities and try to provide learning targets within context.

communicative
의사소통의

[kəˈmjuːnɪkətɪv]

relating to the exchange of information or news
(syn) interactive, expressive
(e.g.) The teacher's goal was to design **communicative** activities.

infiniteness
비정형성, 시제 · 인칭의 변화를 갖지 않는 성질

[ɪnˈfɪnɪtnəs]

the property of being non-finite and lacking tense/agreement marking
(syn) non-finiteness, tenselessness
(e.g.) The ungrammaticality results from the **infiniteness** of the embedded clause.

multimodal
다중 양식의

[ˌmʌltiˈmoʊdl]

characterized by several different modes of activity or occurrence
(syn) multisensory, mixed-mode
(e.g.) If various **multimodal** resources are available, my students will be able to express their ideas more creatively.

embed
(단단히) 박아 넣다, 삽입하다

[ɪmˈbed]

to fix (an object) firmly and deeply in a surrounding mass; to insert
(syn) insert, implant
(e.g.) The online platform allows students to incorporate photos and graphics or **embed** videos into their work.

reorder
재정렬하다, 다시 주문하다

[ˌriːˈɔːrdər]

to arrange (something) in a different or new sequence; to place an order for the same goods again
(syn) rearrange, reorganize
(e.g.) The teacher asked students to **reorder** the sentences to make a clear paragraph.

staged authenticity
연출된 진정성

[steɪdʒd ɔːθentɪˈsɪti]

a constructed version of cultural "realness" presented to tourists
(syn) performed authenticity, curated authenticity
(e.g.) The cultural experience remains **staged authenticity**, shaped by tourist expectations.

cadence
운율, 억양, (말의) 강약

[ˈkeɪdns]

a modulation or inflection of the voice; a sequence of notes or chords comprising the close of a musical phrase
(syn) rhythm, meter, tempo
(e.g.) The speaker's voice had a pleasing **cadence** that captivated the audience.

contiguous
인접한, 근접한

[kənˈtɪgjuəs]

sharing a common border; touching
(syn) adjacent, bordering, proximate
(e.g.) The two states are **contiguous**, sharing a long border.

consonant
자음

[ˈkɒnsənənt]

a basic speech sound in which the breath is at least partly obstructed
(syn) non-vowel
(e.g.) The indefinite article 'a' is used before a word that begins with a **consonant** sound.

syllable
음절

[ˈsɪləbl]

a unit of pronunciation having one vowel sound, with or without surrounding consonants
(syn) phonetic unit, beat
(e.g.) The suffix appears to avoid the repetition of /l/ in the final **syllable**.

DAY
06

foot

음보(音步), 강세를 기준으로 한 영어의 리듬 단위

[fʊt]

stress unit, rhythmic unit

(syn) metrical foot

(e.g.) In 'fourteen men,' the rightmost **foot** receives the primary stress, causing a stress-shift.

dissimilation

이화 (현상)

[dɪˌsɪmɪˈleɪʃən]

a phonological process in which two sounds that are too similar become less alike

(syn) differentiation, phonological process

(e.g.) Repeated segments in proximity are sometimes repaired by means of **dissimilation**.

segment

부분, 단편

[ˈsegmənt]

each of the parts into which something is or may be divided

(syn) section, portion

(e.g.) It is not unusual for a **segment** to appear repeatedly in a word.

morpheme

형태소

[ˈmɔːrfiːm]

a meaningful morphological unit of a language that cannot be further divided

(syn) linguistic unit

(e.g.) The past-tense **morpheme** is realized in three different phonetic forms.

suffix

접미사

[ˈsʌfɪks]

an affix that is added at the end of a word

(syn) ending, postposition

(e.g.) The -al **suffix** appears in the form of -ar to avoid the repetition of /l/.

repetition
반복

[ˌrepəˈtɪʃn]

the action of repeating something that has already been said or written
(syn) recurrence, reiteration
(e.g.) The -al suffix appears in the form -al to avoid the **repetition** of /l/.

seclusion
격리, 은둔

[sɪˈkluːʒn]

the state of being private and away from other people
(syn) isolation, solitude, privacy
(e.g.) He sought **seclusion** in the mountains to focus on his writing

ambiguity
모호함, 중의성

[ˌæmbɪˈgjuːəti]

the quality of being open to more than one interpretation
(syn) vagueness, obscurity
(e.g.) The sentence created **ambiguity** because it could be understood in two ways.

scope
범위

[skoʊp]

the extent of the area or subject matter that something deals with or to which it is relevant
(syn) range, extent
(e.g.) The teacher narrowed the **scope** of the topic to make it easier to discuss.

semantically
의미론적으로

[sɪˈmæntɪkli]

relating to meaning in language or logic
(syn) meaningfully, interpretively
(e.g.) Two sentences can look similar but differ **semantically** in meaning.

DAY
06

surface structure
표면 구조

['sɜːrfɪs 'strʌktʃər]

the structure of a sentence as it is pronounced or written, regardless of its underlying meaning
(syn) explicit form, linear order
(e.g.) The **surface structure** of the sentence hides its deeper grammatical relations.

reverse
뒤집다, 반대로 하다, 되돌리다

['riːvɜːrs]

to change something to its opposite, or return it to an earlier state
(syn) undo, invert
(e.g.) When the stress pattern was **reversed** in the phrase, the pronunciation shifted to keep natural English rhythm.

modal
양태의, 조동사

['moʊdl]

expressing possibility, necessity, or contingency (e.g., must, can, will)
(syn) auxiliary
(e.g.) Consider the two **modal** auxiliaries in relation to the negative.

variant forms
이형태, 형태소가 환경에 따라 달라지는 실현형

['vɛəriənt fɔːrmz]

different phonetic realizations of a single morpheme
(syn) alternate forms
(e.g.) Past-tense endings show several **variant forms** depending on the final consonant.

proposition
명제

[ˌprɒpə'zɪʃən]

a statement or idea that expresses a judgment or opinion; what a sentence conveys as meaning
(syn) statement, assertion, claim
(e.g.) Linguists analyze **propositions** to understand how meaning is structured in sentences.

transitive
타동사의

['trænzətɪv]

(of a verb or verb construction) taking a direct object
(e.g.) The Case-less NP problem can be solved by moving it to the object position of a **transitive** verb.

Case-less
격이 없는

['keɪsləs]

(in linguistics) lacking a grammatical case
(syn) uncased, without case
(e.g.) The ungrammaticality indicates that the NP the team is **Case-less**.

anomalous
변칙적인, 이례적인

[ə'nɑːmələs]

deviating from what is standard, normal, or expected
(syn) abnormal, irregular, atypical
(e.g.) Scientists observed an **anomalous** reading on the sensor.

DAY
06

expletive
(필요 없는) 덧붙이는 말·구

['eksplətɪv]

a word or phrase that serves to fill out a sentence or metrical line without adding to the sense
(syn) filler, placeholder
(e.g.) The **expletive** it, as a meaningless placeholder, can make the sentence grammatical.

placeholder
자리 표시자

['pleɪsˌhoʊldər]

a piece of text or an image that indicates where content should be inserted
(syn) marker, substitute
(e.g.) The expletive it is a meaningless **placeholder**.

unmarked
표적이 없는, 보통의

[ʌnˈmɑːrkt]

(in linguistics) the normal, expected, or default form of a word or structure
(syn) typical, default
(e.g.) In English, it is more typical, more frequent, so **unmarked**, for the person who experiences emotional feelings to appear in the subject position.

conjunction
접속사

[kənˈdʒʌŋkʃən]

a word used to connect clause or sentence
(syn) connective, link
(e.g.) We should incorporate coordinating and subordinating **conjunctions** into the syllabus.

coordinating
등위의, 조정하는

[koʊˈɔːrdɪneɪtɪŋ]

serving to connect grammatical units of equal status
(syn) linking, balancing
(e.g.) **Coordinating** conjunctions such as and and but were listed in the grammar section.

subordinating
종속적인

[səˈbɔːrdɪneɪtɪŋ]

placing in a lower rank or position; (in grammar) connecting a subordinate clause to a main clause
(syn) dependent, secondary
(e.g.) The grammar section listed **subordinating** conjunctions such as when and unless.

coordinative
대등하게 연결하는, 협력적인

[koʊˈɔːrdɪnətɪv]

serving to coordinate; of or involving coordination
(syn) connective, linking, collaborative
(e.g.) **Coordinative** conjunctions like "and" and "but" join elements of equal grammatical rank.

assessment 평가

[əˈsesmənt]

the evaluation or estimation of the nature, quality, or ability of someone or something
(syn) evaluation, appraisal
(e.g.) Item discrimination was part of the classroom **assessment** workshop.

principle 원리, 원칙

[ˈprɪnsəpl]

a fundamental truth or proposition that serves as the foundation for a system of belief or behavior
(syn) fundamental, rule
(e.g.) The issues they discuss are related to one of the **principles** of language assessment.

efficacy 효능, 유효성

[ˈefɪkəsi]

the ability to produce a desired or intended result
(syn) effectiveness, utility, potency
(e.g.) The **efficacy** of the new drug is still under investigation.

cater to (요구·기호를) 충족시키다, 맞추다

[ˈkeɪtər tuː]

to provide what is desired or demanded, often to satisfy a specific audience
(syn) serve, accommodate
(e.g.) The tourism industry continually **caters to** visitors searching for an authentic experience.

consistency 일관성

[kənˈsɪstənsi]

the quality of always behaving or being the same
(syn) uniformity, steadiness
(e.g.) Internal **consistency** was measured by Cronbach's alpha.

DAY
06

extent
정도, 규모

[ɪk'stent]

the degree to which something has spread or is comprehensive
(syn) scope, scale
(e.g.) The **extent** to which test takers' performances on this test are consistent is acceptable.

validated
검증된, 입증된

['vælɪdeɪtɪd]

shown or confirmed to be true, accurate, or possessing a required quality
(syn) confirmed, authenticated
(e.g.) The test scores were examined by correlation with the scores of the ERAT developed and **validated** by a well-known testing agency.

facility
(테스트 항목의) 용이도

[fə'sɪləti]

(in psychometrics) the degree to which an item is easy
(syn) easiness, item difficulty
(e.g.) Item difficulty (i.e., item **facility**) was measured by calculating the proportion of test takers who got the item correct.

proportion
비율, 비례

[prə'pɔːrʃn]

a part, share, or number considered in comparative relation to a whole
(syn) ratio, fraction
(e.g.) Item difficulty was measured by calculating the **proportion** of test takers who got the item correct.

discrimination
변별(력)

[dɪ,skrɪmɪ'neɪʃən]

the ability to distinguish between different groups or objects (in testing: the ability of an item to distinguish between high and low scorers)
(syn) differentiation, distinction
(e.g.) Item **discrimination** was assessed by item-total correlation.

commendable 칭찬할 만한, 훌륭한

[kəˈmendəbl]

deserving praise
(syn) praiseworthy, admirable, laudable
(e.g.) Her efforts to organize the charity event were truly **commendable**.

miskeying 오답 처리

[mɪsˈkiːɪŋ]

the error of incorrectly assigning the correct answer to a multiple-choice item
(syn) wrong key, scoring error
(e.g.) Item 3 should be carefully investigated in terms of the probability of **miskeying**.

anthropology 인류학

[ˌænθrəˈpɒlədʒi]

the study of humankind, in particular its societies and cultures
(syn) ethnology
(e.g.) The **anthropology** of tourism often overemphasizes the role of image consumers.

pilot testing 파일럿 테스트, 예비 시험

[ˈpaɪlət ˌtɛstɪŋ]

a small-scale trial run used to check whether a test, project, or procedure works properly before full implementation
(syn) trial run, preliminary testing
(e.g.) The assessment team conducted **pilot testing** to identify unclear items before administering the full exam.)

2024

DAY

07

유희태 일반영어
⑤ 기출 VOCA 30days

connective device	○○○	static	○○○
authenticity	○○○	erosion	○○○
aesthetic	○○○	degraded	○○○
artisan	○○○	virtual	○○○
intangible	○○○	recognition	○○○
tangible	○○○	audiovisual	○○○
overemphasize	○○○	ethical	○○○
craving	○○○	controversy	○○○
ingenious	○○○	empirical	○○○
intrusion	○○○	enterprise	○○○
intercultural	○○○	apparent	○○○
reinforcing	○○○	expedite	○○○
evolutionary	○○○	complexity	○○○
tenet	○○○	deduce	○○○
equilibrium	○○○	demands	○○○
reliable	○○○	locating	○○○
alter	○○○	inferencing	○○○
manipulator	○○○	methodology	○○○
receiver	○○○	exposure	○○○
disassociated	○○○	facilitate	○○○
potentially	○○○	detection	○○○
yield	○○○	prominent	○○○
digital	○○○	noticeable	○○○
analog	○○○	component	○○○
algorithm	○○○	correspond	○○○
encoded	○○○	appreciate	○○○
finite	○○○	outward	○○○
numerical	○○○	vibrant	○○○
representation	○○○	awaken	○○○
proctor	○○○	transformative	○○○

connective device

연결 장치, 아이디어를 논리적으로 연결하는 표현

[kəˈnɛktɪv dɪˈvaɪs]

a linguistic element such as a conjunction and adverb used to link ideas and improve coherence
(syn) linking device, cohesive tie
(e.g.) Students need more **connective devices** to make their business writing coherent.

authenticity

진정성, 진짜임

[ˌɔːθenˈtɪsəti]

the quality of being genuine or true
(syn) genuineness, validity
(e.g.) The tourist is continually in search of **authentic** experience.

aesthetic

미적인, 미학적인

[iːsˈθetɪk]

concerned with beauty or the appreciation of beauty
(syn) artistic, visual
(e.g.) The artisan developed an **aesthetic** view that satisfied his own cultural identity.

artisan

장인, 숙련공

[ˈɑːrtəzn]

a worker skilled in a trade, especially one that involves making things by hand
(syn) craftsperson, maker
(e.g.) The longer an **artisan** was in the business of producing "tourist art," the more he developed an aesthetic.

intangible

만질 수 없는, 무형의

[ɪnˈtændʒəbl]

unable to be touched or grasped; not having physical presence
(syn) abstract, elusive
(e.g.) Cultural products include tangible and **intangible** creations.

tangible
지나치게 강조하다 만질 수 있는, 유형의

[ˈtændʒəbl]

perceptible by touch; clear and definite
(syn) physical, concrete
(e.g.) Use tasks that require students to produce concrete and **tangible** outcomes.

overemphasize
지나치게 강조하다

[ˌoʊvərˈemfəsaɪz]

to place too much emphasis on something
(syn) exaggerate, overstress
(e.g.) Semiotics **overemphasize** the role of image consumers at the expense of the process of image creation.

craving
갈망, 열망

[ˈkreɪvɪŋ]

a powerful desire for something
(syn) longing, yearning
(e.g.) The tourist industry caters to this **craving** by using ingenuous ways.

DAY
07

ingenious
솔직 담백한, 기발한

[ɪnˈdʒiːniəs]

cleverly and originally devised
(syn) inventive, clever
(e.g.) The tourist industry caters to this craving by using evermore **ingenious** ways to let the tourist gaze.

intrusion
침범, 방해

[ɪnˈtruːʒn]

the action of thrusting or forcing in
(syn) encroachment, interruption
(e.g.) Most tourists prefer not to think about the numerous human **intrusions** (e.g., ski lifts).

intercultural 이문화 간의

[ˌɪntərˈkʌltʃərəl]

relating to or existing between two or more cultures
(syn) cross-cultural, bicultural
(e.g.) The goal of the course is to help students develop **intercultural** competence.

reinforcing 강화하는

[ˌriːɪnˈfɔːrsɪŋ]

strengthening or supporting something
(syn) strengthening, confirming
(e.g.) Teachers should avoid **reinforcing** associations between nationalities and cultures.

evolutionary 진화의

[ˌevəˈluːʃəneri]

relating to the process of biological evolution
(syn) developmental, adaptive
(e.g.) At an **evolutionary** equilibrium, both signalers and receivers must benefit.

tenet 주의, 교리

[ˈtenɪt]

a principle or belief, especially one of the main principles of a religion or philosophy
(syn) doctrine, principle
(e.g.) A central **tenet** of signaling theory is that both signalers and receivers must benefit.

equilibrium 균형, 평형

[ˌiːkwɪˈlɪbriəm]

a state of balance
(syn) balance, stability
(e.g.) As the population approached an evolutionary **equilibrium**, reliable signaling would disappear.

reliable

신뢰할 수 있는

[rɪˈlaɪəbl]

able to be trusted; consistently good in quality or performance
(syn) trustworthy, dependable
(e.g.) **Reliable** signaling would disappear altogether.

alter

(성질·모양·크기 등을) 바꾸다, 변경하다

[ˈɔːltər]

to change the character or composition of something
(syn) modify, transform
(e.g.) A signal is a behavior or structure that **alters** the actions of other organisms.

manipulator

조종자

[məˈnɪpjuleɪtər]

a percon or organism that controls or influences skillfully or unfairly
(syn) controller, influencer
(e.g.) Krebs and Dawkins describe animal signaling as an arms race between **manipulators** (signalers) and mind-readers (receivers).

receiver

수신자, (신호의) 수용자

[rɪˈsiːvər]

an organism that detects a signal
(syn) recipient, detector
(e.g.) Dishonesty occurs when a **receiver** registers X from a signaler.

disassociated

분리된, 연관성이 끊어진

[ˌdɪsəˈsoʊʃieɪtɪd]

detached or disconnected from something else
(syn) separated, detached
(e.g.) Dishonest communication occurs when a signal becomes **disassociated** from the signaler's ability or need.

potentially

잠재적으로, 어쩌면

[pəˈtenʃəli]

with the capacity to develop into something in the future
(syn) possibly, maybe
(e.g.) Dishonesty **potentially** delivers notable rewards.

DAY

07

yield
양보하다, 내어주다

[jiːld]

to surrender possession of (something); to supply or bear (a product or result)
(syn) surrender, concede
(e.g.) A weak individual might convince others to **yield** resources.

digital
디지틸의

[ˈdɪdʒɪtl]

relating to or denoting information expressed in numerical form
(syn) computerized, electronic
(e.g.) A phone produces a **digital** representation of an object.

analog
아날로그의

[ˈænɔːlɔːg]

relating to or denoting a mechanism in which data is represented by measurable physical quantities
(syn) non-digital
(e.g.) Our parents' **analog** photos have degraded over time.

algorithm
알고리즘

[ˈælgərɪðəm]

a process or set of rules to be followed in calculations or other problem-solving operations
(syn) procedure, computation
(e.g.) Digital representations are often encoded by **algorithms**.

encoded
암호화된, 부호화된

[ɪnˈkoʊdɪd]

converted into a coded form
(syn) ciphered, digitized
(e.g.) Digital representations are **encoded** by algorithms.

finite
유한한, 한정된

[ˈfaɪnaɪt]

having limits or bounds (in linguistics: a verb form that shows tense)
(syn) limited, restricted
(e.g.) The phone produces a digital representation using a **finite** set of symbols.

numerical
숫자의, 수의

[nuːˈmerɪkl]

relating to or expressed as a number or numbers
(syn) quantitative, mathematical
(e.g.) The camera divides our face into a **numerical** grid.

representation
표현, 표상

[ˌreprɪzenˈteɪʃn]

the action of speaking or acting on behalf of someone or the way something is shown
(syn) depiction, image
(e.g.) When we paint on canvas we create a purely physical **representation**.

proctor
(지문 내에서) 음운 변화를 보이는 예시 단어

[ˈprɑːktər]

a lexical item used to illustrate consonant alternation under suffixation
(syn) example word, model item
(e.g.) Words like *torture* and *proctor* show the change in final consonants when suffixes are added.

static
정적인, 고정된

[ˈstætɪk]

lacking in movement, action, or change
(syn) fixed, unmoving
(e.g.) Rather than being something **static**, this digital representation can be manipulated.

erosion
침식, 약화

[ɪˈroʊʒn]

the gradual destruction of something
(syn) degradation, deterioration
(e.g.) Digital representations can be stored for long periods of time without **erosion** of information.

DAY

07

degraded
손상된, 저하된

[dɪˈɡreɪdɪd]

reduced in quality or value
(syn) deteriorated, impaired
(e.g.) Unlike analog photos which have **degraded** over time, the digital image will remain the same.

virtual
가상의

[ˈvɜːrtʃuəl]

almost or nearly as described, but not literally or actually; carried out or existing using computer technology
(syn) simulated, digital
(e.g.) When teachers use this **virtual** reality simulation app, they can invite their students into the virtual space.

recognition
인식, 인지

[ˌrekəɡˈnɪʃn]

the action or process of recognizing or being recognized
(syn) identification, awareness
(e.g.) Students can use voice **recognition** software to bridge the gap between oral and written language.

audiovisual
시청각의

[ˌɔːdiəʊˈvɪʒuəl]

using both sight and sound, typically in the form of slides or video
(syn) multimedia, A/V
(e.g.) Teachers should utilize different types of **audiovisual** aids.

ethical
윤리적인, 도덕적인

[ˈeθɪkl]

relating to moral principles
(syn) moral, principled
(e.g.) All researchers must follow a strict set of **ethical** guidelines when conducting studies.

controversy
논란, 논쟁

[ˈkɒntrəvɜːrsi]

a prolonged public disagreement or heated discussion
(syn) dispute, argument
(e.g.) The new policy caused **controversy** among teachers and parents.

empirical

경험적인, 실증적인

[ɪmˈpɪrɪkl]

based on, concerned with, or verifiable by observation or experience
(syn) experimental, observational
(e.g.) The scientist collected **empirical** data to support her research findings.)

enterprise

사업, 새로운 시도

[ˈentərˌpraɪz]

a purposeful business venture or undertaking involving initiative
(syn) venture, undertaking
(e.g.) He sold his horse and started an independent **enterprise** of his own.

apparent

분명한, 명백한

[əˈpærənt]

clearly visible or understood; obvious
(syn) evident, distinct
(e.g.) It is **apparent** that my students misunderstood the acts my utterances performed.

expedite

신속히 처리하다, 촉진하다

[ˈekspɪdaɪt]

to make an action or process happen more quickly
(syn) accelerate, facilitate
(e.g.) The new software was designed to **expedite** data analysis.

DAY

07

complexity

복잡성

[kəmˈpleksəti]

the state of being intricate or complicated
(syn) intricacy, complication
(e.g.) The level of task difficulty is impacted by the **complexity** of vocabulary and grammar.

deduce

추론하다, 연역하다

[dɪˈdjuːs]

to reach a conclusion through reasoning or logical inference
(syn) infer, conclude
(e.g.) From the evidence, the scientist **deduced** that the species had adapted to colder climates.

demands
구체적인 요구 (사항), 요청들

[dɪˈmændz]
pressing requirements or burdens
(syn) requirements, burdens
(e.g.) Task difficulty is impacted by the processing **demands** of a task.

locating
찾아내기, 위치를 파악하기

[ˈloʊkeɪtɪŋ]
discovering the exact place or position of something
(syn) finding, positioning
(e.g.) Processing demands include **locating** information and inferencing.

inferencing
추론하기

[ˈɪnfərɪnsɪŋ]
the process of deducing or concluding information
(syn) deduction, reasoning
(e.g.) Processing demands include locating information and **inferencing**.

methodology
방법론, 연구 방법

[ˌmeθəˈdɒlədʒi]
a system of methods used in a particular area of study or activity
(syn) approach, procedure
(e.g.) His research **methodology** combines quantitative and qualitative data.

exposure
노출, 접하게 함

[ɪkˈspoʊʒər]
the state of being subjected to something
(syn) contact, experience
(e.g.) Teachers need to increase the frequency of **exposure** to certain words and phrases.

facilitate
용이하게 하다, 촉진하다

[fəˈsɪlɪteɪt]
to make an action or process easy or easier
(syn) aid, assist
(e.g.) The frequency of exposure helps to **facilitate** noticing and detection.

detection
발견, 감지

[dɪˈtekʃən]

the action or process of identifying the presence of something
(syn) recognition, sensing
(e.g.) The frequency of exposure helps to facilitate noticing and **detection**.

prominent
눈에 잘 띄는, 두드러진

[ˈprɒmɪnənt]

standing out so as to be easily seen; important or famous
(syn) conspicuous, noticeable
(e.g.) The term is defined as how **prominent** or easy a certain input is to hear or read.

noticeable
눈에 띄는, 현저한

[ˈnoʊtɪsəbl]

easily observed; attracting attention
(syn) visible, prominent
(e.g.) Features that are more prominent or easier may be more **noticeable** and will attract attention.

component
구성 요소, 부품

[kəmˈpoʊnənt]

a part that makes up a whole
(syn) element, factor
(e.g.) The teacher trainer explained the **components** of the Item Analysis table.

correspond
일치하다, 부합하다

[ˌkɒrɪˈspɒnd]

to be in agreement or conformity with
(syn) match, align
(e.g.) I need to choose the components that do NOT **correspond** to the teachers' ideas.

appreciate
이해하다, 가치를 인식하거나 고마움을 느끼다

[əˈpriːʃɪeɪt]

to recognize the value or significance of something; to be grateful for something
(syn) recognize, value, be grateful for
(e.g.) Students gradually **appreciate** the importance of meaningful interaction in language learning.

outward
바깥의, 외형적인

['aʊtwərd]

directed toward or relating to the outside or surface of something
(syn) external, exterior, outside
(e.g.) The building's **outward** appearance was simple but elegant.

vibrant
활기찬, 생기 있는

['vaɪbrənt]

full of life or excitement
(syn) lively, animated
(e.g.) Her freedom ultimately awakens in her a **vibrant** state of being.

awaken
일깨우다, 각성시키다

[ə'weɪkənz]

to arouse a feeling or realization
(syn) stir, rouse
(e.g.) Her freedom ultimately **awakens** in her a sense of freedom.

transformative
변화시키는, 변형적인

[træns'fɔːrmətɪv]

causing a marked change in someone or something
(syn) altering, revolutionary
(e.g.) The woman experiences a **transformative** change both in her location and social status.

유희태 일반영어

⑤ 기출 VOCA 30days

flourish	○○○	administrator	○○○
sparse	○○○	arrangement	○○○
grandiose	○○○	by-product	○○○
staged	○○○	cognates	○○○
interplay	○○○	compliment	○○○
wriggling	○○○	consensus	○○○
warily	○○○	context	○○○
lag	○○○	decent	○○○
hollow	○○○	discursive	○○○
solitude	○○○	macroeconomic	○○○
personification	○○○	appropriate	○○○
monologue	○○○	preoccupied	○○○
vocalize	○○○	hierarchical	○○○
voice recognition	○○○	framed	○○○
aspiring	○○○	intercourse	○○○
irremediably	○○○	excursion	○○○
undertaking	○○○	tractable	○○○
autonomous	○○○	prenatal	○○○
farmhand	○○○	threshold effect	○○○
saloon	○○○	multi-layered	○○○
haul	○○○	negotiation	○○○
rubbish	○○○	novice	○○○
irreplaceable	○○○	outcome	○○○
assert	○○○	utilitarian	○○○
meticulously	○○○	parallelism	○○○
intentionally	○○○	individualized	○○○
steadily	○○○	viewpoint	○○○
permissive	○○○	compendium	○○○
investigated	○○○	proximity	○○○
essence	○○○	recall	○○○

flourish
번창하다, 잘 자라다

['flɜːrɪʃ]

to grow or develop in a healthy or vigorous way
(syn) thrive, prosper
(e.g.) While tourism research has begun to **flourish**, the studies dealing with expressive culture are relatively sparse.

sparse
드문, 희박한

[spɑːrs]

thinly dispersed or scattered
(syn) scant, infrequent
(e.g.) The studies dealing with tourism and expressive culture are relatively **sparse**.

grandiose
웅장한, 거창한

['grændiəʊs]

impressive and imposing in appearance or style, especially pretentiously so
(syn) magnificent, imposing
(e.g.) The Alps offer a **grandiose** physical environment.

staged
연출된, 계획된

[steɪdʒd]

organized and presented as a show
(syn) performed, orchestrated
(e.g.) The whole event felt **staged**, not natural at all.

interplay
상호 작용

['ɪntərpleɪ]

the way in which two or more things affect each other
(syn) interaction, connection
(e.g.) There's a strong **interplay** between light and shadow in this photo.

wriggling
꿈틀거리는

['rɪglɪŋ]

twisting or moving from side to side
(syn) squirming, twisting
(e.g.) The baby was **wriggling** in her arms.

warily
조심스럽게

['weərəli]

carefully and with attention
(syn) cautiously, carefully
(e.g.) He stepped **warily** into the dark room.

lag
뒤처지다

[læg]

to move or develop more slowly than others
(syn) trail, fall behind
(e.g.) Our team **lags** behind in technology.

hollow
움푹한 곳, 골짜기

['hɒloʊ]

a small valley or dip in the ground
(syn) dip, pit
(e.g.) The stream runs through a **hollow** between the hills.

solitude
고독, 외로움

['sɑːlɪtuːd]

the state of being alone, often peacefully
(syn) loneliness, isolation
(e.g.) She enjoys the **solitude** of early mornings.

personification
의인화

[pərˌsɒnɪfɪˈkeɪʃn]

giving human qualities to something non-human
(syn) embodiment, anthropomorphism
(e.g.) The poem uses the **personification** of the wind to show emotion.

monologue
독백

['mɒnəlɒg]

a long speech by one person
(syn) soliloquy, speech
(e.g.) Mr. Jung played a **monologue** to his students in class.

DAY

08

vocalize
말로 표현하다, 소리 내다

['voʊkəlaɪz]
to utter or say (something)
(syn) express, articulate
(e.g.) I usually ask my students to **vocalize** these goals together.

voice recognition
음성 인식, 말소리를 분석하여 문자나 명령으로 변환하는 기술

[ˌvɔɪs ˌrɛkəgˈnɪʃən]
technology that converts spoken language into text or commands
(syn) speech recognition, speech-to-text
(e.g.) With **voice recognition**, learners can record themselves and instantly see which words they mispronounced.

aspiring
야심 있는, 포부가 큰

[əˈspaɪərɪŋ]
having a strong desire and determination to achieve something
(syn) ambitious, driven
(e.g.) The **aspiring** young artist moved to the city to follow her dreams.

irremediably
고칠 수 없게, 회복 불가능하게

[ˌɪrɪˈmiːdiəbli]
in a way that cannot be fixed or corrected
(syn) incurably, hopelessly
(e.g.) He was **irremediably** proud of his achievements, blind to his own faults.

undertaking
(어렵지만 도전적인) 일, 사업

['ʌndərteɪkɪŋ]
an important or difficult task or project
(syn) enterprise, venture
(e.g.) Building the bridge was a massive **undertaking** that took five years.

autonomous
자율적인, 독립적인

[ɔːˈtɒnəməs]
acting freely and independently, without control by others
(syn) independent, self-governing
(e.g.) The company allows each branch to make **autonomous** decisions.

farmhand | 농장 일꾼

['fɑːrmhænd]

a worker on a farm
(syn) laborer, farm worker
(e.g.) My father worked as a **farmhand** until he was thirty-four years old.

saloon | (과거의) 술집, 선술집

[sə'luːn]

a public room or building formerly used for a specified purpose; a bar
(syn) pub, bar
(e.g.) In town he drank beer and stood about in Ben Head's **saloon**.

haul | (무거운 것을) 운반하다, 나르다

[hɔːl]

to pull or drag with effort or force
(syn) carry, transport
(e.g.) I don't want to be carrying nobody's rubbish or **haul** people's rubbish.

rubbish | 쓰레기

['rʌbɪʃ]

waste material; refuse
(syn) garbage, trash
(e.g.) I can get you on the **rubbish** if you want to work.

irreplaceable | 대체할 수 없는

[ˌɪrɪ'pleɪsəbl]

impossible to replace if lost or damaged
(syn) unique, essential
(e.g.) Lyons insists that music is an essential and **irreplaceable** part of his life.

assert | 주장하다, 단언하다

[ə's3ːrt]

to state a fact or belief confidently and forcefully
(syn) insist, maintain
(e.g.) She **asserts** that everyone has the right to equal treatment.

DAY
08

meticulously
세심하게, 꼼꼼하게

[məˈtɪkjələsli]
in a very careful and detailed way
(syn) thoroughly, carefully
(e.g.) He **meticulously** checked every reference before submitting his paper.

intentionally
의도적으로, 고의로

[ɪnˈtenʃənəli]
done on purpose; deliberately
(syn) deliberately, purposefully
(e.g.) The writer **intentionally** left the ending open to interpretation.

steadily
꾸준히, 점차

[ˈstedɪli]
in a consistent or gradual way
(syn) gradually, progressively
(e.g.) The patient's health **steadily** improved over several weeks.

permissive
관대한, 허용을 많이 하는

[pərˈmɪsɪv]
allowing many behaviors that others might restrict
(syn) tolerant
(e.g.) A **permissive** environment encourages creativity.

investigated
조사된, 연구된

[ɪnˈvestɪɡeɪtɪd]
formally examined or inquired into
(syn) examined, researched
(e.g.) Item 3 should be carefully **investigated** in terms of the probability of miskeying.

essence
본질, 핵심

[ˈesns]
the intrinsic nature or indispensable quality of something
(syn) core, heart
(e.g.) The numbers make up the **essence** of our digital image.

administrator
관리자, 행정 담당자

[əd'mɪnɪstreɪtər]

a person responsible for running a business, organization, etc.
(syn) manager, executive
(e.g.) **Administrators** are responsible for securing the necessary resources for the test.

arrangement
준비, (합의된) 약속

[ə'reɪndʒmənt]

plans or preparation made for a future event
(syn) plans, agreement
(e.g.) Mr. Garner agreed to the **arrangement** with Halle.

by-product
부산물, 부수적으로 생기는 결과

['baɪ ˌprɒdʌkt]

a secondary result, often unexpected or unintended
(syn) consequence, side effect
(e.g.) Image creation is a **by-product** of the tourist industry.

cognates
동족어

['kɒgneɪts]

words that have a common origin (and often similar form and meaning)
(syn) relatives, related words
(e.g.) One listening strategy is identifying **cognates**.

compliment
칭찬

['kɒmplɪmənt]

a polite expression of praise or admiration
(syn) praise, flattery
(e.g.) Since I made a **compliment**, I expected a simple thank-you from the student.

consensus
의견 일치, 합의

[kən'sensəs]

general agreement
(syn) agreement, accord
(e.g.) The most popular design principles utilize **consensus**-building activities.

DAY

08

context
맥락, 상황

['kɒntekst]

the circumstances that form the setting for an event or idea
(syn) background, framework
(e.g.) I try to provide learning targets within **context**.

decent
괜찮은, 품위 있는

['diːsnt]

of an acceptable standard; good
(syn) acceptable, respectable
(e.g.) Lyons said he can't find no **decent** job.

discursive
담론적인, 논증적인

[dɪ'skɜːrsɪv]

proceeding by reasoned argument rather than intuition; relating to extended verbal expression
(syn) analytical, expository
(e.g.) The researcher adopted a **discursive** approach to examine the ideological function of language.

macroeconomic
거시경제의

[ˌmækroʊˌiːkə'nɒmɪk]

relating to large-scale economic factors such as national productivity or interest rates
(e.g.) The paper investigates the **macroeconomic** consequences of fiscal decentralization.

appropriate
전용하다, 도용하다

[ə'proʊprieɪt]

to take something for one's own use, typically without permission
(syn) usurp, commandeer
(e.g.) The state **appropriated** local resources for industrial expansion.

preoccupied
몰두한, 사로잡힌

[priˈɒkjupaɪd]

absorbed in thought; mentally engaged to the exclusion of other things
(syn) absorbed, engrossed
(e.g.) The critic was **preoccupied** with questions of authenticity in postmodern art.

hierarchical
위계적인, 계층적인

[ˌhaɪəˈrɑːrkɪkl]

arranged in levels of rank or authority
- (syn) stratified, tiered
- (e.g.) The company maintains a **hierarchical** management structure resistant to reform.

framed
(틀에 넣어) 만들어진, 짜인

[freɪmd]

constructed, conceived, or planned
- (syn) shaped, formulated
- (e.g.) I believe that lesson goals should be **framed** from the students' perspective.

intercourse
교류, 교제

[ˈɪntərkɔːrs]

communication or dealings between individuals or groups
- (syn) exchange, communication
- (e.g.) He drove into town to spend a few hours in social **intercourse**.

excursion
짧은 여행, 소풍, 탐방,

[ɪkˈskɜːʒn]

a short journey, especially for leisure or study
- (syn) itinerary, expedition
- (e.g.) The field linguistics team planned an **excursion** to collect dialect samples.

tractable
다루기 쉬운, 유순한

[ˈtræktəbl]

easily managed or influenced; malleable
- (syn) manageable, compliant
- (e.g.) The data proved surprisingly **tractable** for computational analysis.

prenatal
출산 전의, 태아기의

[priˈneɪtl]

relating to the period before birth; during or relating to pregnancy
- (syn) maternal, antenatal
- (e.g.) The study focused on **prenatal** nutrition and fetal development.

DAY
08

threshold effect
임계 효과, 일정 수준을 넘은 뒤에 급격한 변화가 나타나는 현상

[ˈθrɛʃhoʊld ɪˈfɛkt]
a phenomenon in which noticeable change occurs only after a critical level is reached
(syn) critical-mass effect, tipping-point effect
(e.g.) Learners often exhibit a **threshold effect** in speaking development after sufficient exposure and practice.

multi-layered
다층적인

[ˈmʌlti ˈleɪərd]
having many layers or levels
(syn) multi-level, complex
(e.g.) I think a **multi-layered** syllabus would be most appropriate.

negotiation
협상, 교섭

[nɪˌɡoʊʃiˈeɪʃn]
discussion aimed at reaching an agreement
(syn) bargaining, discussion
(e.g.) Unit 2 focuses on Business **Negotiation**.

novice
초보자, 미숙한 사람

[ˈnɒvɪs]
a person new to or inexperienced in a field or situation
(syn) beginner, amateur
(e.g.) Ms. Min, a **novice** middle school English teacher, conducted a survey.

outcome
결과, 성과

[ˈaʊtkʌm]
the way a thing turns out; a consequence
(syn) result, consequence
(e.g.) Use tasks that require students to produce concrete and tangible **outcomes**.

utilitarian
실용적인, 공리주의적인

[juːˌtɪlɪˈtɛəriən]
designed for usefulness over beauty; related to utilitarian philosophy
(syn) practical, functional
(e.g.) The building has a **utilitarian** design focused on efficiency.

parallelism
유사성, 병행

[ˈpærəlelɪzəm]

the state of being parallel or corresponding in some way
(syn) similarity, correspondence
(e.g.) The unexpected **parallelism** between passive and raising predicates can be accounted for.

individualized
개별화된

[ˌɪndɪˈvɪdʒuəlaɪzd]

tailored to the specific needs or characteristics of a particular person
(syn) personalized, customized
(e.g.) The program provides **individualized** feedback to support each learner's progress.

viewpoint
관점, 시각

[ˈvjuːpɔɪnt]

a particular attitude or position from which something is considered
(syn) perspective, outlook
(e.g.) The novel presents history from a distinctly feminist **viewpoint**.

compendium
요약서, 작품집

[kəmˈpendiəm]

a concise but comprehensive collection of information or works
(syn) portfolio, anthology
(e.g.) The museum published a **compendium** of modern art criticism.

DAY
08

proximity
근접, 가까움

[prɒkˈsɪməti]

nearness in space, time, or relationship
(syn) closeness, vicinity
(e.g.) Repeated segments in **proximity** are sometimes repaired.

recall
기억해 내다, 회상하다

[rɪˈkɔːl]

to bring (a fact, event, or situation) back into one's mind
(syn) recollect, remember
(e.g.) I **recall** a couple of examples in particular.

2023

DAY

09

유희태 일반영어

⑤ 기출 VOCA 30days

referential	○○○	vicious	○○○
snippet	○○○	delicate	○○○
unsettling	○○○	archaic	○○○
volatility	○○○	inconsistency	○○○
faith	○○○	unequivocal	○○○
constant flux	○○○	suppress	○○○
discretion	○○○	ambiguous	○○○
confound	○○○	conjectural	○○○
intrinsic	○○○	presumably	○○○
extrinsic	○○○	adhere	○○○
contingency	○○○	prolonged	○○○
adverse	○○○	discrepancy	○○○
vulnerability	○○○	transcend	○○○
tenacity	○○○	resort	○○○
eminent	○○○	drastic	○○○
intrapersonal	○○○	deter	○○○
stifle	○○○	pervasive	○○○
divulge	○○○	precedent	○○○
recondite	○○○	commence	○○○
subtle	○○○	elaboration	○○○
paradoxical	○○○	consequence	○○○
predicament	○○○	articulate	○○○
reminiscence	○○○	exhaustive	○○○
reliance	○○○	concrete	○○○
resigned	○○○	adequate	○○○
disdain	○○○	obsess	○○○
humiliation	○○○	practical	○○○
sorrow	○○○	diminish	○○○
pity	○○○	allocate	○○○
trivial	○○○	elucidate	○○○

referential
지시하는, 참조의

[ˌrefəˈrenʃl]

relating to or referring to something
(syn) indicative, denotative
(e.g.) I like to ask **referential** questions that are more related to the students' life.

snippet
단편, 토막

[ˈsnɪpɪt]

a small piece of something
(syn) fragment, extract
(e.g.) The **snippet** from the front of the text was only a few lines.

unsettling
불안하게 하는, 동요시키는

[ʌnˈsetlɪŋ]

causing worry or anxiety; disturbing
(syn) disturbing, alarming, bothersome
(e.g.) The letter's vague message had an **unsettling** effect on him.

volatility
변동성, 불안정성

[ˌvɒləˈtɪləti]

the quality of changing quickly and unpredictably
(syn) instability, unpredictability, turbulence
(e.g.) Investors stayed cautious because of the recent market **volatility**.

faith
신뢰, 믿음

[feɪθ]

strong trust or confidence
(syn) trust, confidence
(e.g.) With automation bias, our **faith** in software becomes stronger than our trust in our senses.

constant flux
끊임없는 변화

[ˌkɒnstənt flʌks]

continual change or movement
(syn) continual shift
(e.g.) Inuit hunters track snow formations that remain in **constant flux**.

discretion
재량, 신중함

[dɪˈskreʃn]

the right or ability to decide something; careful judgment
(syn) judgment, freedom of choice, prudence
(e.g.) The manager handled the issue at her own **discretion**.

confound
당황하게 하다, 뒤섞다

[kənˈfaʊnd]

to confuse or surprise someone
(syn) perplex, bewilder, confuse
(e.g.) The sudden change in data **confounded** the researchers.

intrinsic
본질적인, 내재적인

[ɪnˈtrɪnzɪk]

belonging naturally; essential
(syn) inherent, innate, fundamental
(e.g.) Curiosity is an **intrinsic** part of learning.

extrinsic
외재적인, 외적인

[ekˈstrɪnsɪk]

coming from outside rather than from within
(syn) external, acquired, irrelevant
(e.g.) Grades are an **extrinsic** form of motivation for students.

contingency
우발성, 우발 사건

[kənˈtɪndʒənsi]

a possible event that may happen in the future
(syn) eventuality, possibility, chance
(e.g.) The company prepared a **contingency** plan for emergencies.

adverse
불리한, 해로운

[ˈædvɜːrs]

having a harmful or negative effect
(syn) unfavorable, detrimental, negative
(e.g.) The new law had an **adverse** impact on small businesses.

vulnerability
취약성

[ˌvʌlnərəˈbɪləti]

the state of being open to harm or attack
(syn) susceptibility, weakness, exposure
(e.g.) This software has a serious **vulnerability** to cyberattacks.

DAY
09

tenacity
끈기, 불굴의 정신

[təˈnæsəti]
persistent determination and strength in continuing despite difficulties
(syn) perseverance, endurance
(e.g.) Her **tenacity** helped her finish the project even when everyone else gave up.

eminent
탁월한, 저명한

[ˈemɪnənt]
highly distinguished or respected in a particular field
(syn) distinguished, notable
(e.g.) She studied under an **eminent** scholar who was known worldwide for his research.

intrapersonal
내적 관계의

[ˌɪntrəˈpɜːrsənl]
relating to one's inner thoughts, feelings, and self-awareness
(syn) introspective, self-reflective
(e.g.) The course focuses on **intrapersonal** skills such as self-reflection and emotional awareness.

stifle
억누르다, 억압하다

[ˈstaɪfl]
to suppress or hold back the expression or development of something
(syn) restrain, suppress
(e.g.) Strict rules can **stifle** students' creativity if they are not applied carefully.

divulge
누설하다, 폭로하다

[daɪˈvʌldʒ]
to reveal private or sensitive information intentionally
(syn) reveal, disclose
(e.g.) He refused to **divulge** any details about the investigation.

recondite
난해한, 심오한

[ˈrekəndaɪt]
dealing with obscure or difficult-to-understand ideas
(syn) abstruse, esoteric
(e.g.) The professor's lecture covered **recondite** theories that many students struggled to understand.

subtle | 미묘한, 감지하기 힘든

['sʌtl]

delicate and precise in meaning or expression; not obvious or easy to perceive; cleverly indirect
(syn) delicate, faint, nuanced
(e.g.) There was a **subtle** shift in the character's tone that hinted at his hidden anger.

paradoxical | 역설적인, 모순적인

[ˌpærə'dɒksɪkl]

seeming to contradict itself or defy logic, yet possibly containing a deeper truth
(syn) contradictory, self-refuting, illogical
(e.g.) It is **paradoxical** that the pursuit of happiness often leads to greater frustration.

predicament | 곤경, 처지, 궁지

[prɪ'dɪkəmənt]

a difficult, unpleasant, or embarrassing situation that is hard to escape from
(syn) dilemma, difficult situation, plight
(e.g.) The financial crisis left the entire family in a severe **predicament** with no easy solution.

reminiscence | 추억, 회상

[ˌremɪ'nɪsns]

the act of recalling past experiences or events, often with affection or nostalgia
(syn) recollection, remembrance
(e.g.) The old man's story was filled with gentle **reminiscence** about his youth.

DAY
09

reliance | 의존

[rɪ'laɪəns]

dependence on something
(syn) dependence
(e.g.) **Reliance** on GPS has weakened hunters' ability to navigate independently.

resigned
체념한, 단념한

[rɪ'zaɪnd]

having accepted something unpleasant or unavoidable without protest

(syn) acquiescent, submissive, fatalistic

(e.g.) He gave a **resigned** shrug, knowing he could not change the long-established policy.

disdain
경멸, 무시

[dɪs'deɪn]

a strong feeling of contempt or scorn toward something considered unworthy of respect

(syn) contempt, scorn, haughtiness

(e.g.) The critic viewed the popular novel with intellectual **disdain**.

humiliation
굴욕, 창피

[hjuːˌmɪli'eɪʃn]

the painful feeling of embarrassment or shame caused by loss of dignity or respect

(syn) embarrassment, disgrace, shame

(e.g.) The character endured a public **humiliation** that she would never forget.

sorrow
슬픔, 비애

['sɒroʊ]

a feeling of deep distress or grief caused by loss, disappointment, or misfortune

(syn) grief, sadness, woe

(e.g.) A wave of profound **sorrow** washed over the war veteran as he recalled his youth.

pity
연민, 동정

['pɪti]

a feeling or sadness and compassion caused by the suffering and misfortune of others

(syn) sympathy, compassion, mercy

(e.g.) The old man's desperate situation evoked sincere **pity** from the onlookers.

trivial
사소한, 하찮은

['trɪviəl]

of little importance or value; insignificance in meaning or consequence
(syn) unimportant, minor, insignificant
(e.g.) They spent hours debating **trivial** details instead of the core issue.

vicious
잔인한, 사악한, 악순환의

['vɪʃəs]

having or showing a deliberate intention to cause harm; characterized by violence or cruelty; producing harmful and self-perpetuating effects
(syn) cruel, malicious, savage
(e.g.) The poverty and lack of education created a **vicious** circle that was difficult to break.

delicate
섬세한, 연약한

['delɪkət]

requiring care; easily damaged
(syn) subtle, fragile
(e.g.) The painter used **delicate** strokes.

archaic
고대의, 구식의

[ɑːrˈkeɪɪk]

belonging to an earlier historical period; no longer in common use or outdated in style or language
(syn) obsolete, outdated
(e.g.) The play's dialogue is full of **archaic** expressions that reflect its medieval setting.

DAY
09

inconsistency
불일치, 모순

[ˌɪnkənˈsɪstənsi]

lack of harmony or coherence
(syn) contradiction
(e.g.) Fred noticed but didn't mention Bill's **inconsistency**.

unequivocal
명확한, 모호하지 않은

[ˌʌnɪˈkwɪvəkl]

leaving no doubt or uncertainty; expressed in a clear, direct, and decisive manner
(syn) explicit, categorical
(e.g.) The principal gave an **unequivocal** statement that discrimination would not be tolerated.

suppress
억누르다, 억압하다

[səˈprɛs]

to hold down or prevent expression
(syn) restrain
(e.g.) Automation can **suppress** the struggles that once shaped human skill.

ambiguous
애매한, 중의적인

[æmˈbɪgjuəs]

open to more than one interpretation or having an unclear meaning
(syn) equivocal, indefinite, cryptic
(e.g.) The essay's conclusion was highly **ambiguous**, inviting various interpretations.

conjectural
추측에 의한, 가설적인

[kənˈdʒektʃərəl]

based on guesswork, incomplete evidence, or speculation rather than certainty
(syn) speculative, hypothetical
(e.g.) His theory remains purely **conjectural** until more data are collected.

presumably
아마, 짐작건대

[prɪˈzuːməbli]

used to express that something is assumed or likely to be true based on available facts
(syn) probably, likely, supposedly
(e.g.) **Presumably**, the library will be closed on the national holiday.

adhere
(규칙을) 고수하다, 충실히 지키다, 들러붙다

[əd'hɪər]

to stick firmly to a surface or to follow a rule, principle, or belief closely and faithfully

(syn) stick to, abide by, comply

(e.g.) All members must strictly **adhere** to the ethical standards of the profession.

prolonged
오랜 기간의

[prə'lɔːŋd]

continuing for a long time

(syn) extended

(e.g.) Inuit skills were shaped by **prolonged** struggles with winds, stars, and tides.

discrepancy
불일치, 차이

[dɪ'skrepənsi]

a difference or inconsistency between two or more facts, statements, or accounts

(syn) difference, inconsistency, variance

(e.g.) The audit revealed a significant **discrepancy** between the recorded sales and the inventory.

transcend
초월하다, 넘어서다

[træn'send]

to go beyond or rise above the limits of something, especially ordinary experience or understanding

(syn) surpass, outdo, excel

(e.g.) Great art has the power to **transcend** time and culture.

DAY
09

resort
(수단에) 의지하다, 기대다

[rɪ'zɔːrt]

to turn to or make use of something, especially as a final or less desirable option

(syn) turn to, fall back on, utilize

(e.g.) When his patience ran out, he had no choice but to **resort** to drastic measures.

drastic
과감한, 급격한

['dræstɪk]

extreme or having a strong and far-reaching effect
(syn) extreme, severe, radical
(e.g.) To cut costs, the company decided to implement **drastic** structural changes.

deter
막다, 단념시키다

[dɪ't3ːr]

to prevent or discourage someone from doing something by making it difficult or risky
(syn) prevent, discourage, dissuade
(e.g.) Strict assessment criteria may **deter** learners from taking communicative risks.

pervasive
만연한, 스며드는

[pər'veɪsɪv]

spreading widely throughout an area or a group of people
(syn) widespread, prevalent, permeating
(e.g.) The sense of anxiety was **pervasive** throughout the city during the lockdown.

precedent
선례, 판례

['presɪdənt]

an earlier or decision that severs as an example or rule for future cases
(syn) model, example, standard
(e.g.) The court's decision set an important legal **precedent** for environmental protection.

commence
시작하다, 개시하다

[kə'mens]

to begin or start something, especially in a formal or official way
(syn) begin, initiate, launch
(e.g.) The ceremony will **commence** promptly at 10 o'clock in the main hall.

elaboration
상세한 설명, 정교화

[ɪˌlæbəˈreɪʃn]
the process of developing or presenting something in greater detail or complexity
(syn) refinement, development, detailed explanation
(e.g.) The report requires further **elaboration** on the methodology used.

consequence
결과, 중요성

[ˈkɒnsɪkwens]
a result or effect of an action or condition; the significance or importance of something
(syn) result, outcome, importance
(e.g.) Ignoring the warning could have serious **consequences**.

articulate
분명히 표현하다, 명확하게 말하다

[ɑːrˈtɪkjuleɪt]
to express thoughts, ideas, or feelings clearly and effectively in speech or writing
(syn) express, enunciate, verbalize
(e.g.) She was highly skilled at **articulating** complex ideas simply.

exhaustive
철저한, 완전한

[ɪɡˈzɔːstɪv]
including all possibilities or aspects; leaving nothing out
(syn) comprehensive, thorough, all-inclusive
(e.g.) The researcher conducted an **exhaustive** analysis of the data set.

concrete
구체적인, 실질적인

[ˈkɒnkriːt]
real, specific, and not abstract; able to be perceived or measured
(syn) tangible, definite, factual
(e.g.) The report needs **concrete** evidence to support its argument.

adequate
충분한, 적절한

[ˈædɪkwət]
satisfactory or acceptable in quality or quantity
(syn) sufficient, enough, satisfactory
(e.g.) The results were not **adequate** to confirm the hypothesis.

DAY 09

obsess
집착하다

[əb'sɛs]

to focus excessively on something
(syn) fixate
(e.g.) Slow reading makes people **obsess** over each tiny feature of a text.

practical
실용적인, 실제적인

['præktɪkl]

concerned with the actual use or application of ideas rather than theory; useful and effective in real situations.
(syn) utilitarian, sensible, realistic
(e.g.) The workshop focused on providing students with **practical** job-seeking skills.

diminish
줄어들다, 약해지다

[dɪ'mɪnɪʃ]

to make or become smaller, weaker, or less important in degree or intensity
(syn) lessen, decrease, reduce
(e.g.) The severity of the symptoms began to **diminish** after the medication was administered.

allocate
할당하다, 배분하다

['æləkeɪt]

to distribute or assign resources, duties, or time for a particular purpose
(syn) assign, distribute, designate
(e.g.) The government decided to **allocate** more funds to public education.

elucidate
설명하다, 명료하게 하다

[ɪ'luːsɪdeɪt]

to make something clear by explaining it in detail or clarifying complex ideas
(syn) clarify, explain, illuminate
(e.g.) Could you please **elucidate** the complex relationship between the two variables?

유희태 일반영어
⑤ 기출 VOCA 30days

dismantle	○○○	temperance	○○○
corroborate	○○○	ubiquitous	○○○
hinder	○○○	tunnel vision	○○○
highlight	○○○	venture out	○○○
oblige	○○○	zephyr	○○○
sanction	○○○	alleviate	○○○
sever	○○○	benevolent	○○○
unprecedented	○○○	cynical	○○○
venerable	○○○	detrimental	○○○
warrant	○○○	empathy	○○○
shrink	○○○	fall victim to	○○○
arduous	○○○	formulated problem	○○○
barren	○○○	heterogeneous	○○○
concordancer	○○○	indispensable	○○○
coercion	○○○	mitigate	○○○
discount	○○○	negligible	○○○
eloquent	○○○	contemporary	○○○
fiasco	○○○	precarious	○○○
hazard	○○○	profound	○○○
hospitable	○○○	sustain	○○○
impartial	○○○	turbulent	○○○
juxtapose	○○○	terrain	○○○
lament	○○○	wrestle with	○○○
intuition	○○○	conjecture	○○○
nostalgia	○○○	existential	○○○
linking word	○○○	engagement	○○○
observer	○○○	innate	○○○
quandary	○○○	perceptive	○○○
recalcitrant	○○○	generative	○○○
sycophant	○○○	skill-integration	○○○

dismantle
해체하다, 분해하다

[dɪsˈmæntl]

to take apart or remove
(syn) disassemble
(e.g.) Overreliance on automation can **dismantle** our ability to act independently.

corroborate
입증하다, 확증하다

[kəˈrɒbəreɪt]

to confirm or support with evidence
(syn) verify, confirm
(e.g.) Some results were not **corroborated** by other sources.

hinder
방해하다, 막다

[ˈhɪndər]

to create obstacles that make progress or achievement more difficult
(syn) obstruct, impede, delay
(e.g.) Lack of funding continues to **hinder** the development of the project.

highlight
강조하다, 눈에 띄게 표시하다

[ˈhaɪlaɪt]

to emphasize or draw attention to
(syn) accentuate
(e.g.) When using a negative stem, teachers should **highlight** the negative word.

oblige
의무를 지우다, 강요하다

[əˈblaɪdʒ]

to make someone do something by law, rule, or moral duty
(syn) compel, require, bind
(e.g.) Regulations now **oblige** all companies to report their environmental impact.

sanction
(n) 제재, (v) 승인하다

[ˈsæŋkʃən]

(n) a penalty imposed for disobedience; (v) to give official permission or approval
(syn) (n) penalty, embargo; (v) authorize, approve
(e.g.) Economic **sanctions** were imposed against the aggressor nation.

sever
전례... 단절하다, 끊다

['sevər]

to cut or break off
(syn) disconnect
(e.g.) Computer automation **severs** the ends from the means.

unprecedented
전례 없는

[ʌn'presɪdentɪd]

never having happened or existed before
(syn) unparalleled, exceptional, unique
(e.g.) The stock market experienced an **unprecedented** surge in trading volume.

venerable
존경할 만한, 숭고한

['venərəbl]

deserving deep respect because of age, wisdom, or character
(syn) respected, revered, admirable
(e.g.) The **venerable** scholar delivered the opening address at the conference.

warrant
정당화하다, 보증하다

['wɔːrənt]

to justify or make something necessary; to guarantee the truth or validity of something
(syn) justify, guarantee, merit
(e.g.) The gravity of the situation does not **warrant** such an extreme reaction.

shrink
줄어들다, 축소되다

[ʃrɪŋk]

to become smaller or narrower
(syn) contract
(e.g.) During tunnel vision, the world seems to **shrink** and context disappears.

arduous
고된, 몹시 힘든

['ɑːrdʒuəs]

requring great effort and persistence; very difficult and tiring
(syn) difficult, taxing, grueling
(e.g.) Climbing the mountain was an **arduous** task that tested their endurance.

DAY

10

barren
척박한, 불모의

['bærən]

too empty or poor to support life
(syn) desolate, infertile
(e.g.) Inuit hunters navigate **barren** Arctic terrain with few landmarks.

concordancer
콘코던서(용례 검색 도구)

[kənˈkɔːrdænsər]

a tool that shows real examples of how words are used
(syn) corpus tool
(e.g.) Students searched for do and make expressions by referencing an online **concordancer**.

coercion
강압, 강제

[koʊˈɜːrʒn]

the act of forcing someone to do something through threats or pressure
(syn) force, compulsion, duress
(e.g.) The contract was deemed invalid because it was signed under **coercion**.

discount
무시하다, 평가절하하다

['dɪskaʊnt]

to ignore or dismiss as unimportant
(syn) disregard
(e.g.) Automation bias makes us **discount** information from our own senses.

eloquent
유창한, 설득력 있는

['eləkwənt]

expressing ideas clearly, effectively, and persuasively in speech or writing
(syn) articulate, fluent, persuasive
(e.g.) His farewell speech was surprisingly **eloquent** and heartfelt.

fiasco
대실패, 큰 실수

[fiˈæskoʊ]

a complete and embarrassing failure
(syn) failure, disaster, debacle
(e.g.) The launch of the new product was an embarrassing **fiasco**.

hazard

위험, 위험 요소

['hæzərd]

a potential source of danger
(syn) risk
(e.g.) GPS routes can lead hunters onto thin ice or other **hazards** a skilled navigator would avoid.

hospitable

환대하는, 친절한

[hɒ'spɪtəbl]

friendly and welcoming to guests or strangers
(syn) welcoming, gracious, friendly
(e.g.) The villagers were incredibly **hospitable** to the travelers.

impartial

공정한, 편견 없는

[ɪm'pɑːrʃl]

treating all sides or people equally without bias or favorism
(syn) unbiased, neutral, objective
(e.g.) It is crucial for a judge to remain completely **impartial**.

juxtapose

병치하다, 나란히 놓다

[ˌdʒʌkstə'poʊz]

to place different things side by side for comparison or contrast
(syn) place side-by-side, contrast
(e.g.) The painting **juxtaposes** bright, vibrant colors with deep, dark shadows.

lament

한탄하다, 슬퍼하다

[lə'ment]

to express deep grief, sorrow, or regret
(syn) mourn, grieve, bewail
(e.g.) The poet is **lamenting** for a lost era of peace.

intuition

직관

[ˌɪntu'ɪʃən]

immediate understanding without reasoning
(syn) instinct
(e.g.) GPS reliance weakens the Inuit hunters' **intuition** for changing conditions.

DAY

10

nostalgia
향수, 그리움

[nɒˈstældʒə]

sentimental longing for the past, often associated with happy memories

(syn) yearning, reminiscence, homesickness

(e.g.) Listening to the old songs filled her with **nostalgia** for her youth.

linking word
접속어, 연결어

[ˈlɪŋkɪŋ wɜːrd]

a word that shows logical relationships between ideas

(syn) connector

(e.g.) To fix organization problems, Jinhee used **linking words** like *but* and *then*.

observer
관찰자

[əbˈzɜːrvər]

someone who watches rather than acts

(syn) spectator

(e.g.) Automation turns us from actors into **observers**.

quandary
딜레마, 곤경

[ˈkwɒndəri]

a state of uncertainty or confusion over what to do in a difficult situation

(syn) dilemma, predicament, impasse

(e.g.) The ethical **quandary** facing the doctor was deeply unsettling.

recalcitrant
저항하는, 다루기 힘든

[rɪˈkælsɪtrənt]

stubbornly resisting authority, control, or convention

(syn) defiant, uncooperative, refractory

(e.g.) The **recalcitrant** student refused to follow the teacher's instructions.

sycophant
아첨꾼

[ˈsɪkəfənt]

a person who flatters or acts obsequiously toward someone powerful to gain advantage

(syn) flatterer, toady, bootlicker

(e.g.) The manager was surrounded by **sycophants** who always praised his decisions.

temperance
절제, 금주

['tempərəns]

moderation and self-control, especially in eating or drinking
(syn) moderation, restraint, sobriety
(e.g.) She lived her life with remarkable **temperance** and discipline.

ubiquitous
어디에나 있는, 편재하는

[juːˈbɪkwɪtəs]

existing or present everywhere at the same time
(syn) omnipresent, pervasive, universal
(e.g.) In the modern world, mobile phones have become truly **ubiquitous**.

tunnel vision
터널 시야, 편협한 시야

['tʌnəl ˌvɪʒən]

a narrowed perception that excludes context
(syn) narrow focus
(e.g.) A lack of background knowledge can cause **tunnel vision** in learners.

venture out
과감히 나가다, 모험적으로 밖으로 나서다

['vɛntʃər aʊt]

to go out into a place that may involve risk, difficulty, or uncertainty
(syn) go forth, set out
(e.g.) Inuit hunters have **ventured out** across miles of ice and tundra for thousands of years in search of game.

zephyr
미풍

['zefər]

a soft, gentle breeze, often used poetically
(syn) breeze, gentle wind
(e.g.) A cool **zephyr** provided a pleasant relief from the afternoon heat.

alleviate
완화하다, 경감하다

[əˈliːvieɪt]

to make pain, difficulty, or burden less severe or more bearable
(syn) ease, mitigate, relieve
(e.g.) Medications were prescribed to **alleviate** the patient's constant pain.

DAY
10

benevolent
자비로운, 인정 많은

[bə'nevələnt]

showing kindness and goodwill; motivated by a desire to help others
(syn) kind, charitable, benign
(e.g.) The organization relies on the support of **benevolent** donors.

cynical
냉소적인, 회의적인

['sɪnɪkl]

believing that people act only out of selfish motives; distrustful of sincerity or integrity
(syn) pessimistic, skeptical, distrustful
(e.g.) After years of political disappointment, the public became increasingly **cynical**.

detrimental
해로운, 손해를 입히는

[ˌdetrɪ'mentl]

causing harm, damage, or injury to someone or something
(syn) harmful, damaging, adverse
(e.g.) Excessive exposure to the sun is **detrimental** to skin health.

empathy
공감

['empəθi]

the ability to understand and share another person's feeling or experiences
(syn) compassion, understanding, fellow feeling
(e.g.) A good counselor must possess a high degree of **empathy** for their clients.

fall victim to
~의 희생양이 되다

[fɔːl 'vɪktɪm tuː]

to be harmed or negatively affected by something
(syn) suffer from
(e.g.) Many users **fall victim to** automation bias when they unquestioningly accept computer output.

formulated problem

명확히 제시된 문제

['fɔːrmjʊleɪtɪd 'prɒbləm]

a clearly stated issue in an assessment item

(syn) defined problem

(e.g.) Good selected-response items must present a single clearly **formulated problem**.

heterogeneous

이질적인, 다양한

[ˌhetərəˈdʒiːniəs]

consisting of parts or elements that are different from each other

(syn) diverse, varied, mixed

(e.g.) The class was made up of a **heterogeneous** group of students from various countries.

indispensable

필수적인, 없어서는 안 될

[ˌɪndɪˈspensəbl]

absolutely necessary; essential and not to be replaced

(syn) essential, crucial, necessary

(e.g.) The project manager is an **indispensable** member of the team.

mitigate

완화시키다, 경감시키다

['mɪtɪgeɪt]

to make something less severe, harsh, or painful

(syn) alleviate, ease, lessen

(e.g.) Emergency funds were released to **mitigate** the effects of the drought.

negligible

무시해도 좋은, 하찮은

['neglɪdʒəbl]

so small or unimportant as to be not worth considering

(syn) insignificant, trivial, minor

(e.g.) The cost increase was **negligible** compared to the overall budget.

DAY

10

contemporary
현대의, 현재의

[kən'tempərəri]

belonging to or occurring in the present; modern in character or style
(syn) modern, current, present-day
(e.g.) The museum features **contemporary** works by emerging artists.

precarious
불안정한, 위태로운

[prɪ'keəriəs]

not securely held or in position; dangerously uncertain or unstable
(syn) unstable, risky, perilous
(e.g.) The climber was balanced on a **precarious** ledge hundreds of feet high.

profound
심오한, 깊은

[prə'faʊnd]

very great or intense; deeply meaningful
(syn) deep, significant
(e.g.) Automation raises **profound** questions about what defines human identity.

sustain
유지하다, 지속하다

[sə'steɪn]

to support or keep something going over time; to endure without giving way
(syn) maintain, support, endure
(e.g.) The country needs to **sustain** its economic growth for the next decade.

turbulent
격변하는, 격동의

['tɜːrbjələnt]

characterized by disorder, conflict, or great change
(syn) chaotic, volatile, tumultuous
(e.g.) The 1960s were a **turbulent** period in world history.

terrain
지형, 지세

[təˈreɪn]

the physical features of a landscape

(syn) landscape, ground

(e.g.) Inuit hunters navigate barren Arctic **terrain** with few landmarks.

wrestle with
씨름하다, 고군분투하다

[ˈrɛsəl wɪð]

to struggle with difficulty or complexity

(syn) grapple with

(e.g.) We become who we are by **wrestling with** difficult tasks.

conjecture
추측, 짐작

[kənˈdʒektʃər]

an opinion or conclusion formed on the basis of incomplete information

(syn) speculation, guess, hypothesis

(e.g.) The theory remains merely a **conjecture** until further research is conducted.

existential
실존적인

[ˌɛgzɪˈstɛnʃəl]

relating to human existence or purpose

(e.g.) Automation forces us to face an **existential** question about what defines us.

engagement
참여, 몰입

[ɛnˈgeɪdʒmənt]

active involvement or attention

(syn) participation

(e.g.) Complacency reduces **engagement** and makes us inattentive to our surroundings.

innate
선천적인, 타고난

[ɪˈneɪt]

existing naturally or inborn; present from birth rather than acquired

(syn) inborn, inherent, natural

(e.g.) Humans have an **innate** capacity for language learning.

DAY

10

perceptive 통찰력 있는, 감지하는

[pərˈseptɪv]

having or showing the ability to notice and understand things quickly or clearly
(syn) discerning, insightful
(e.g.) A **perceptive** reader can detect subtle shifts in tone and meaning.

generative 생성적인, 생산력 있는

[ˈdʒenərətɪv]

capable of producing or creating something new; often used in linguistic or cognitive contexts
(syn) creative, productive
(e.g.) Chomsky's theory of **generative** grammar transformed modern linguistics.

skill-integration 기술 통합

[skɪl ˌɪntəˈɡreɪʃn]

the instructional approach of teaching by combining the four language skills (listening, speaking, reading, writing) in integrated tasks
(syn) integrated skills, multi-skill approach
(e.g.) The project-based learning approach naturally promotes **skill-integration**.

mnemonic	○○○	pursue	○○○
construct	○○○	investigate	○○○
process-oriented	○○○	analyze	○○○
criterion-referenced	○○○	implication	○○○
norm-referenced	○○○	phenomenon	○○○
validity	○○○	abstraction	○○○
guideline	○○○	manipulate	○○○
distractor	○○○	hypothesize	○○○
plausible	○○○	relevance	○○○
elicit	○○○	inherent	○○○
distinct	○○○	distort	○○○
cultural capsule	○○○	biased	○○○
interactive	○○○	unintended	○○○
automation bias	○○○	spontaneous	○○○
acquire	○○○	denotational	○○○
phonological	○○○	indelible	○○○
assimilation	○○○	cursory	○○○
voicing	○○○	inattentive	○○○
onset	○○○	deft	○○○
coda	○○○	pensive	○○○
host society	○○○	ailment	○○○
argument	○○○	ease	○○○
predicate	○○○	convoluted	○○○
thematic role	○○○	rely on	○○○
agent	○○○	referencing	○○○
countable	○○○	elusive	○○○
movement	○○○	assiduous	○○○
embedded	○○○	decorum	○○○
coherence	○○○	forthright	○○○
integrate	○○○	complacency	○○○

mnemonic
기억술의, 연상 기호의

[nɪˈmɒnɪk]

a technique or device designed to aid memory
- (syn) memory aid, suggestive device
- (e.g.) Students often use **mnemonic** devices like acronyms to memorize lists of words.

construct
(심리적) 개념, 구성체

[ˈkɒnstrʌkt]

an abstract concept defined within a theory (e.g., intelligence, fluency)
- (syn) concept, idea
- (e.g.) Fluency is a complex **construct** that is difficult to measure directly.

process-oriented
과정 중심의

[ˈproʊses ˈɔːriəntɪd]

emphasizing developmental steps and procedures rather than only the final product
- (syn) developmental, procedural
- (e.g.) The writing course employs a **process-oriented** approach, emphasizing drafting and revision.

criterion-referenced
준거 지향의

[kraɪˈtɪəriən ˈrefərənst]

assessing performance against fixed standards or criteria, not in comparison to other test-takers
- (syn) standards-based, absolute
- (e.g.) Passing the exam is based on meeting the predetermined **criterion-referenced** standard.

norm-referenced
규준 지향의

[nɔːrm ˈrefərənst]

assessing performance by comparing a test-taker's score with those of a reference group
- (syn) relative, competitive
- (e.g.) Unlike a criterion-referenced test, this exam is **norm-referenced** to rank students.

validity
타당도

[vəˈlɪdəti]

the degree to which a test actually measures what it claims to measure

(syn) accuracy, legitimacy

(e.g.) We must ensure that the test has strong **validity** to measure reading comprehension accurately.

guideline
지침, 기준

[ˈgaɪdlaɪn]

a general rule, principle, or recommendation intended to guide actions or decisions

(syn) rule, principle, directive

(e.g.) All test developers must strictly adhere to the item writing **guideline**.

distractor
오답지

[dɪˈstræktər]

a plausible but incorrect option in a multiple-choice item

(syn) foil, incorrect option

(e.g.) The item was revised to ensure all **distractors** were equally plausible.

plausible
그럴듯한, 타당해 보이는

[ˈplɔːzəbl]

appearing reasonable or credible; likely to be true

(syn) credible, reasonable, believable

(e.g.) The incorrect options must be **plausible** to test-takers who lack the target knowledge.

elicit
(반응, 대답을) 끌어내다

[ɪˈlɪsɪt]

to draw out a response, idea, or information from someone

(syn) extract, draw out, evoke

(e.g.) The teacher used controversial questions to **elicit** a lively discussion.

distinct

별개의, 독특한

[dɪ'stɪŋkt]

clearly separate and different from others
(syn) separate, unique, marked
(e.g.) Each group chose one **distinct** aspect of the holiday to research for their presentation.

cultural capsule

문화 소개 자료

['kʌltʃər 'kæpsjuːl]

a concise instructional text that highlights one aspect of the target culture with factual detail
(syn) culture note, short report
(e.g.) Students wrote a **cultural capsule** about table manners in Korea.

interactive

상호 작용하는

[ˌɪntər'æktɪv]

involving mutual action or influence among participants or systems
(syn) communicative, participatory
(e.g.) The new language lab features an **interactive** virtual reality program.

automation bias

자동화 과신 편향

[ˌɔːtə'meɪʃən baɪəs]

trusting computer output too much and ignoring other information
(syn) tech overreliance
(e.g.) **Automation bias** makes people ignore their own eyes and ears when the computer provides wrong data.

acquire

습득하다, 얻다

[ə'kwaɪər]

to gain or develop knowledge, a skill, or an ability
(syn) obtain, gain
(e.g.) Learners must seek background knowledge elsewhere if they wish to **acquire** it.

phonological 음운론적인

[ˌfoʊnəˈlɒdʒɪkl]

relating to the sound system and patterns of a language
(syn) phonetic, linguistic
(e.g.) The choice of a particular allomorph is often determined by **phonological** conditions.

assimilation 동화(현상)

[əˌsɪməˈleɪʃn]

the process of absorbing, integrating, or becoming similar to something else; in linguistics, the way a sound changes to become more like a neighboring sound.
(syn) sound change, harmonization
(e.g.) The change of /n/ to /m/ before a labial consonant is an example of **assimilation**.

voicing 유성음화

[ˈvɔɪsɪŋ]

the use of vocal fold vibration in producing a sound
(syn) sonority, vocalization
(e.g.) The difference between /t/ and /d/ is a contrast in **voicing**.

onset (음절의) 초성, 두음

[ˈɒnset]

the consonant(s) preceding the vowel (nucleus) within a syllable
(syn) initial sound, beginning
(e.g.) A syllable is structurally divided into the **onset** and the rhyme.

coda (음절의) 종성, 꼬리

[ˈkoʊdə]

the consonant(s) following the vowel (nucleus) within a syllable
(syn) ending, tail
(e.g.) Syllables without a **coda** are called open syllables.

host society 호스트 사회, 이민자 · 관광객을 받아들이는 지역 사회

[hoʊst səˈsaɪəti]

the community that receives outsiders such as tourists or migrants
(syn) receiving society
(e.g.) Tourist pressure can reshape the **host society**'s cultural practices.

argument 논항

['ɑːrgjəmənt]

a required phrase or noun phrase that completes the meaning of a predicate
(syn) complement, required phrase
(e.g.) The verb *give* requires three **arguments**: an agent, a theme, and a recipient.

predicate 술어

['predɪkət]

the clausal part that contains the verb and states something about the subject
(syn) verb phrase, assertion
(e.g.) The verb and its arguments together form the core **predicate** of the sentence.

thematic role 의미 역할

[θiːˈmætɪk roʊl]

a semantic function (e.g., Agent, Theme, Goal) assigned to NPs within a clause
(syn) semantic role, Θ-role
(e.g.) Changing the voice of a verb often changes the **thematic role** assigned to the subject.

agent 행위자

['eɪdʒənt]

the participant that initiates or performs the action of the verb
(syn) initiator, doer
(e.g.) In the active sentence, the subject is assigned the **agent** thematic role.

countable 가산의

['kaʊntəbəl]

able to be counted as individual units
(syn) enumerable
(e.g.) Students identified which nouns were **countable** and uncountable.

movement

(구문) 이동

['muːvmənt]

the displacement of a constituent from its base position to a surface position

(syn) displacement, shift

(e.g.) Wh-questions are formed through the **movement** of the wh-phrase to the sentence-initial position.

embedded

내포된, 삽입된

[ɪmˈbedɪd]

occurring as a subordinate clause within a larger clause

(syn) nested, inserted

(e.g.) The structure involves an **embedded** question within the main clause.

coherence

일관성, 통일성

[koʊˈhɪrəns]

the property of a text in which ideas are logically connected and unified

(syn) consistency, unity, clarity

(e.g.) The student's essay lacked **coherence** due to poor transitions between paragraphs.

integrate

통합하다, 합치다

['ɪntɪɡreɪt]

to combine parts into a whole so they function together

(syn) blend, merge, unify

(e.g.) The teacher aimed to **integrate** multiple language skills into a single project.

pursue

추구하다, 쫓다

[pərˈsuː]

to strive for or follow something over time; to continue with an activity or goal

(syn) seek, follow, strive for

(e.g.) She **pursued** academic excellence by dedicating herself to the degree program.

investigate 조사하다, 연구하다

[ɪnˈvestɪɡeɪt]

to conduct a systematic inquiry to uncover facts and evidence
(syn) examine, research, explore
(e.g.) I first **investigated** my own teaching to identify ways to improve classroom practice.

analyze 분석하다

[ˈænəlaɪz]

to examine methodically in order to explain, interpret, or evaluate
(syn) examine, dissect, study
(e.g.) After we **analyzed** the results, we confirmed the effectiveness of the method.

implication 영향, 함의

[ˌɪmplɪˈkeɪʃn]

the possible effect or meaning that follows from a situation or statement
(syn) consequence, ramification, suggestion
(e.g.) We discussed the **implications** of the new policy for school operations.

phenomenon 현상

[fəˈnɒmɪnən]

an observable event or fact, especially one that invites explanation
(syn) occurrence, happening, event
(e.g.) There are several interesting **phenomena** in the process of language acquisition.

abstraction 추상 개념, 구체적 형태 없이 개념화된 것

[æbˈstrækʃən]

a general idea removed from specific instances
(syn) concept, notion
(e.g.) Justice is often treated as an **abstraction**.

manipulate 조작하다, 능숙하게 다루다

[məˈnɪpjuleɪt]

to control unfairly for one's advantage or to handle skillfully
(syn) exploit, handle, operate
(e.g.) He **manipulated** the information to tilt the situation in his favor.

hypothesize
가설을 세우다

[haɪˈpɒθəsaɪz]

to propose a tentative explanation that can be tested or argued
(syn) speculate, theorize, postulate
(e.g.) The researchers **hypothesized** that environmental changes trigger species migration.

relevance
적합성, 관련성

[ˈreləvəns]

the degree of connection something has to the matter at hand
(syn) pertinence, applicability, bearing
(e.g.) The **relevance** of these data is crucial to the final conclusions.

inherent
내재하는, 고유의

[ɪnˈherənt]

existing as a permanent or essential attribute of something
(syn) intrinsic, innate, built-in
(e.g.) Every language has **inherent** difficulties and complexities.

distort
왜곡하다

[dɪˈstɔːrt]

to twist or misrepresent the shape or meaning of something
(syn) misrepresent, twist, bias
(e.g.) The media sometimes **distort** facts and sway public opinion.

biased
편향된, 선입견이 있는

[ˈbaɪəst]

showing unfair preference or prejudice for or against something
(syn) prejudiced, partial, subjective
(e.g.) The judge was criticized for being **biased** against the defendant.

unintended
의도하지 않은

[ˌʌnɪnˈtendɪd]

not planned or meant to happen
(syn) accidental, unexpected, unforeseen
(e.g.) His remarks had serious **unintended** consequences.

spontaneous
자발적인, 즉흥적인

[spɒnˈteɪniəs]

arising from inner impulse without preplanning or external prompting
(syn) impulsive, unprompted, extemporaneous
(e.g.) The teacher encouraged **spontaneous** student responses during problem-solving.

denotational
지시적인 의미의

[ˌdiːnoʊˈteɪʃənəl]

relating to the literal dictionary meaning
(syn) literal
(e.g.) Students must know a lexical item's written form, spoken form, and **denotational** meaning.

indelible
지워지지 않는, 잊을 수 없는

[ɪndélǝbl]

impossible to remove or forget; making a lasting impression
(syn) permanent, enduring, unforgettable, ineradicable
(opp) erasable, temporary, fleeting
(e.g.) The trip left an **indelible** memory in their hearts.

cursory
대충하는, 피상적인

[kə́ːrsəri]

done quickly and without attention to detail or thoroughness
(syn) hasty, superficial, perfunctory
(opp) careful, thorough, meticulous
(e.g.) She gave the report only a **cursory** glance before the meeting.

inattentive
부주의한, 주의를 기울이지 않는

[ˌɪnəˈtɛntɪv]

not paying enough attention
(syn) distracted
(e.g.) Automation complacency makes us **inattentive** to what is happening around us.

deft
솜씨 좋은, 능숙한

[deft]

skillful and quick in one's movements or actions
(syn) skillful, adept, nimble, agile
(opp) clumsy, awkward, inept
(e.g.) The chef's **deft** movements impressed the apprentices.

pensive

깊은 생각에 잠긴, 수심 어린

[pénsɪv]

engaged in serious or deep thought, often with a touch of sadness

(syn) reflective, thoughtful, melancholy, contemplative

(opp) carefree, lighthearted, frivolous

(e.g.) He sat by the window in a **pensive** mood after the funeral.

ailment

경미한 질환, 문제

[ˈeɪlmənt]

a minor illness or cognitive problem

(syn) disorder, complaint

(e.g.) Automation complacency and bias are described as cognitive **ailments** that make us error-prone.

ease

완화하다, 편하게 하다

[iːz]

to make something less severe, serious, or painful

(syn) alleviate, moderate, diminish

(opp) aggravate, intensify, worsen

(e.g.) New laws were introduced to **ease** environmental damage.

convoluted

복잡한, 뒤얽힌

[kánvəlùːtɪd]

extremely complex and difficult to follow or understand

(syn) complicated, intricate, tangled, elaborate

(opp) simple, straightforward, clear

(e.g.) The plot was so **convoluted** that few viewers understood it fully.

rely on

~에 의존하다

[rɪˈlaɪ ɒn]

to depend on someone or something

(syn) depend on

(e.g.) Modern hunters increasingly **rely on** computer-generated maps.

referencing

참고하기, 인용하기

[ˈrɛfərənsɪŋ]

consulting a source for examples or information

(syn) consulting

(e.g.) Students found more examples of do and make by **referencing** an online concordancer.

elusive
이해하기 어려운, 달아나는

[ilúːsiv]
difficult to find, catch, or achieve; hard to grasp or define clearly
(syn) evasive, intangible, subtle, slippery
(opp) obvious, clear, definite
(e.g.) The meaning of true happiness can be **elusive** to many people.

assiduous
근면한, 끈기 있는

[əsídʒuəs]
showing great care and perseverance in doing something
(syn) diligent, persistent, industrious, attentive
(opp) lazy, negligent, careless
(e.g.) Her **assiduous** study habits helped her win a scholarship.

decorum
단정함, 예의 바름

[dɪkɔ́ːrəm]
behavior in keeping with good taste and propriety
(syn) propriety, etiquette, politeness, civility
(opp) rudeness, impropriety, vulgarity
(e.g.) The teacher emphasized **decorum** during formal presentations.

forthright
솔직한, 거리낌 없는

[fɔːrθràit]
direct and outspoken; straightforward and honest
(syn) candid, frank, blunt, outspoken
(opp) evasive, reserved, deceitful
(e.g.) She was **forthright** in expressing her disagreement.

complacency
자만, 안이함

[kəmˈpleɪsənsi]
a false sense of security leading to inattention
(syn) self-satisfaction
(e.g.) Automation **complacency** occurs when a machine lulls us into believing everything is secure.

2022

DAY

12

excerpt	○○○	lullaby	○○○
mortised	○○○	loophole	○○○
gouge	○○○	bogus	○○○
neglect	○○○	epiphany	○○○
pruning	○○○	hamper	○○○
corrosion	○○○	facework	○○○
chisel	○○○	dominating	○○○
opaque	○○○	assault	○○○
minutia	○○○	dismiss	○○○
melancholy	○○○	punctuality	○○○
rigorous	○○○	predator	○○○
obscure	○○○	intestine	○○○
vitality	○○○	secrete	○○○
reduction	○○○	pigment	○○○
regression	○○○	compress	○○○
formulate	○○○	squirt	○○○
prestige	○○○	pseudomorph	○○○
convergence	○○○	decoy	○○○
virtually	○○○	mollusc	○○○
tasteless	○○○	taxonomic	○○○
doublespeak	○○○	luminescent	○○○
inflated	○○○	rigid	○○○
extraordinary	○○○	predetermined	○○○
genuine	○○○	affix	○○○
counterfeit	○○○	syntax	○○○
jargon	○○○	derivation	○○○
profundity	○○○	ellipsis	○○○
co-construct	○○○	annotate	○○○
allude	○○○	isomorphic	○○○
chump	○○○	syllabic	○○○

excerpt
발췌, 인용구

['ɛksɜ:rpt]

a short extract from a film, broadcast, piece of music, or writing
(syn) extract, passage
(e.g.) Read the **excerpt** and follow the directions to complete the commentary.

mortised
암숫구멍이 난

['mɔ:rtɪst]

cut with a hole or recess to fit another piece
(syn) jointed
(e.g.) The carpenter fitted the door into a **mortised** frame.

gouge
파내다, 도려내다

[gaʊdʒ]

to cut or scoop out a hole or shape
(syn) scoop, hollow
(e.g.) He accidentally **gouged** a mark in the table with his screwdriver.

neglect
방치, 태만

[nɪ'glɛkt]

the state of being uncared for or ignored
(syn) inattention, disregard
(e.g.) The garden was full of weeds after months of **neglect**.

pruning
전정, 가지치기

['pru:nɪŋ]

cutting off dead or overgrown branches to help plants grow
(syn) trimming, clipping
(e.g.) Regular **pruning** keeps the trees healthy.

corrosion
부식

[kə'roʊʒən]

the gradual damage caused by a chemical reaction, often rust
(syn) decay, deterioration
(e.g.) The metal fence showed signs of **corrosion** after the rain.

chisel 끌

['tʃɪzəl]

a tool used for cutting or shaping wood or stone
(syn) cutter, blade
(e.g.) He used a **chisel** to carve his initials into the wood.

opaque 불투명한, 이해하기 어려운

[oʊ'peɪk]

not clear or easy to see through or understand
(syn) cloudy, unclear
(e.g.) The glass was **opaque**, so no one could see inside.

minutia 세부 사항

[mɪ'nuːʃiˌa]

the small, precise, or trivial detail of something
(syn) trifle, fine point
(e.g.) He struggled with screw holes, splinters, opaque instructions,
minutiae of metal.

melancholy 우울감

['mɛlənkəli]

a feeling of pensive sadness, typically with no obvious cause
(syn) sadness, gloom
(e.g.) The narrator creates a sense of **melancholy** by focusing on
parts of the property that are in a state of decay.

rigorous 엄격한, 정밀한

['rɪgərəs]

extremely thorough, exhaustive, or accurate
(syn) meticulous, strict
(e.g.) Fashion criticism should be **rigorous**, clearly stated, and
historically informed.

obscure 모호한, 이해하기 어려운

[əb'skjʊr]

not clearly expressed or easily understood
(syn) vague, ambiguous
(e.g.) Criticism should not be unnecessarily **obscure** (as current
art criticism often is).

vitality
활력

[vaɪˈtæləti]

the state of being strong and active; energy
- (syn) vigor, exuberance
- (e.g.) It should look for **vitality** and boldness, and distinguish the original from the derivative.

reduction
축소, 감소

[rɪˈdʌkʃən]

the act of making something smaller or less
- (syn) decrease, lowering
- (e.g.) Tunnel vision can come from a **reduction** in background knowledge.

regression
퇴보

[rɪˈgrɛʃən]

a return to a former or less developed state
- (syn) decline, deterioration
- (e.g.) Criticism should track a designer's development or point out standstill or **regression**.

formulate
정립하다, 만들어내다

[ˈfɔːrmjəleɪt]

to create or devise methodically
- (syn) articulate, express
- (e.g.) As Pierre Bourdieu **formulated** it, "Taste classifies, and it classifies the classifier."

prestige
명성, 위신

[preˈstiːʒ]

widespread respect and admiration felt for someone or something
- (syn) status, reputation
- (e.g.) Writing criticism is about putting your **prestige** and your very identity at risk.

convergence
수렴, 집중

[kənˈvɜːrdʒəns]

the process or state of meeting or coming together
- (syn) agreement, conformity
- (e.g.) There will usually be a high degree of **convergence** between critics in their judgments.

virtually
사실상, 거의

['vɜːrtʃuəli]

almost entirely; nearly
(syn) practically, almost
(e.g.) It would be surprising if a critic argued that a designer has **virtually** no aesthetic merit.

tasteless
저속한, 무감각한

['teɪstlɪs]

lacking in taste and refinement
(syn) vulgar, gauche
(e.g.) One might prefer one designer and even find a certain collection plain **tasteless**.

doublespeak
이중화법

['dʌbəlˌspiːk]

language used to make the bad seem good or the basic profound
(syn) euphemism
(e.g.) "Revenue enhancement" through "user fees" is an example of **doublespeak**.

inflated
과장된, 부풀려진

[ɪnˈfleɪtɪd]

excessively or highly exaggerated
(syn) exaggerated, bombastic
(e.g.) **Inflated** language is designed to make the ordinary seem extraordinary.

extraordinary
비범한

[ɪkˈstrɔːrdəneri]

beyond what is usual, ordinary, regular, or established
(syn) exceptional, remarkable
(e.g.) Inflated language is designed to make the ordinary seem **extraordinary**.

genuine
진짜의, 진정한

['dʒɛnjuɪn]

truly what it is purported to be; authentic
(syn) real, authentic
(e.g.) Cheap material could be described as "**genuine** imitation leather."

counterfeit 위조의, 가짜의

['kaʊntərfɪt]

made in exact imitation of something valuable or important with the intention to deceive or defraud

(syn) fake, bogus

(e.g.) A glass stone could be described as a "real **counterfeit** diamond."

jargon 전문 용어

['dʒɑːrgən]

specialized language used by a professional group

(syn) terminology, lingo

(e.g.) **Jargon** as doublespeak occurs when professional language is used with people not "in-the-know."

profundity 심오함

[prə'fʌndəti]

deep insight or great depth of knowledge or thought

(syn) depth, reconditeness

(e.g.) The use of jargon may be to give an air of **profundity**, authority, and prestige.

co-construct 공동 구성하다

[ˌkoʊkən'strʌkt]

to build or create something together with another person or group

(syn) collaborate, build jointly

(e.g.) Conversation is **co-constructed** by two or more people, unfolding dynamically in real time.

allude 넌지시 언급하다

[ə'luːd]

to suggest or call attention to indirectly; to hint at

(syn) hint, refer

(e.g.) It is often thought desirable not to **allude** to the original marriage at all.

chumph 바보, 얼간이

[tʃʌmp]

a foolish or easily deceived person
(syn) fool, dupe
(e.g.) I only wish I'd known about your custom before, Stevens, it certainly made me look like a **chump**.

lullaby 자장가

['lʌləbaɪ]

a quiet, gentle song sung to send a child to sleep
(syn) cradle song
(e.g.) I thought maybe Mami had sung me **lullabies** she'd learned from wives stationed at the embassy.

loophole (법률 등의) 허점

['luːphoʊl]

an ambiguity or inadequacy in the law or a set of rules
(syn) flaw, evasion
(e.g.) I fought back tears, thinking maybe there was a little **loophole**, maybe just maybe I could be the one exception.

bogus 가짜의, 위조의

['boʊɡəs]

not genuine or true; false
(syn) fake, counterfeit
(e.g.) The speaker was thinking of all those notebooks filled with **bogus** poems she'd have to burn.

epiphany (문득 깨닫는) 계시, 통찰

[ɪ'pɪfəni]

a moment of sudden and great revelation or realization
(syn) realization, revelation
(e.g.) When she saw "Chiquita Banana" on TV, the speaker had an **epiphany** that her dream did not need to be hampered.

hamper 방해하다

['hæmpər]

to hinder or impede the movement or progress of
(syn) obstruct, impede
(e.g.) The speaker realized her dream did not need to be **hampered** by her roots.

facework
체면 관리 행위

['feɪswɜːrk]

the various ways to deal with conflict and face
(syn) image management
(e.g.) The various ways to deal with conflict and face are called **facework** or facework strategies.

dominating
지배적인

['dɑːmɪneɪtɪŋ]

having a commanding influence on
(syn) controlling, assertive
(e.g.) **Dominating** facework is an effort to control the conflict situation.

assault
공격하다, 비난하다

[ə'sɔːlt]

to make a physical or verbal attack on someone
(syn) attack, abuse
(e.g.) A dominating facework behavior is to **assault** the other verbally.

dismiss
묵살하다

[dɪs'mɪs]

to treat as unworthy of serious consideration
(syn) disregard, ignore
(e.g.) An avoiding facework behavior is to **dismiss** the conflict that threatens the other's face.

punctuality
시간 엄수

[ˌpʌŋktʃu'æləti]

the quality or habit of being on time
(syn) promptness, timeliness
(e.g.) In his culture, **punctuality** is highly important and making others wait is regarded as inconsiderate.

predator
포식자

['prɛdətər]

an animal that preys on others
(syn) hunter, carnivore
(e.g.) Many species of octopus and squid exhibit a behavior that enables them to escape from **predators**.

intestine

장(腸)

[ɪnˈtɛstɪn]

the lower part of the digestive tract

(syn) gut, bowel

(e.g.) In the region of their **intestines**, the animals have a special sac-like organ.

secrete

분비하다

[sɪˈkriːt]

to produce and discharge (a substance)

(syn) exude, discharge

(e.g.) The gland **secretes** a brown or black liquid rich in the pigment melanin.

pigment

색소

[ˈpɪgmənt]

a substance that gives color to something

(syn) colorant, dye

(e.g.) The black liquid is rich in the **pigment** melanin.

compress

압축하다

[kəmˈprɛs]

to flatten or press together

(syn) squeeze, condense

(e.g.) When threatened, the animal has the ability to **compress** the ink sac and squirt a jet of liquid.

squirt

뿜어내다

[skwɜːrt]

to eject a liquid in a thin, forceful stream

(syn) spray, jet

(e.g.) The animal can **squirt** a jet of the liquid from its anus.

pseudomorph

가짜 형상

[ˈsuːdəˌmɔːrf]

a false shape or form; specifically, the ink cloud formed to resemble the animal

(syn) false image, dummy

(e.g.) The cloud of ink forms a dummy squid termed a **pseudomorph**, which attracts the predator.

decoy
(v) 유인하다, (n) 유인물

['diːkɔɪ]

to lure or entice someone or something into a trap
(syn) lure, tempt
(e.g.) The ink-dummy serves to **decoy** a bird predator while the slug made its escape.

mollusc
연체동물

['mɑːləsk]

an invertebrate of a large phylum that includes snails, slugs, mussels, and octopuses
(syn) invertebrate
(e.g.) Squid and octopus are **molluscs**, taxonomic relatives of the garden slug and snail.

taxonomic
분류학적인

[ˌtæksə'nɑːmɪk]

relating to or concerned with the classification of things
(syn) classification-based
(e.g.) Squid and octopus are molluscs, **taxonomic** relatives of the garden slug and snail.

luminescent
발광성의

[ˌluːmɪ'nɛsənt]

emitting light not caused by heat
(syn) glowing, phosphorescent
(e.g.) Deep-water squid secrete a **luminescent** ink, creating a brief flash of light.

rigid
경직된, 융통성 없는

['rɪdʒɪd]

unable to bend or be forced out of shape; not flexible
(syn) stiff, inflexible
(e.g.) The conversation program seemed too **rigid** in that he could only practice at designated times.

predetermined 미리 정해진

[ˌpriːdɪˈtɜːrmɪnd]

established or decided in advance
(syn) preset, prearranged
(e.g.) The program was too rigid with **predetermined** contents.

affix 접사

[ˈæfɪks]

a morpheme that is attached to a word stem
(syn) prefix, suffix
(e.g.) The tense-**affix**, such as -ed or -s, forms an independent head (T).

syntax 통사론, 구문론

[ˈsɪntæks]

the arrangement of words and phrases to create well-formed sentences
(syn) grammar, sentence structure
(e.g.) In English **syntax**, the subject usually comes before the verb.

derivation 파생, 도출

[ˌdɛrɪˈveɪʃən]

the process of forming a word from another word or base
(syn) formation, origin
(e.g.) The **derivation** of the ungrammatical sentence involves crossing too many bounding nodes.

ellipsis 생략

[ɪˈlɪpsɪs]

the omission from speech or writing of a word or words that can be understood from contextual clues
(syn) deletion, omission
(e.g.) VP-**ellipsis** is assumed to be licensed when the verb phrase is isomorphic to its antecedent.

annotate

주석을 달다

['ænə,teɪt]

to add notes that explain or comment on a text

(syn) comment on, mark up

(e.g.) Teachers often ask students to **annotate** texts to highlight important ideas.

isomorphic

동형의

[,aɪsə'mɔːrfɪk]

corresponding or similar in form or relations

(syn) identical in form, corresponding

(e.g.) VP-ellipsis is licensed when the verb phrase is **isomorphic** to that of its antecedent.

syllabic

음절을 이루는

[sɪ'læbɪk]

forming a syllable, especially a consonant that acts as the nucleus

(syn) vocalic, core-forming

(e.g.) It is usual to indicate that a consonant is **syllabic** by means of a small vertical mark.

유희태 일반영어

⑤ 기출 VOCA 30days

feature	○○○	adjunct	○○○
obstruent	○○○	decode	○○○
sonorant	○○○	redundancy	○○○
approximant	○○○	correlation	○○○
resonance	○○○	substitution	○○○
neutralize	○○○	inflection	○○○
error-prone behavior	○○○	phonotactic	○○○
trochaic	○○○	revert	○○○
aspirated	○○○	unwarranted	○○○
cohesion	○○○	complex onset	○○○
presuppose	○○○	entail	○○○
lexical	○○○	transcribe	○○○
coherent	○○○	accompany	○○○
genre	○○○	locus	○○○
norm	○○○	depict	○○○
milieu	○○○	inconsiderate	○○○
paradigm	○○○	legitimize	○○○
rigor	○○○	nominal	○○○
reactive	○○○	panorama	○○○
pre-emptive	○○○	retrospection	○○○
metalanguage	○○○	adamant	○○○
recast	○○○	callous	○○○
schema	○○○	candid	○○○
spectral	○○○	discern	○○○
complementizer	○○○	decontextualize	○○○
subjacency	○○○	tendency	○○○
constraint	○○○	mature	○○○
coordination	○○○	resolute	○○○
ongoing	○○○	enigmatic	○○○
complement	○○○	astound	○○○

feature
(변별) 자질, 특징

['fiːtʃər]

a distinct element or characteristic; a distinctive trait in phonology
(syn) trait, characteristic
(e.g.) Voicing is an important **feature** that distinguishes sounds.

obstruent
장애음

['ɑːbstruənt]

a consonant sound made by blocking or restricting airflow
(syn) consonant (stop/fricative)
(e.g.) The sound /p/ is an **obstruent**.

sonorant
공명음

['sɑːnərənt]

a sound produced with free airflow, such as vowels or nasals
(syn) non-obstruent
(e.g.) The sound /m/ is a **sonorant**.

approximant
접근음

[ə'prɑːksɪmənt]

a sound made when two articulators come close but without friction
(syn) glide, liquid
(e.g.) The sound /w/ in *we* is an **approximant.**

resonance
공명, 울림

['rezənəns]

the quality in a sound of being deep, full, and reverberating
(syn) reverberation, vibration
(e.g.) The **resonance** of the vowel /a/ makes it stand out in singing.

neutralize
중화시키다

['nuːtrəlaɪz]

to eliminate the distinction between two sounds
(syn) negate, counteract
(e.g.) The contrast between the two liquids is **neutralized** after alveolar obstruents.

error-prone behavior

오류 발생이 쉬운 행동

['ɛrər proʊn bə'heɪvjər]

behavior that easily leads to mistakes
(syn) mistake-prone tendency
(e.g.) Complacency and bias can make us display **error-prone behavior** when relying on computers.

trochaic

강약격의, 트로카이의

[troʊ'keɪɪk]

a metrical foot consisting of a stressed syllable followed by an unstressed syllable
(syn) falling rhythm
(e.g.) Here we are going to refer to foot, which is **trochaic** in English.

aspirated

기식음화된

['æspəreɪtɪd]

pronounced with an accompanying puff of breath
(syn) breathed
(e.g.) Voiceless stops are **aspirated** when they are followed by a stressed vowel.

cohesion

응집성

[koʊ'hiːʒən]

the grammatical and lexical links that bind a text together
(syn) unity, connectedness
(e.g.) For conversational discourse to be successful, the participants have to achieve **cohesion**.

presuppose

전제하다

[ˌpriːsə'poʊz]

to require a preceding element in a discourse for interpretation
(syn) assume, imply
(e.g.) A cohesive relation is one in which the interpretation of one element **presupposes** another.

lexical
어휘의

['lɛksɪkəl]

relating to the words or vocabulary of a language

(syn) vocabulary-based

(e.g.) **Lexical** cohesive devices include the use of synonyms and repetition.

coherent
통일성 있는

[koʊˈhɪrənt]

logically connected; forming a unified whole

(syn) consistent, logical

(e.g.) The talk becomes more **coherent** when the speakers are talking to topic.

genre
장르

['ʒɑːnrə]

a socially recognized way of using language for a particular purpose

(syn) category, type

(e.g.) A genre-based writing instruction involves students in an in-depth analysis of texts in the **genre**.

norm
규범

[nɔːrm]

a standard or pattern, especially of social behavior

(syn) standard, rule

(e.g.) Genre represents the **norms** of different kinds of writing shared among people within a community.

milieu
환경, 사회적 배경

[miːˈljɜː]

a person's social or cultural setting; the context in which something occurs

(syn) environment, sphere

(e.g.) The novel reflects the artistic **milieu** of early twentieth-century Paris.

paradigm

모범, 전형, 이론적 틀

['pærədaɪm]

a typical example or framework that shapes thought or practice
(syn) model, archetype
(e.g.) The researcher proposed a new **paradigm** for understanding second-language acquisition.

rigor

엄밀함, 철저함

['rɪgər]

the quality of being extremely thorough, careful, and precise
(syn) strictness, exactness
(e.g.) The study was praised for its **rigor** and methodological consistency.

reactive

반응적인

[ri'æktɪv]

acting in response to a situation
(syn) responsive, consequential
(e.g.) **Reactive** focus on form arises out of some problem in a participant's production.

pre-emptive

선제적인

[ˌpriː'ɛmptɪv]

taking action before someone else does
(syn) anticipatory, proactive
(e.g.) **Pre-emptive** focus on form is where participants make a particular form the topic even though no problem has arisen.

metalanguage

메타언어

[ˌmɛtə'læŋgwɪdʒ]

language used to discuss language
(syn) linguistic terminology
(e.g.) The teacher directly corrects the error by formally correcting it or by using **metalanguage**.

recast

재진술

[ri'kæst]

an implicit type of corrective feedback that rephrases a student's incorrect utterance

(syn) rephrase, reformulation

(e.g.) The teacher responds to a student's error by means of a **recast** or a clarification request.

schema

배경지식, 스키마, 도식

['ski:mə]

a conceptual framework or mental structure for organizing and interpreting information

(syn) framework, mental model

(e.g.) I usually have pre-reading discussion time to activate **schemata**.

spectral

유령 같은, 스펙트럼의

['spɛktrəl]

relating to or resembling a ghost; also relating to a spectrum in scientific or linguistic contexts

(syn) ghostly, phantom, ethereal

(e.g.) The novel's atmosphere is filled with **spectral** images that blur the line between reality and illusion.

complementizer

보문사

['kɒmplɪməntaɪzər]

a function word that introduces a complement clause

(syn) subordinator

(e.g.) In many sentences, the **complementizer** "that" can be omitted without changing the meaning of the clause.

subjacency

인접 조건

[ˌsʌbdʒeɪsənsi]

a syntactic constraint that restricts movement to be local

(syn) locality principle

(e.g.) The sentence is a violation of **subjacency** because the wh-phrase crosses over three bounding nodes.

constraint
제약, 제한

[kənˈstreɪnt]

a restriction or limitation

(syn) limitation, restriction

(e.g.) Subjacency is a syntactic **constraint** that restricts movement to be local.

coordination
등위 연결

[koʊˌɔːrdɪˈneɪʃən]

the joining of constituents that are of the same type and perform the same syntactic function

(syn) linking, conjoining

(e.g.) **Coordination** is possible when two constituents share the same type of syntactic function.

ongoing
계속 진행 중인

[ˈɒnˌɡoʊɪŋ]

continuing to happen; still developing

(syn) continuing, persistent

(e.g.) The teacher's **ongoing** investigation of her teaching practice improved her lessons.

complement
보어

[ˈkɑːmpləmənt]

a word or group of words that completes the meaning of a verb, adjective, or other element

(syn) necessary element, argument

(e.g.) A **complement** can be conjoined by another complement, but not with an adjunct.

adjunct
부가어, 수식어

[ˈædʒʌŋkt]

a word or phrase that constitutes an optional addition to a sentence

(syn) modifier, optional element

(e.g.) If a complement is combined with an **adjunct**, ungrammaticality results.

decode 해독하다

[diːˈkoʊd]

to convert a coded message back into its original form; understand written or spoken language

(syn) decipher, interpretate

(e.g.) Bottom-up processing is the processing of individual elements for the **decoding** of language input.

redundancy 중복, 과잉

[rɪˈdʌndənsi]

the state of being unnecessarily repeated or used more than needed

(syn) repetition, duplication

(e.g.) Good writing avoids **redundancy** by removing repeated ideas.

correlation 상관관계, 연관성

[ˌkɔːrəˈleɪʃn]

a mutual relationship or connection between two or more things

(syn) association, interrelation

(e.g.) Researchers found a strong **correlation** between reading habits and vocabulary growth.

substitution 대체

[ˌsʌbstɪˈtuːʃən]

the action of replacing someone or something with another person or thing

(syn) replacement

(e.g.) Grammatical cohesive devices include reference, **substitution**, ellipsis, and conjunction.

inflection 굴절

[ɪnˈflɛkʃən]

a change in the form of a word to express a grammatical function

(syn) modification, variation

(e.g.) The test focuses on the correct **inflection** of adjectives for comparatives and superlatives.

phonotactic 음운 규칙의

[ˌfoʊnəˈtæktɪk]

relating to the sound patterns that are permitted in a language
(syn) sound-pattern related
(e.g.) Speakers simply reject nonsense words that violate English **phonotactic** rules.

revert 되돌아가다, 복귀하다

[rɪˈvɜːrt]

to return to (a previous state, practice, or topic)
(syn) return, go back
(e.g.) The program ensures students do not **revert** to relying solely on bottom-up processing.

unwarranted 부당한, 불필요한

[ʌnˈwɔːrəntɪd]

not justified or authorized
(syn) unjustified, uncalled-for
(e.g.) The use of jargon in criticism can be considered **unwarranted** when it aims to obscure rather than clarify.

complex onset 복잡한 음절 초두군

[ˈkɒmpleks ˈɒnˌsɛt]

a syllable beginning with two or more consonants
(syn) consonant cluster beginning
(e.g.) Words with a **complex onset**, like *shliz*, can still sound English-like if they follow phonotactic rules.

entail 수반하다, 필요로 하다

[ɪnˈteɪl]

to involve (something) as a necessary or inevitable part or consequence
(syn) involve, require
(e.g.) The new reading activity may **entail** additional preparation time for the teacher.

transcribe 전사하다

[trænˈskraɪb]

to put thoughts, speech, or data into written or printed form
(syn) write down, render
(e.g.) Researchers had to **transcribe** all the recorded conversations to analyze the students' errors.

accompany
동반하다, 함께하다

[əˈkʌmpəni]

to go somewhere with (someone) as a companion or escort
(syn) attend, escort
(e.g.) I could create a listening task **accompanied** by a note-taking sheet.

locus
(특정 활동의) 중심지, 소재

[ˈloʊkəs]

a particular position, place, or focus of activity
(syn) center, point
(e.g.) The **locus** of the grammatical error was identified in the use of the past tense.

depict
묘사하다, 그리다

[dɪˈpɪkt]

to represent by a drawing, painting, or other art form
(syn) portray, describe
(e.g.) The sequenced pictures in the task **depict** a scene for the students to describe using superlatives.

inconsiderate
경솔한, 사려 깊지 못한

[ˌɪnkənˈsɪdərət]

thoughtlessly causing hurt or inconvenience to others
(syn) thoughtless, selfish
(e.g.) Making others wait is regarded as **inconsiderate** in Ken's culture.

legitimize
정당화하다, 합법화하다

[lɪˈdʒɪtəmaɪz]

to make something acceptable, reasonable, or officially valid
(syn) validate, authorize, sanction
(e.g.) The new evidence helped **legitimize** the theory that had long been dismissed.

nominal
명목상의, 아주 적은

[ˈnɒmɪnəl]

existing in name only or very small in amount
(syn) token, insignificant, minimal
(e.g.) Despite its **nominal** cost, the service offered remarkable quality.

panorama
전경, 전체적 모습

[ˌpænəˈræmə]

a comprehensive or broad view of a situation, series of events, or subject

(syn) overview, prospect, landscape

(e.g.) The novel offers a vivid **panorama** of life in a rapidly changing society.

retrospection
회고, 반추

[ˌretrəˈspɛkʃən]

the act of looking back on or reviewing past events or situations

(syn) recollection, remembrance, reflection

(e.g.) In moments of quiet **retrospection**, she reconsidered the choices that shaped her life.

adamant
단호한, 확고한

[ǽdəmənt]

refusing to be persuaded or to change one's mind

(syn) resolute, firm, unwavering, determined

(opp) flexible, yielding, compliant

(e.g.) He was **adamant** about finishing the project on his own terms.

callous
냉담한, 무정한

[kǽləs]

showing or having an insensitive and cruel disregard for others

(syn) heartless, unfeeling, insensitive, unsympathetic

(opp) compassionate, empathetic, kind

(e.g.) The manager's **callous** remark hurt everyone in the meeting.

candid
솔직한, 허심탄회한

[kǽndɪd]

truthful and straightforward; frank and honest in expression

(syn) frank, sincere, open, forthright

(opp) deceitful, guarded, evasive

(e.g.) He gave a **candid** answer about his failures in business.

discern

식별하다, 인식하다

[dɪsə́ːrn]

to perceive or recognize something clearly, especially something not obvious
- (syn) detect, distinguish, perceive, identify
- (opp) overlook, ignore, miss
- (e.g.) It was difficult to **discern** truth from rumor in the report.

decontextualize

맥락에서 분리하다

[ˌdiːkənˈtɛkstʃuəˌlaɪz]

to remove something from its original context, making it harder to interpret
- (syn) isolate, detach
- (e.g.) Reading too slowly can **decontextualize** words and lead to tunnel vision.

tendency

경향

['tɛndənsi]

a usual or repeated behavior or pattern
- (syn) inclination, habit
- (e.g.) English speakers have a strong **tendency** to maintain regular rhythm in speech.

mature

성숙해지다

[məˈtʊə(r)]

to develop fully in mind or body
- (syn) grow, develop
- (e.g.) Students need time to **mature** as writers, especially when learning to organize ideas logically.

resolute

확고한, 단호한

[rézəlùːt]

admirably purposeful, determined, and unwavering
- (syn) determined, steadfast, unwavering, firm
- (opp) indecisive, weak, hesitant
- (e.g.) She remained **resolute** in defending her principles despite criticism.

enigmatic

수수께끼 같은, 불가사의한

[ènigmǽtik]

mysterious and difficult to understand
- (syn) puzzling, cryptic, obscure, inscrutable
- (opp) clear, obvious, transparent
- (e.g.) His **enigmatic** smile left everyone wondering about his true feelings.

astound

깜짝 놀라게 하다

[əstáund]

to shock or greatly surprise someone
- (syn) amaze, astonish, stun, startle
- (opp) bore, calm, expect
- (e.g.) The magician's final trick **astounded** the entire audience.

DAY

13

2021

DAY

14

유희태 일반영어

5 기출 VOCA 30days

discourse	○○○	degenerative	○○○
netiquette	○○○	subdued	○○○
spectrum	○○○	dissonance	○○○
discrepant	○○○	confine	○○○
yardstick	○○○	dichotomy	○○○
integrity	○○○	reversion	○○○
exquisite	○○○	equate	○○○
outstrip	○○○	subsume	○○○
citation	○○○	cultivation	○○○
forlorn	○○○	abnormality	○○○
draggled	○○○	transnational	○○○
puzzled	○○○	acumen	○○○
makeweight	○○○	mobilize	○○○
obliged	○○○	relic	○○○
foreboding	○○○	differentiate	○○○
luring	○○○	arcane	○○○
nervously	○○○	axiom	○○○
vicinity	○○○	polarized	○○○
diphthong	○○○	ethos	○○○
monophthong	○○○	evince	○○○
generalization	○○○	enact	○○○
contrast	○○○	transmission	○○○
phenomena	○○○	aural	○○○
category	○○○	reconstruction	○○○
monitor	○○○	reinterpretation	○○○
rhetorically	○○○	anomaly	○○○
indice	○○○	viability	○○○
successively	○○○	synthetic	○○○
indoctrination	○○○	concurrently	○○○
improperly	○○○	inadequate	○○○

discourse
담화, 토론, 언어

['dɪskɔːrs]

written or spoken communication or debate; a formal discussion of a topic
(syn) conversation, communication
(e.g.) Political **discourse** often involves heated debate on social issues.

netiquette
네티켓 (네트워크 에티켓)

['netɪket]

the correct or acceptable way of communicating on the Internet
(syn) online manners
(e.g.) Students must follow proper **netiquette** when posting in the online forum.

spectrum
스펙트럼, 범위

['spɛktrəm]

a wide range of related ideas, qualities, or activities
(syn) range, scale
(e.g.) The study examined a broad **spectrum** of learning strategies.

discrepant
모순된, 상반된

[dɪ'skrepənt]

showing a lack of agreement or harmony between facts or ideas
(syn) conflicting, divergent
(e.g.) The witnesses gave **discrepant** accounts of what happened.

yardstick
기준, 척도

['jɑːrdstɪk]

a standard used for comparison or measurement
(syn) benchmark, gauge
(e.g.) Customer satisfaction is often used as a **yardstick** for company performance.

integrity

진실성, 완전성

[ɪnˈtegrəti]

the state of being honest and having strong principles; structural or moral soundness
(syn) honesty, probity, unity
(e.g.) The bridge's **integrity** must be tested regularly to ensure safety.

exquisite

매우 아름다운, 정교한

[ˈekskwɪzɪt]

extremely beautiful and delicate
(syn) superb, magnificent
(e.g.) The artist captured the **exquisite** details of the landscape.

outstrip

능가하다, 뛰어넘다

[aʊtˈstrɪp]

to go faster, further, or be better than someone or something
(syn) surpass, outperform, eclipse
(e.g.) The company's sales continued to **outstrip** all market predictions.

citation

인용, 언급

[saɪˈteɪʃən]

a reference to a source or an acknowledgment of another's words or ideas
(syn) quotation, reference
(e.g.) The researcher included every **citation** carefully according to the required format.

forlorn

쓸쓸해 보이는, 버려진

[fərˈlɔːrn]

pitifully sad and abandoned or lonely
(syn) despondent, abandoned
(e.g.) She held the **forlorn** little piece of money out to her.

draggled

흙에 더럽혀진, 축 늘어진

[ˈdrægəld]

wet and dirty from being trailed along the ground
(syn) muddy, soiled
(e.g.) She was wearing **draggled**, once fine clothes.

puzzled   어리둥절한, 당황한

[ˈpʌzld]

unable to understand; perplexed
(syn) bewildered, confused
(e.g.) The woman looked **puzzled** and good-natured all at once.

makeweight   부충물, 덤

[ˈmeɪkweɪt]

something added to complete a required weight
(syn) addition, filler
(e.g.) I'll throw in two for **makeweight**.

obliged   감사하는, 고마워하는

[əˈblaɪdʒd]

indebted or grateful (for a service or favor)
(syn) grateful, thankful
(e.g.) I am much **obliged** to you for your kindness.

foreboding   불길한 예감, 전조

[fɔːrˈboʊdɪŋ]

a feeling that something bad is going to happen
(syn) apprehension, dread
(e.g.) There's something **foreboding** in the air.

luring   유혹하는, 매혹적인

[ˈloərɪŋ]

powerfully attractive or tempting; enticing
(syn) attractive, tempting
(e.g.) The sound was **luring** them toward the danger outside.

nervously   초조하게, 불안하게

[ˈnɜːrvəsli]

in an uneasy or fearful way; with nervousness
(syn) anxiously, agitatedly
(e.g.) Felicity turns off the radio **nervously**.

vicinity
근처, 부근

[vɪˈsɪnəti]

the area near or surrounding a particular place
(syn) proximity, neighborhood
(e.g.) The search has narrowed to the immediate **vicinity** of Muldoon Manor.

diphthong
이중 모음

[ˈdɪfθɔːŋ]

a sound formed by the combination of two vowels in a single syllable
(syn) gliding vowel
(e.g.) /ou/ is realized as a **diphthong** [ou].

monophthong
단일 모음

[ˈmɒnəfθɔːŋ]

a vowel in which the tongue position does not change
(syn) pure vowel
(e.g.) /ou/ is realized as a **monophthong** [o].

generalization
일반화

[ˌdʒenərəlaɪˈzeɪʃn]

a general statement or concept obtained by inference from specific cases
(syn) abstraction, principle
(e.g.) One could make a **generalization** as in (3).

contrast
대조, 대비

[ˈkɒntræst]

the state of being strikingly different from something else
(syn) difference, distinction
(e.g.) It cannot explain the **contrast** between (4) and (5).

phenomena
현상

[fəˈnɒmɪnə]

plural of phenomenon; a fact or situation that is observed to exist or happen
(syn) occurrences, events
(e.g.) To account for some syntactic **phenomena**.

DAY
14

category

범주, 분류

['kætəgɔːri]

a class or division of people or things regarded as having particular shared characteristics
(syn) class, group
(e.g.) We can resort to phrasal **categories** such as VP, TP, CP.

monitor

감시하다, 감독하다

['mɒnɪtər]

to observe and check the progress or quality of (something)
(syn) track, oversee
(e.g.) She argued persuasively that the supervisory line should **monitor** the whole production schedule.

rhetorically

수사적으로, 설득의 기술로

[rɪ'tɒrɪkli]

in a manner intended to persuade or impress, often using effective language
(syn) eloquently, persuasively
(e.g.) The speaker argued **rhetorically**, using vivid examples and careful pacing.

indice

지표, 척도

['ɪndɪs]

a numerical or symbolic measure used to represent conditions or trends
(syn) indicator, measure, benchmark
(e.g.) Economic **indices** show a steady improvement in global trade.

successively

연속적으로, 잇따라

[sək'sɛsɪvli]

in sequence; one after another without interruption
(syn) sequentially, consecutively
(e.g.) The lights flashed **successively**, creating a smooth transition across the stage.

indoctrination
주입식 교육, 세뇌

[ɪnˌdɒktrɪˈneɪʃən]

the process of teaching someone to accept a set of beliefs uncritically

(syn) conditioning, inculcation

(e.g.) The film explores how political **indoctrination** can shape collective identity.

improperly
부적절하게, 틀리게

[ɪmˈprɒpərli]

in a way that is not suitable or correct

(syn) incorrectly, inappropriately

(e.g.) The equipment stopped working because it had been **improperly** installed.

degenerative
퇴행성의, 악화되는

[dɪˈdʒɛnərətɪv]

characterized by progressive decline or deterioration

(syn) deteriorative, regressive

(e.g.) The report warned of a **degenerative** trend in urban infrastructure.

subdued
차분한, 눌린

[səbˈdjuːd]

quiet and controlled; lacking intensity or energy

(syn) restrained, muted

(e.g.) Her voice was **subdued**, but her words carried deep emotion.

dissonance
불협화음, 불일치

[ˈdɪsənəns]

a lack of harmony or agreement between ideas or elements

(syn) discord, incongruity

(e.g.) The film's eerie **dissonance** between sound and image created tension.

confine
제한하다, 가두다

[kənˈfaɪn]

to keep something or someone within limits or in a particular place
(syn) restrict, limit
(e.g.) The teacher reminded students not to **confine** their ideas to the examples given in the book.

dichotomy
이분법, 양분

[daɪˈkɒtəmi]

a division or contrast between two things that are represented as being entirely different
(syn) duality, polarity
(e.g.) The novel explores the **dichotomy** between freedom and responsibility.

reversion
복귀, 되돌아감

[rɪˈvɜːrʒən]

a return to a previous state, condition, or form
(syn) regression, relapse
(e.g.) The country's **reversion** to isolationist policies surprised many observers.

equate
동일시하다

[iˈkweɪt]

to consider one thing as being the same as another
(syn) identify with, regard as equal
(e.g.) Some students mistakenly **equate** high test scores with true language ability.

subsume
포함하다, 통합하다

[səbˈsjuːm]

to include or absorb into a larger or more general category
(syn) incorporate, encompass
(e.g.) Artistic innovation is often **subsumed** under broader cultural trends.

cultivation
배양, 함양

[ˌkʌltɪ'veɪʃən]

the process of improving or developing something, especially through sustained care or education
(syn) refinement, nurturing
(e.g.) The **cultivation** of moral character was central to ancient philosophy.

abnormality
비정상, 이상

[ˌæbnɔːr'mæləti]

a condition that deviates from what is typical
(syn) irregularity, deviation
(e.g.) In phonology, even a slight **abnormality** in sound patterning can affect how native speakers judge the well-formedness of a word.

DAY
14

transnational
초국가적인, 국경을 초월한

[ˌtrænz'næʃənl]

extending beyond or operating across national boundaries
(syn) global, cross-border
(e.g.) The summit addressed **transnational** challenges such as migration and climate change.

acumen
통찰력, 감각

['ækjʊmən]

the ability to make quick and accurate judgments or decisions
(syn) insight, discernment
(e.g.) His scientific **acumen** made him one of the leading figures in modern research.

mobilize
동원하다, 활용하다

['moʊbəlaɪz]

to organize and bring into action or use for a particular purpose
(syn) deploy, activate
(e.g.) The campaign aimed to **mobilize** public support for environmental reform.

relic

유물, 잔재

['rɛlɪk]

surviving object or custom from an earlier time, often carrying historical or symbolic meaning

(syn) remnant, vestige

(e.g.) The museum displayed **relics** of early human craftsmanship.

differentiate

구분하다, 차별화하다

[ˌdɪfəˈrɛnʃieɪt]

to recognize or express the difference between two or more things

(syn) distinguish, demarcate

(e.g.) It's important to **differentiate** genuine curiosity from superficial interest.

arcane

난해한, 비밀스러운

[ɑːrˈkeɪn]

understood by only a few people with specialized knowledge; mysterious

(syn) esoteric, abstruse

(e.g.) The scholar's **arcane** terminology made his lecture difficult for beginners.

axiom

공리, 자명한 원리

['æksiəm]

a statement or principle accepted as true without proof; foundational truth

(syn) postulate, maxim

(e.g.) Ethics is often built upon philosophical **axioms** about human nature.

polarized

양극화된, 대립된

['poʊləraɪzd]

divided into two sharply contrasting groups or sets of opinions

(syn) divided, antithetical

(e.g.) The debate grew increasingly **polarized** as emotions heightened.

ethos

정신, 기풍

[ˈiːθɒs]

the characteristic spirit, values, or guiding beliefs of a culture or community
(syn) spirit, culture
(e.g.) The novel reflects the **ethos** of postwar disillusionment.

evince

분명히 나타내다, 드러내다

[ɪˈvɪns]

to reveal the presence of a quality, feeling, or attitude clearly
(syn) demonstrate, manifest
(e.g.) Her calm tone **evinced** a quiet confidence.

enact

제정하다, 시행하다

[ɪˈnækt]

to make a law or put an idea formally into action
(syn) establish, implement
(e.g.) The committee voted to **enact** new regulations on data privacy.

transmission

전달, 전파

[trænzˈmɪʃən]

the process of passing something from one person, place, or generation to another
(syn) dissemination, communication
(e.g.) The **transmission** of cultural values often occurs through shared stories.

aural

청각의

[ˈɔːrəl]

relating to the ear or the sense of hearing
(syn) auditory, acoustic
(e.g.) Transferring **aural** information.

reconstruction

재구성, 복원

[ˌriːkənˈstrʌkʃən]

the act of rebuilding or reinterpreting something from existing elements or fragments
(syn) restoration, reassembly
(e.g.) The historian devoted years to the **reconstruction** of the destroyed manuscript.

reinterpretation
재해석, 새로운 해석

[ˌriːɪnˌtɜːrprɪˈteɪʃən]

the process of understanding something in a different or updated way

(syn) reexamination, revision

(e.g.) The myth has undergone **reinterpretation** in light of modern psychology.

anomaly
이례, 변칙

[əˈnɒməli]

irregularity or deviation from what is standard or expected

(syn) exception, aberration

(e.g.) Astronomers noted several **anomalies** in the planet's orbit.

viability
생존 가능성, 실행 가능성

[ˌvaɪəˈbɪləti]

the ability to work effectively or continue to exist

(syn) practicality, operability

(e.g.) The **viability** of the new energy model remains uncertain.

synthetic
종합적인, 인공적인

[sɪnˈθetɪk]

made by combining different elements; artificial or contrived

(syn) composite, fabricated

(e.g.) The lab developed a **synthetic** compound to replace natural rubber.

concurrently
동시에, 병행하여

[kənˈkʌrəntli]

happening or existing at the same time

(syn) simultaneously, synchronously

(e.g.) Two reforms were implemented **concurrently** across the provinces.

inadequate
부적절한, 불충분한

[ɪnˈædɪkwət]

not enough or not suitable for a particular purpose

(syn) insufficient, deficient

(e.g.) Their **inadequate** response led to widespread criticism.

MEMO

2021

DAY

15

interwoven	○○○	reincarnation	○○○
durability	○○○	lucrative	○○○
arbitration	○○○	eccentric	○○○
ordinance	○○○	exclude	○○○
momentum	○○○	categorical	○○○
reclusive	○○○	kowtow	○○○
lucidity	○○○	contrary	○○○
recruit	○○○	adorn	○○○
Third Culture Kids	○○○	dimple	○○○
formative	○○○	metaphor	○○○
undeniable	○○○	consult	○○○
alienation	○○○	resemblance	○○○
initiate	○○○	metrical	○○○
diaspora	○○○	emerge	○○○
amplify	○○○	alteration	○○○
ancillary	○○○	deletion	○○○
persistence	○○○	medial	○○○
structuralist	○○○	prime	○○○
eliminate	○○○	locative	○○○
inflectional	○○○	inversion	○○○
sequence	○○○	preposing	○○○
relational	○○○	postposing	○○○
precedence	○○○	reflexive	○○○
derivative	○○○	framework	○○○
kinetics	○○○	optimization	○○○
particle	○○○	configuration	○○○
determinant	○○○	applicability	○○○
conciliate	○○○	encapsulation	○○○
facetiously	○○○	retrieval	○○○
babble	○○○	appraise	○○○

interwoven
얽혀 있는, 밀접히 관련된

[ˌɪntərˈwoʊvən]

closely connected or combined in a complex way
(syn) intertwined, entangled
(e.g.) Memory and imagination are **interwoven** in the act of storytelling.

durability
내구성, 지속성

[ˌdjʊərəˈbɪləti]

the ability to withstand wear, pressure, or damage
(syn) endurance, permanence
(e.g.) The **durability** of the structure reflects exceptional engineering.

arbitration
중재, 조정

[ˌɑːrbɪˈtreɪʃən]

the process of resolving a dispute outside the courts by an impartial third party
(syn) mediation, adjudication
(e.g.) The contract required disputes to be settled through **arbitration**.

ordinance
조례, 규정

[ˈɔːrdɪnəns]

an authoritative law or decree enacted by a government or institution
(syn) edict, mandate
(e.g.) Local **ordinances** now restrict construction near heritage sites.

momentum
탄력, 추진력

[moʊˈmentəm]

the driving force gained by the development of a process or course of events
(syn) impetus, drive
(e.g.) The movement gained **momentum** after widespread public support.

reclusive

은둔한, 세상과 떨어진

[rɪˈkluːsɪv]

avoiding social contact; preferring isolation
(syn) solitary, withdrawn
(e.g.) The **reclusive** poet lived in near-complete silence for decades.

lucidity

명료함, 투명성

[luːˈsɪdəti]

clarity of expression or thought; the quality of being easy to understand
(syn) clarity, coherence
(e.g.) Her writing is admired for its **lucidity** and precision.

recruit

신입, 신참

[rɪˈkruːt]

a person newly enlisted or joining an organization
(syn) newcomer, entrant
(e.g.) But then what do these **recruits** really matter.

DAY
15

Third Culture Kids

제3문화 아이들

[θɜːrd\ ˈkʌltʃər\ kɪdz]

children raised in a culture other than their parents' culture (or the culture of their passport country)
(syn) TCKs
(e.g.) Children in this situation are called "**Third Culture Kids**" (TCKs).

formative

형성하는, 발달상의

[ˈfɔːrmətɪv]

serving to form something, especially having a profound influence on a person's development
(syn) influential, developmental
(e.g.) Especially during their **formative** years.

undeniable

부인할 수 없는

[ˌʌndɪˈnaɪəbl]

unable to be denied or disputed
(syn) indisputable, unquestionable
(e.g.) **Undeniable** challenges.

alienation
소외, 이탈

[ˌeɪliəˈneɪʃn]

a state of being isolated from a group, activity, or sense of meaning
(syn) estrangement, detachment
(e.g.) Modern technology can create profound **alienation** despite global connectivity.

initiate
시작하다, 개시하다

[ɪˈnɪʃieɪt]

to begin something or cause it to start
(syn) begin, launch
(e.g.) The school will **initiate** a new program to improve students' writing skills next semester.

diaspora
이산, 흩어짐

[daɪˈæspərə]

the dispersion of people from their original homeland or community
(syn) dispersion, scattering
(e.g.) The cultural identity of a **diaspora** is often sustained through shared memory and language.

amplify
확대하다, 강화하다

[ˈæmplɪfaɪ]

to increase the intensity or impact of something
(syn) intensify, heighten
(e.g.) Social media tends to **amplify** both solidarity and conflict.

ancillary
보조적인, 부수적인

[ˈænsɪləri]

providing support to the main system or structure
(syn) supplementary, subsidiary
(e.g.) The museum developed **ancillary** programs to complement its main exhibition.

persistence 지속성, 집요함

[pər'sɪstəns]

the continued existence or endurance of something despite obstacles

(syn) endurance, tenacity

(e.g.) The **persistence** of linguistic patterns reveals deep cultural continuity.

structuralist 구조주의적인

['strʌktʃərəlɪst]

relating to the theory that phenomena are best understood as systems of interrelated elements

(syn) systemic, formalist

(e.g.) A **structuralist** reading interprets myths as symbolic networks of opposition.

DAY

15

eliminate 제거하다, 없애다

[ɪ'lɪmɪneɪt]

to remove something completely

(syn) remove, get rid of

(e.g.) Revising the flawed question helped **eliminate** confusion for the test takers.

inflectional 굴절의

[ɪn'flekʃənl]

relating to changes in form that express grammatical relationships

(syn) declensional, morphological

(e.g.) Languages differ widely in their use of **inflectional** endings to mark tense and case.

sequence 연속, 순서

['siːkwəns]

an ordered series of related elements or events

(syn) succession, progression

(e.g.) The ritual unfolded in a precise **sequence** of gestures and chants.

relational
관계적인

[rɪˈleɪʃənl]   concerning the way in which entities are connected or associated
(syn) interactive, correlative
(e.g.) Identity is a **relational** construct shaped by social perception.

precedence
우선권, 선행

[ˈpresɪdəns]   the condition of being considered more important than something
else; priority
(syn) priority, primacy
(e.g.) In moral decisions, human dignity should take **precedence**
over efficiency.

derivative
파생적인, 독창성 없는

[dɪˈrɪvətɪv]   something that originates from another source; lacking originality
(syn) secondary, imitative
(e.g.) His theory, though **derivative**, clarified earlier philosophical
arguments.

kinetics
운동학, 동력학

[kɪˈnɛtɪks]   the study of motion and the forces that cause it
(syn) dynamics, motion science
(e.g.) The sculpture captures a sense of **kinetics**, as if the metal
were alive with movement.

particle
입자, 미세 요소

[ˈpɑːrtɪkəl]   a minute portion of matter or linguistic unit with functional
meaning
(syn) element, fragment
(e.g.) Subatomic **particles** behave in ways that challenge
classical logic.

determinant
결정 요인

[dɪˈtɜːrmɪnənt]

a factor that decisively affects the nature or outcome of something
(syn) influence, catalyst
(e.g.) Access to education remains a key **determinant** of economic mobility.

conciliate
달래다, 화해시키다

[kənˈsɪlieɪt]

to gain goodwill or reduce hostility between opposing sides
(syn) appease, reconcile
(e.g.) The mediator worked to **conciliate** rival factions before negotiations collapsed.

facetiously
경박하게, 우스꽝스럽게

[fəˈsiːʃəsli]

treating serious issues with deliberately inappropriate humor
(syn) jokingly, flippantly
(e.g.) Smiling **facetiously** into the candlelight.

babble
재잘거리다

[ˈbæbəl]

to talk rapidly and excitedly in a way that is difficult to understand
(syn) prattle, chatter
(e.g.) As the others **babbled** about reincarnation.

reincarnation
환생

[ˌriːɪnkɑːrˈneɪʃn]

the rebirth of a soul in a new body
(syn) transmigration, rebirth
(e.g.) Babbled about **reincarnation**.

lucrative
수익성이 좋은, 돈이 되는

[ˈluːkrətɪv]

producing a great deal of profit
(syn) profitable, remunerative
(e.g.) Architects who wanted a **lucrative** business.

eccentric
괴짜, 기인

[ɪkˈsentrɪk]

a person of unconventional and slightly strange views or behavior
(syn) oddball, individualist
(e.g.) I am prepared to put up with an **eccentrics**.

exclude
제외하다

[ɪkˈskluːd]

to leave something or someone out; to prevent participation
(syn) leave out, omit
(e.g.) In the revised version, unnecessary details were **excluded** to make the item clearer.

categorical
범주적인, 단정적인

[ˌkætəˈɡɒrɪkəl]

unconditional and explicit, leaving no room for doubt
(syn) absolute, definitive
(e.g.) The manager gave a **categorical** refusal, making it clear that the decision would not be changed.

kowtow
굽실거리다

[ˌkaʊˈtaʊ]

to act in an excessively subservient manner
(syn) grovel, defer
(e.g.) They don't have to **kowtow** to anybody.

contrary
반대되는, 고집 센

[ˈkɒntreri]

opposed to what is expected; perversely inclined to disagree
(syn) opposite, rebellious
(e.g.) Just for being their **contrary** little selves.

adorn
장식하다

[əˈdɔːrn]

to make more beautiful or attractive
(syn) decorate, embellish
(e.g.) The desiguer **adorned** the dress with flowers before my eye.

dimple
잔물결이 일다

['dɪmpl]

to form small depressions or ripples on the surface
(syn) ripple
(e.g.) I saw the **dimpling** river pass.

metaphor
은유

['metəfɔːr]

a figure of speech in which a word or phrase is applied to an object or action that it does not literally denote
(syn) figure of speech, analogy
(e.g.) **Metaphor** can in one way be defined as a figure of speech.

consult
상담하다, 자문을 구하다

[kən'sʌlt]

to ask someone for information or advice
(syn) seek advice from, ask
(e.g.) Before revising the test items, the teacher decided to **consult** a more experienced colleague.

DAY
15

resemblance
유사성, 닮음

[rɪ'zembləns]

the state of being similar to something or someone
(syn) similarity, likeness
(e.g.) In order to imply a **resemblance**.

metrical
율격의, 운문적인

['mɛtrɪkəl]

relating to the measured rhythm or pattern of a poetic or musical composition
(syn) rhythmic, cadenced
(e.g.) The poem's **metrical** balance mirrors the harmony of its theme.

emerge
나타나다, 드러나다

[i'mɜːrdʒ]

to come out or become visible; to become known
(syn) appear, arise
(e.g.) After reviewing the students' drafts, several common problems **emerged** in their organization and vocabulary use.

alteration
변화, 수정

[ˌɔːltəˈreɪʃən]

a change made to something
(syn) modification, adjustment
(e.g.) The plan needed a small **alteration** before everyone agreed to it.

deletion
삭제

[dɪˈliːʃn]

the action or process of deleting or erasing something
(syn) removal, effacement
(e.g.) Foot structure can change due to [ə]-**deletion**.

medial
중간의

[ˈmiːdiəl]

situated in the middle
(syn) middle, central
(e.g.) [ə] in a **medial** stressless syllable can be deleted.

prime
(v) 준비시키다, 미리 영향을 주다, (a) 가장 중요한, 최고의

[praɪm]

(v) to make someone ready for something, especially by giving information in advance; (a) also used to mean the best or most important part
(syn) prepare, condition
(e.g.) Teachers often **prime** students with background knowledge before starting a difficult reading passage.

locative
처소의, 위치의

[ˈloʊkətɪv]

indicating place or location
(syn) positional, spatial
(e.g.) **Locative** inversion involves the preposing of a locative phrase.

inversion
도치

[ɪnˈvɜːrʒn]

the reversal of the normal order of words
(syn) reversal, transposition
(e.g.) Locative **inversion**.

preposing 전치

[pri:ˈpoʊzɪŋ]

the moving of a phrase to the front of a sentence
(syn) fronting, initial placement
(e.g.) Involves the **preposing** of a locative phrase.

postposing 후치

[poʊstˈpoʊzɪŋ]

the moving of a phrase to the end of a sentence
(syn) postponing, end-placement
(e.g.) And the **postposing** of the subject after the verb.

reflexive 반성적인, 되비치는

[rɪˈfleksɪv]

directed back on itself; self-referential
(syn) introspective, self-referent
(e.g.) The essay took a **reflexive** tone, questioning its own assumptions.

framework 체계, 골격

[ˈfreɪmwɜːrk]

a supporting structure or underlying set of principles
(syn) system, schema
(e.g.) The policy was developed within a new ethical **framework**.

optimization 최적화

[ˌɒptɪmaɪˈzeɪʃn]

the process of making a system as effective or functional as possible
(syn) maximization, enhancement
(e.g.) Continuous **optimization** improved the model's predictive accuracy.

configuration 구성, 배치

[kənˌfɪɡjəˈreɪʃn]

the arrangement or pattern of elements within a system or structure
(syn) layout, composition
(e.g.) The device failed because of an unstable **configuration**.

DAY

15

applicability 적용 가능성

[əˌplɪkəˈbɪləti]

the quality of being relevant or suitable for a particular use or situation
(syn) relevance, suitability
(e.g.) The study examined the **applicability** of the method to real-world teaching.

encapsulation 포함, 요약

[ɪnˌkæpsjʊˈleɪʃn]

the act of expressing or containing something within a concise or bounded form
(syn) containment, summary
(e.g.) The essay serves as an **encapsulation** of the author's broader philosophy.

retrieval 회상, 검색

[rɪˈtriːvəl]

the act of recalling or recovering information from memory or storage
(syn) recall, recollection
(e.g.) Vocabulary **retrieval** is faster when the target words are contextually meaningful.

appraise 평가하다

[əˈpreɪz]

to assess the value or quality of
(syn) evaluate, assess
(e.g.) These three constructs can be applied to **appraise** written or spoken language skill.

MEMO

DAY

16

유희태 일반영어
⑤ 기출 VOCA 30days

ratio	○○○	displace	○○○
tally	○○○	skepticism	○○○
skim	○○○	monopoly	○○○
calibration	○○○	predecessor	○○○
enunciation	○○○	reciprocal	○○○
homophone	○○○	manifest	○○○
palate	○○○	presume	○○○
gustatory	○○○	ramification	○○○
olfactory	○○○	attenuated	○○○
hue	○○○	undermine	○○○
intervention	○○○	ingenuity	○○○
revulsion	○○○	irrevocable	○○○
semiotics	○○○	protocol	○○○
corpus	○○○	frugal	○○○
collocation	○○○	regulation	○○○
authentic	○○○	explicate	○○○
audacious	○○○	rhetoric	○○○
stimulus	○○○	display	○○○
numbness	○○○	epistemology	○○○
dissuade	○○○	proliferate	○○○
coerce	○○○	confluence	○○○
unfathomable	○○○	haphazard	○○○
incisive	○○○	divine	○○○
quintessential	○○○	extraneous	○○○
cardinal	○○○	constitutive	○○○
understate	○○○	resonate	○○○
repertoire	○○○	stagnant	○○○
unanimous	○○○	violate	○○○
prerequisite	○○○	surmise	○○○
proponent	○○○	reiterate	○○○

ratio
비율

[ˈreɪʃioʊ]

the quantitative relationship between two amounts
(syn) proportion, fraction
(e.g.) Calculating the **ratio** of independent and dependent clauses.

tally
집계하다, 기록하다

[ˈtæli]

to calculate or count up
(syn) count, total
(e.g.) **Tallying** the number of different verbs used.

skim
훑어 읽다

[skɪm]

to read (something) quickly so as to note only the important points
(syn) glance, scan
(e.g.) Tasks Ss to **skim** the text.

calibration
보정, 정밀 조정

[ˌkælɪˈbreɪʃn]

the act of fine-tuning an instrument, model, or process for precision and accuracy
(syn) alignment, standardization
(e.g.) The research model required constant **calibration** to maintain data reliability.

enunciation
명료한 발음, 분명한 진술

[ɪˌnʌnsiˈeɪʃn]

the act of pronouncing words distinctly or expressing an idea clearly and formally
(syn) articulation, declaration
(e.g.) The professor's careful **enunciation** of each term underscored its conceptual weight.

homophone
동음이의어

[ˈhɒməfoʊn]

each of two or more words having the same pronunciation but different meanings, origins, or spelling
(syn) homonym, sound-alike
(e.g.) "Palette" is a **homophone** for the term "palate".

palate
구개, 미각

['pælət]

the roof of the mouth; a person's ability to discern different flavors
(syn) roof of the mouth, taste
(e.g.) **Palate**: signifying both the roof of the mouth and the sense of taste.

gustatory
미각의

['gʌstətɔːri]

relating to taste or the sense of taste
(syn) taste-related, culinary
(e.g.) **Gustatory** compositions.

olfactory
후각의

[ɒl'fæktəri]

relating to the sense of smell
(syn) smell-related, nasal
(e.g.) The stimuli... and the **olfactory** sense generate taste.

hue
색조, 색깔

[hjuː]

a color or shade
(syn) color, tint
(e.g.) Just as the primary **hues** generate all others.

intervention
개입

[ˌɪntər'venʃn]

the action or process of intervening
(syn) involvement, intercession
(e.g.) Taste also requires the **intervention** of the brain.

revulsion
혐오감, 역겨움

[rɪ'vʌlʃn]

a sense of disgust and loathing
(syn) disgust, abhorrence
(e.g.) The pleasure or **revulsion** generated.

DAY

16

semiotics 기호학

[ˌsemiˈɒtɪks]

the study of signs and symbols and their interpretation
(syn) sign theory, meaning study
(e.g.) This process might be defined as the "**semiotics**" of taste.

corpus 코퍼스 (언어 자료 집합)

[ˈkɔːrpəs]

a collection of texts of written or spoken language presented in electronic form
(syn) text body, language data
(e.g.) A **corpus** is a collection of texts.

collocation 연어

[ˌkɒləˈkeɪʃn]

the habitual juxtaposition of a particular word with another word or words with a frequency greater than chance
(syn) word partnership, co-occurrence
(e.g.) The phrase "heavy rain" is a natural **collocation**, but "strong rain" sounds strange.

authentic 진짜의, 실제의

[ɔːˈθentɪk]

of undisputed origin; genuine
(syn) genuine, real
(e.g.) **Authentic** example sentences.

audacious 대담한, 무모한

[ɔːˈdeɪʃəs]

showing a willingness to take surprisingly bold risks
(syn) daring, intrepid
(e.g.) The company launched an **audacious** plan to colonize Mars.

stimulus 자극, 유인

[ˈstɪmjələs]

something that rouses activity or energy in someone or something
(syn) incentive, spur
(e.g.) Economic **stimulus** measures were introduced to revive growth.

numbness
무감각, 둔함

['nʌmnəs]

the state of lacking feeling or responsiveness
(syn) insensitivity, deadness
(e.g.) He felt a strange **numbness** after hearing the tragic news.

dissuade
단념하게 하다

[dɪ'sweɪd]

to persuade someone not to do something
(syn) deter, discourage
(e.g.) She was **dissuaded** from quitting her job by her mentor.

coerce
강요하다

[koʊ'ɜːrs]

to force to act in an involuntary way by pressure or threats
(syn) compel, pressure
(e.g.) The witness was **coerced** into giving false testimony.

unfathomable
헤아릴 수 없는

[ʌn'fæðəməbl]

impossible to measure or understand fully
(syn) impenetrable, inscrutable
(e.g.) The ocean's depths remain largely **unfathomable** to humans.

DAY
16

incisive
예리한, 통찰력 있는

[ɪn'saɪsɪv]

sharply analytical and clear-thinking
(syn) penetrating, acute
(e.g.) Her **incisive** analysis revealed flaws in the argument.

quintessential
전형적인, 본질적인

[ˌkwɪntɪ'senʃəl]

representing the perfect example of something
(syn) archetypal, classic
(e.g.) Shakespeare is the **quintessential** English playwright.

cardinal
가장 중요한

['kɑːrdɪnl]

fundamental and central
(syn) principal, primary
(e.g.) Honesty is a **cardinal** virtue in any profession.

understate
절제하다, 축소해서 말하다.

[ˌʌndərˈsteɪt]
to express in a restrained, subtle way
(syn) subdue, restrain
(e.g.) Her **understated** elegance impressed the guests.

repertoire
레퍼토리, 목록

[ˈrepərtwɑːr]
a stock of plays, dances, or pieces that a company or a performer is prepared to perform
(syn) collection, stock
(e.g.) The band added several new songs to their **repertoire**.

unanimous
만장일치의

[juːˈnænɪməs]
(of two or more people) fully in agreement
(syn) agreed, united
(e.g.) The jury reached a **unanimous** verdict.

prerequisite
필수 조건

[ˌpriːˈrekwɪzɪt]
a thing that is required as a prior condition for something else to happen or exist
(syn) necessity, requirement
(e.g.) A good attitude is a **prerequisite** for success.

proponent
지지자

[prəˈpoʊnənt]
a person who advocates a theory, proposal, or course of action
(syn) supporter, advocate
(e.g.) He is a strong **proponent** of environmental protection.

displace
옮기다, 대체하다, 쫓아내다

[dɪsˈpleɪs]
to force something or someone out of its place; to replace something with another
(syn) replace, remove
(e.g.) New technology can **displace** traditional classroom routines, sometimes creating challenges for teachers.

skepticism 회의론, 의심

['skeptɪsɪzəm]

a skeptical attitude; doubt as to the truth of something
(syn) doubt, distrust
(e.g.) The claims were met with a great deal of **skepticism**.

monopoly 독점

[mə'nɒpəli]

the exclusive possession or control of the supply or trade in a commodity or service
(syn) control, dominance
(e.g.) The company has a virtual **monopoly** on the market.

predecessor 전임자, 앞서 있던 것

['predəsesər]

a person who held a job or office before the current holder; a thing that has been followed or replaced by another
(syn) forerunner, antecedent
(e.g.) The new model is significantly faster than its **predecessor**.

DAY
16

reciprocal 상호 간의

[rɪ'sɪprəkl]

given, felt, or done in return
(syn) mutual, corresponding
(e.g.) They have a **reciprocal** agreement to help each other.

manifest 명백한, 분명한

['mænɪfest]

clear or obvious to the eye or mind
(syn) apparent, overt
(e.g.) Her disappointment was **manifest** in her tone of voice.

presume 추정하다

[pɹɪ'zjuːm]

to suppose something is true without full proof
(syn) assume, suppose
(e.g.) We cannot **presume** that students understand the rule until they use it correctly in their writing.

ramification
파생적 결과, 여파

[ˌræmɪfɪˈkeɪʃn]

a complex or unwelcome consequence
(syn) implication, outcome
(e.g.) The new policy has several unexpected social **ramifications**.

attenuated
약화된, 희석된

[əˈtenjueɪtɪd]

weakened in force, effect, or value
(syn) diluted, weakened
(e.g.) The drug's effect was **attenuated** by prolonged exposure.

undermine
손상시키다, 약화시키다

[ˌʌndərˈmaɪn]

to damage or weaken gradually
(syn) compromise, impair
(e.g.) Constant criticism **undermined** his authority.

ingenuity
독창성, 기발함

[ˌɪndʒəˈnuːəti]

the quality of being clever, original, and inventive
(syn) creativity, inventiveness
(e.g.) The problem required considerable **ingenuity** to solve.

irrevocable
돌이킬 수 없는

[ɪˈrevəkəbl]

not able to be changed, reversed, or recovered; final
(syn) unchangeable, irreversible
(e.g.) The decision was considered **irrevocable**.

protocol
규칙, 절차

[ˈproʊtəkɔːl]

an accepted or official way of doing something
(syn) procedure, guideline
(e.g.) The testing **protocol** requires teachers to follow specific steps when administering the exam.

frugal
검소한

['fruːgl]

sparing or economical with regard to money or food
(syn) thrifty, economical
(e.g.) They led a very **frugal** lifestyle, saving every penny.

regulation
규제, 규정

[ˌregjə'leɪʃən]

a rule or directive made and enforced by an authority to control behavior or processes
(syn) control, guideline, restriction
(e.g.) Stricter **regulation** reduced the use of antibiotics in agriculture.

explicate
설명하다, 해석하다

['eksplɪkeɪt]

to analyze and develop (an idea or principle) in detail
(syn) explain, clarify
(e.g.) The professor was asked to **explicate** the complex theory.

rhetoric
수사학, 웅변술

['retərɪk]

the art of effective or persuasive speaking or writing
(syn) oratory, eloquence
(e.g.) His speech was dismissed as mere political **rhetoric**.

display
보이다, 전시하다

[dɪ'spleɪ]

to show something clearly or make it visible
(syn) show, exhibit
(e.g.) The results were **displayed** on a large screen so that everyone in the workshop could compare the items.

epistemology
인식론

[ɪˌpɪstə'mɒlədʒi]

the theory of knowledge, especially with regard to its methods, validity, and scope
(syn) theory of knowledge
(e.g.) The paper explored the fundamental questions of **epistemology**.

DAY

16

proliferate
증식하다, 급증하다

[prəˈlɪfəreɪt]

to increase rapidly in number; to multiply
(syn) multiply, spread
(e.g.) Rumors about the scandal began to **proliferate**.

confluence
합류, 융합

[ˈkɒnfluːəns]

the junction of two rivers; an act or process of merging
(syn) merging, convergence
(e.g.) The town is located at the **confluence** of two major rivers.

haphazard
무계획적인

[hæpˈhæzərd]

lacking any obvious principle of organization
(syn) random, arbitrary
(e.g.) The books were stacked in a **haphazard** manner on the shelf.

divine
신성한, 신의

[dɪˈvaɪn]

relating to or coming from a god; extremely good or admirable
(syn) sacred, holy, heavenly
(e.g.) Medieval artists used monsters as a medium to visualize the **divine** and the unknown.

extraneous
관련 없는, 외부의

[ɪkˈstreɪniəs]

not essential or relevant
(syn) irrelevant, external
(e.g.) Remove any **extraneous** details to make the essay clearer.

constitutive
구성의, 본질적인

[ˈkɒnstɪtjuːtɪv]

having the power to establish or compose
(syn) structural, essential
(e.g.) Language is **constitutive** of human consciousness.

resonate
울려 퍼지다, 공명하다

['rezəneɪt]

to evoke or suggest images, memories, and emotions; to sound or continue to sound

(syn) echo, reverberate

(e.g.) His speech **resonated** with the audience.

stagnant
정체된, 활발하지 않은

['stægnənt]

(of water or air) not flowing or moving and often having an unpleasant smell; showing no activity or development

(syn) still, motionless

(e.g.) The economy has been **stagnant** for the past few years.

violate
위반하다, 어기다

['vaɪəleɪt]

to break a rule, law, or agreement

(syn) break, infringe

(e.g.) The item **violated** the guideline because it contained more than one possible correct answer.

DAY
16

surmise
추정하다, 짐작하다

[sər'maɪz]

to infer without certain proof

(syn) infer, suppose

(e.g.) From his tone, she **surmised** that he was upset.

reiterate
반복하다

[ri'ɪtəreɪt]

to say something again or a number of times, typically for emphasis or clarity

(syn) repeat, restate

(e.g.) He **reiterated** his commitment to the project.

유희태 일반영어

⑤ 기출 VOCA 30days

sociolinguistic	○○○	mortgage	○○○
solidarity	○○○	stubborn	○○○
cataphoric	○○○	myopia	○○○
illocutionary	○○○	destined	○○○
perlocutionary	○○○	dearly	○○○
transaction	○○○	fault	○○○
pseudo-event	○○○	assess	○○○
mass destruction	○○○	mellow	○○○
insulate	○○○	parlor	○○○
supply	○○○	rosetree	○○○
marginality	○○○	dew	○○○
outskirt	○○○	musing	○○○
rootless	○○○	ammunition	○○○
supercharge	○○○	instinct	○○○
mandate	○○○	offensive	○○○
intriguing	○○○	prototype	○○○
discontinuous	○○○	counterintuitive	○○○
straight forwardly	○○○	clout	○○○
undergo	○○○	irrefutable	○○○
portray	○○○	ostensible	○○○
realistically	○○○	prodigy	○○○
contrived	○○○	preclude	○○○
alternation	○○○	prudent	○○○
distinctive	○○○	heed	○○○
lateral	○○○	ornate	○○○
breakdown	○○○	perennial	○○○
trigger	○○○	rectify	○○○
moderate	○○○	expertise	○○○
acclaim	○○○	invoke	○○○
garner	○○○	saturate	○○○

sociolinguistic | 사회 언어학적인

[ˌsoʊsioʊlɪŋˈɡwɪstɪk]

relating to language as a cultural and social phenomenon
(syn) communal-language
(e.g.) Teachers need to consider **sociolinguistic** factors in interaction.

solidarity | 연대, 결속

[ˌsɑːlɪˈdærəti]

unity or agreement of feeling or action among individuals with a common interest
(syn) unity, harmony
(e.g.) She chose the expression to show **solidarity** with her friend.

cataphoric | 후방 지시적인

[ˌkætəˈfɔːrɪk]

(in linguistics) referring to a later element in the text
(syn) forward-referencing
(e.g.) The sentence contains a **cataphoric** reference.

illocutionary | 발화 의도적인

[ˌɪloʊkjuːˈʃəneri]

the intention or function of a speech act
(syn) functional-meaning
(e.g.) The **illocutionary** force of the statement was a threat.

perlocutionary | 발화 효과적인

[ˌpɜːrloʊkjuːˈʃəneri]

the effect achieved by an utterance on the listener
(syn) resultant-effect
(e.g.) The **perlocutionary** effect of the warning was to stop them.

transaction | 거래, 처리

[trænˈzækʃn]

an instance of buying or selling something; a business deal
(syn) deal, business
(e.g.) They finalized the **transaction** after long negotiations.

pseudo-event
가짜 사건

['sjuːdoʊ ɪ'vent]

an event arranged for the sole purpose of being reported
(syn) staged occurrence, artificial event
(e.g.) The press conference was nothing more than a **pseudo-event**.

mass destruction
대량 파괴

[mæs dɪ'strʌkʃən]

large-scale devastation caused by powerful weapons or forces
(syn) annihilation, devastation
(e.g.) Modern fears of **mass destruction** reflect anxieties shaped by war and technology.

insulate
보호하다, 고립시키다

['ɪnsəleɪt]

to protect (something) by interposing material that prevents the passage of heat or sound; or keep separate
(syn) shield, isolate
(e.g.) He tried to **insulate** himself from the harsh reality.

supply
(v) 공급하다, (n) 공급량

[sə'plaɪ]

to provide something needed; the amount available
(syn) provide, furnish
(e.g.) The program **supplies** students with useful online resources.

DAY
17

marginality
주변성, 비주류

[ˌmɑːrdʒɪ'næləti]

the state of being outside the mainstream or of secondary importance
(syn) peripherality, exclusion
(e.g.) His feeling of **marginality** was due to being far from home.

outskirt
변두리, 외곽

['aʊtskɜːrt]

the outer part of a town or city
(syn) periphery, suburb
(e.g.) They lived on the **outskirts** of the sprawling metropolis.

rootless
뿌리 없는, 정착하지 못한

['ruːtləs]   having no place of permanent residence
(syn) transient, unsettled
(e.g.) She became a **rootless** wanderer after leaving her home country.

supercharge
강화하다, 과부하하다

[ˌsuːpərˈtʃɑːrdʒ]   to enhance or intensify especially in a way that gives it great power
(syn) intensify, augment
(e.g.) The overuse of antibiotics has **supercharged** the process.

mandate
권한, 지시

['mændeɪt]   an official order or commission to do something
(syn) command, directive
(e.g.) A government **mandate** helped lower the prescription rate.

intriguing
흥미로운, 매력적인

[ɪnˈtriːgɪŋ]   arousing great curiosity or interest
(syn) fascinating, captivating
(e.g.) There is an **intriguing** phenomenon in English grammar.

discontinuous
불연속적인

[ˌdɪskənˈtɪnjuəs]   having intervals or interruptions; separated
(syn) separated, interrupted
(e.g.) The quantifier forms a **discontinuous** constituent.

straight forwardly
솔직하게, 간단하게

[ˌstreɪtfɔːrwərdli]   in a simple and direct manner
(syn) directly, simply
(e.g.) This fact can be **straightforwardly** accounted for.

undergo

겪다, 받다

[ˌʌndərˈɡoʊ]

to experience or be subjected to (something, typically a change or unwelcome event)
(syn) experience, sustain
(e.g.) The subject **undergoes** movement to the surface position.

portray

묘사하다, 그리다

[pɔːrˈtreɪ]

to depict (someone or something) in a work of art or literature
(syn) depict, represent
(e.g.) The artist tried to **portray** the scene realistically.

realistically

현실적으로, 사실적으로

[ˌriːəˈlɪstɪkli]

in a way that accurately represents what is natural, true, or practical
(syn) authentically, naturally
(e.g.) You need to portray the characters **realistically**.

contrived

억지로 꾸민 듯한, 부자연스러운

[kənˈtraɪvd]

deliberately created rather than arising naturally or spontaneously
(syn) artificial, forced
(e.g.) The teacher used **contrived** examples in class.

alternation

교대, 번갈아 일어남

[ˌɔːltərˈneɪʃn]

the occurrence of two or more things in turn
(syn) rotation, shift
(e.g.) The rule explains the vowel **alternation** in these words.

distinctive

독특한, 구별되는

[dɪˈstɪŋktɪv]

characteristic of one person or thing, and so serving to distinguish it from others
(syn) characteristic, unique
(e.g.) Voicing is a **distinctive** feature of these phonemes.

DAY

17

lateral
측면의, 옆의

['lætərəl]
of, at, or relatively near a side or edge
(syn) side, peripheral
(e.g.) The sound /l/ is classified as a **lateral** consonant.

breakdown
고장, 실패

['breɪkdaʊn]
a failure of a relationship or system
(syn) failure, collapse
(e.g.) We need to manage communication **breakdowns** effectively.

trigger
촉발하다, 유발하다

['trɪgər]
to cause (an event or situation) to happen or exist
(syn) initiate, prompt
(e.g.) A misunderstanding can **trigger** a negotiation routine.

moderate
보통의, 적당한

['mɑːdərət]
average in amount, intensity, quality, or degree
(syn) average, measured
(e.g.) He achieved only **moderate** fame in his career.

acclaim
찬사, 환호

[ə'kleɪm]
enthusiastic public praise and approval
(syn) praise, recognition
(e.g.) His film received critical **acclaim** but little financial success.

garner
얻다, 모으다

['gɑːrnər]
to gather or collect (something, especially information or approval)
(syn) collect, accumulate
(e.g.) She eventually **garnered** enough grant money to finish the project.

mortgage
주택 융자, 담보 대출

['mɔːrɡɪdʒ]

a legal agreement by which a bank lends money in exchange for taking title to the debtor's property
(syn) loan, debt
(e.g.) They worried about paying off their **mortgage** and loans.

stubborn
완고한, 고집 센

['stʌbərn]

having or showing dogged determination not to change one's attitude or position
(syn) obstinate, tenacious
(e.g.) His **stubborn** myopia prevented him from seeing the truth.

myopia
근시, 통찰력 부족

[maɪˈoʊpiə]

lack of imagination, foresight, or intellectual insight
(syn) shortsightedness, narrow-mindedness
(e.g.) His stubborn **myopia** was his greatest flaw.

destined
~할 운명인

['destɪnd]

predetermined to a certain end or purpose
(syn) fated, predestined
(e.g.) The young man was **destined** for lesser distinctions.

dearly
몹시, 대단히

['dɪərli]

very much; at a great cost
(syn) greatly, deeply
(e.g.) The character loved his partner **dearly** but struggled to express it.

fault
비난하다, 나무라다

['fɔːlt]

to criticize for a fault, especially a minor one
(syn) criticize, blame
(e.g.) The critics often **fault** writer's inability to finish a work.

assess
평가하다

[ə'ses]

to evaluate or estimate the nature, ability, or quality of
(syn) evaluate, judge
(e.g.) The test was designed to **assess** the students' language skills.

mellow
부드러운, 그윽한

['meloʊ]

pleasantly and smoothly rich; softened or matured by age or experience
(syn) soft, gentle
(e.g.) The **mellow** light of the moon filled the parlor.

parlor
응접실, 거실

['pɑːrlər]

a sitting room in a private house
(syn) living room, drawing-room
(e.g.) She saw the moon through the **parlor** window.

rosetree
장미 나무

['roʊzˌtriː]

a rose bush or tree
(syn) rose bush
(e.g.) The dew was heavy upon the **rosetree**.

dew
이슬

[duː]

a tiny drop of water that forms on cool surfaces at night
(syn) moisture, condensation
(e.g.) The **dew** was heavy upon the ground.

musing
사색, 생각

['mjuːzɪŋ]

a period of reflection or thought
(syn) contemplation, reflection
(e.g.) He spent the night in silent **musing** by the window.

ammunition
탄약, (비유) 대응 수단

[ˌæmjəˈnɪʃən]

resources or means used to defend oneself or attack in an argument or conflict
(syn) weaponry, firepower, resources
(e.g.) Doctors are running out of the **ammunition** they need to fight resistant bacteria.

instinct
본능

[ˈɪnstɪŋkt]

an innate, typically fixed pattern of behavior in animals
(syn) intuition, drive
(e.g.) Her maternal **instinct** told her something was wrong.

offensive
불쾌한, 모욕적인

[əˈfensɪv]

causing someone to feel deeply hurt, upset, or angry
(syn) insulting, disrespectful
(e.g.) Students should avoid using overly **offensive** language.

prototype
원형, 시제품

[ˈproʊtətaɪp]

the first or preliminary model of something
(syn) model, archetype
(e.g.) The design was based on the **prototype** from the 1950s.

counterintuitive
직관에 반하는

[ˌkaʊntərɪnˈtuːɪtɪv]

contrary to intuition or to common-sense expectation
(syn) surprising, unexpected
(e.g.) His advice seemed **counterintuitive**, but it worked.

clout
영향력, 힘

[klaʊt]

influence or power, especially in politics or business
(syn) influence, power
(e.g.) The union has considerable political **clout** with local officials.

DAY
17

irrefutable
반박할 수 없는

[ˌɪrɪˈfjuːtəbl]

impossible to deny or disprove
(syn) undeniable, incontestable
(e.g.) The evidence presented was **irrefutable**.

ostensible
표면상의, 겉치레의

[ɑːˈstensəbl]

stated or appearing to be true, but not necessarily so
(syn) apparent, professed
(e.g.) His **ostensible** reason for calling was to check on her health.

prodigy
천재, 신동

[ˈprɑːdɪdʒi]

a young person with exceptional talent or ability
(syn) genius, wonder, phenomenon
(e.g.) Students often admire a **prodigy**, but struggle to learn from one.

preclude
막다, 불가능하게 하다

[prɪˈkluːd]

to prevent from happening; to make impossible
(syn) prevent, rule out
(e.g.) The lack of preparation will **preclude** success.

prudent
신중한, 현명한

[prúːdnt]

acting with or showing care and thought for the future
(syn) cautious, sensible, judicious, wise
(opp) reckless, careless, imprudent
(e.g.) It's **prudent** to double-check all facts before publication.

heed
주의하다, 유념하다

[hiːd]

to pay careful attention to something or someone's advice
(syn) mind, notice, regard, observe
(opp) ignore, disregard, neglect
(e.g.) You should **heed** the warnings before starting the experiment.

ornate

화려한, 장식된

[ɔːrnéɪt]

elaborately decorated or highly ornamented
(syn) elaborate, fancy, embellished, decorative
(opp) plain, simple, unadorned
(e.g.) The **ornate** architecture reflected the wealth of the era.

perennial

영속적인, 지속적인

[pərénial]

lasting or existing for a long or apparently infinite time
(syn) everlasting, enduring, permanent, continual
(opp) temporary, transient, short-lived
(e.g.) Inflation remains a **perennial** concern for economists.

rectify

수정하다, 바로잡다

[réktəfài]

to correct or make something right
(syn) correct, amend, fix, adjust
(opp) damage, worsen, corrupt
(e.g.) The company quickly **rectified** its error in the invoice.

expertise

전문 지식, 전문 기술

[ˌekspɜːrˈtiːz]

specialized knowledge or skill in a particular field
(syn) proficiency, mastery, skill
(e.g.) Students gravitate toward prodigies because their **expertise** seems effortless.

invoke

(권위 · 법 · 이유를) 들다, 호소하다

[ɪnvóuk]

to cite or appeal to (an authority, rule, or reason) in support of an argument
(syn) cite, appeal to, call upon
(opp) ignore, disregard
(e.g.) The author **invokes** recent data to support the claim.

saturate

흠뻑 적시다, 포화시키다

[sǽtʃərèɪt]

to fill completely; to supply beyond capacity
(syn) soak, permeate, flood
(opp) dry, drain
(e.g.) Heavy rains **saturated** the fields overnight.

DAY

17

유희태 일반영어

⑤ 기출 VOCA 30days

work on	○○○	heritage	○○○
workload	○○○	language community	○○○
take part in	○○○	variable	○○○
participatory	○○○	affiliate	○○○
come up with	○○○	articulatory	○○○
get through	○○○	lexicalization	○○○
devise	○○○	institutionalize	○○○
bring about	○○○	approximation	○○○
precipitate	○○○	prescriptive	○○○
keep up with	○○○	respective	○○○
attune	○○○	heuristic	○○○
lay out	○○○	parameter	○○○
go over	○○○	descriptive	○○○
merely	○○○	quantitative	○○○
entirely	○○○	qualitative	○○○
constantly	○○○	substantive	○○○
primary	○○○	dialectical	○○○
medium	○○○	wane	○○○
concise	○○○	withstand	○○○
bicultural	○○○	uphold	○○○
hybrid	○○○	streamline	○○○
generate	○○○	vigilance	○○○
article	○○○	lineage	○○○
periodical	○○○	attest	○○○
aggregate	○○○	confer	○○○
modality	○○○	elude	○○○
thermodynamics	○○○	benign	○○○
competence	○○○	overt	○○○
proficiency	○○○	fabricate	○○○
ethnicity	○○○	ardent	○○○

work on
~에 전념하다, 작업하다

[wɜːrk ɑːn]
to devote effort to developing or improving something
(syn) engage in, focus on
(e.g.) The researcher is **working on** a cross-linguistic study of modality.

workload
업무량

[ˈwɜːrkloʊd]
the amount of work assigned to or expected from a person
(syn) task volume, assignment load
(e.g.) The new online system helped balance teachers' **workloads**.

take part in
참여하다

[teɪk pɑːrt ɪn]
to join or be actively involved in an activity or event
(syn) participate in, engage in
(e.g.) Students **took part in** a discourse analysis workshop.

participatory
참여형의

[pɑːrˈtɪsɪpətɔːri]
involving active participation
(syn) interactive, engaged
(e.g.) The course promotes **participatory** learning through peer feedback.

come up with
(생각·해결책을) 내놓다

[kʌm ʌp wɪð]
to produce or devise an idea or plan
(syn) devise, propose
(e.g.) The linguist **came up with** a new typology of evidential markers.

get through
이겨내다, 통과하다

[get θruː]
to manage to complete or survive something difficult
(syn) overcome, endure
(e.g.) She finally **got through** the demanding oral examination.

devise
고안하다

[dɪˈvaɪz]

to plan or invent a method or system
(syn) formulate, invent
(e.g.) They **devised** a coding scheme for analyzing speech acts.

bring about
초래하다, 야기하다

[brɪŋ əˈbaʊt]

to cause something to happen
(syn) induce, generate
(e.g.) The policy change **brought about** a shift in teaching practices.

precipitate
촉진시키다

[prɪˈsɪpɪteɪt]

to cause to happen suddenly or prematurely
(syn) trigger, prompt
(e.g.) Globalization **precipitated** new forms of linguistic hybridization.

keep up with
뒤처지지 않다

[kiːp ʌp wɪð]

to remain informed or at the same level as others
(syn) stay informed about, follow
(e.g.) Teachers must **keep up with** advances in digital pedagogy.

DAY
18

attune
조율하다, 적응시키다

[əˈtuːn]

to make receptive or responsive
(syn) adjust, adapt
(e.g.) The curriculum was **attuned** to students' communicative needs.

lay out
구성하다, 설명하다

[leɪ aʊt]

to present or plan clearly and systematically
(syn) outline, arrange
(e.g.) The researcher **laid out** the framework in the introduction.

go over — 검토하다

[goʊ ˈoʊvər]

to examine or review carefully
(syn) review, inspect
(e.g.) Let's **go over** the students' pragmatic competence assessments.

merely — 단지, 그저

[ˈmɪrli]

only, simply; and nothing more
(syn) only, solely
(e.g.) Linguistic variation is not **merely** regional but social as well.

entirely — 완전히

[ɪnˈtaɪərli]

completely or wholly
(syn) wholly, fully
(e.g.) The results are not **entirely** consistent with previous findings.

constantly — 끊임없이

[ˈkɑːnstəntli]

continuously, persistently
(syn) continually, repeatedly
(e.g.) Language evolves **constantly** through social interaction.

primary — 주된, 기본의

[ˈpraɪmeri]

of chief importance; main
(syn) main, principal
(e.g.) Vocabulary knowledge is a **primary** predictor of reading ability.

medium — (전달) 매체, 표현 수단

[ˈmiːdiəm]

a means by which something is expressed, communicated, or achieved
(syn) vehicle, channel, instrument
(e.g.) Monsters served as a **medium** for representing the divine and the unknown.

concise

간결한

[kən'saɪs]

giving much information clearly in few words
(syn) succinct, brief
(e.g.) The teacher asked for **concise** summaries of each passage.

bicultural

이중 문화의

[ˌbaɪ'kʌltʃərəl]

combining elements of two cultures
(syn) multicultural, dual-heritage
(e.g.) **Bicultural** identity influences learners' pragmatic choices.

hybrid

혼합된, 복합의

['haɪbrɪd]

composed of mixed elements
(syn) composite, mixed
(e.g.) English today is a **hybrid** language shaped by global contact.

generate

생성하다

['dʒenəreɪt]

to produce or bring into existence
(syn) produce, yield
(e.g.) The model **generates** possible syntactic structures.

DAY

18

article

관사, 논문

['ɑːrtɪkl]

a grammatical determiner; also a scholarly paper
(syn) paper, essay
(e.g.) The **article** explores phonological rules in Korean dialects.

periodical

정기 간행물

[ˌpɪri'ɑːdɪkl]

publishing at regular intervals
(syn) serial, recurring
(e.g.) The study appeared in a leading linguistic **periodical**.

aggregate 총체의

['ægrɪgət]

formed by the collection of units

(syn) combined, collective

(e.g.) The **aggregate** frequency of errors declined over time.

modality 양상, 법성

[moʊ'dæləti]

the grammatical expression of possibility, necessity, etc.

(syn) mood, manner

(e.g.) English **modality** distinguishes between obligation and ability.

thermodynamics 열역학

[,θɜːrmoʊdaɪ'næmɪks]

the branch of physics dealing with heat, energy, and their transformations

(syn) heat physics, energy dynamics

(e.g.) Einstein's class on **thermodynamics** failed to attract many students due to its abstract nature.

competence 능력, 숙달

['kɑːmpɪtəns]

the ability to do something successfully or efficiently

(syn) ability, proficiency

(e.g.) Communicative **competence** integrates linguistic and pragmatic skills.

proficiency 숙련, 능숙

[prə'fɪʃnsi]

high degree of skill or expertise

(syn) expertise, fluency

(e.g.) Language **proficiency** is evaluated through integrated tasks.

ethnicity 민족성

[eθ'nɪsəti]

cultural identity based on shared heritage

(syn) race, heritage

(e.g.) **Ethnicity** often correlates with distinct linguistic patterns.

heritage

유산, 전통

[ˈherɪtɪdʒ]

valued traditions handed down from the past
(syn) legacy, inheritance
(e.g.) Many **heritage** languages face threats of extinction.

language community

언어 공동체

[ˈlæŋgwɪdʒ kəˈmjuːnəti]

a group sharing the same linguistic norms
(syn) speech community, linguistic group
(e.g.) Each **language community** maintains its own discourse conventions.

variable

변수

[ˈveriəbl]

an element that can vary or change
(syn) factor, parameter
(e.g.) The dependent **variable** was test performance.

affiliate

제휴하다, 소속시키다

[əˈfilieɪt]

to officially attach or connect to an organization
(syn) associate, align with
(e.g.) The study was conducted by an institute **affiliated** with the university.

articulatory

조음의

[ɑːrˈtɪkjələˌtɔːri]

relating to the physical production of speech sounds
(syn) phonetic, phonological
(e.g.) **Articulatory** phonetics examines how the tongue and lips move during speech.

lexicalization

어휘화

[ˌleksɪkələˈzeɪʃən]

the process of becoming an established word or expression
(syn) word formation, coinage
(e.g.) The **lexicalization** of internet slang reflects cultural change.

DAY

18

institutionalize 제도화하다

[ˌɪnstɪˈtuːʃənəlaɪz]

to make something part of an established system
(syn) formalize, systematize
(e.g.) Collaborative learning has been **institutionalized** in modern pedagogy.

approximation 근사치, 유사

[əˌprɑːksɪˈmeɪʃn]

a value or form close to the actual one
(syn) similarity, closeness
(e.g.) Learners' interlanguage is an **approximation** of native norms.

prescriptive 규범적인

[prɪˈskrɪptɪv]

enforcing rules about correct language use
(syn) normative, authoritative
(e.g.) **Prescriptive** statements express what ought to be rather than what is.

respective 각자의

[rɪˈspektɪv]

belonging or relating separately to each of two or more things
(syn) individual, particular
(e.g.) Students presented their findings in **respective** groups.

heuristic 발견적인, 발견법의

[hjuˈrɪstɪk]

enabling someone to discover or learn by themselves
(syn) exploratory, self-directed
(e.g.) **Heuristic** learning emphasizes problem-solving through exploration.

parameter 매개변수

[pəˈræmɪtər]

a measurable factor defining a system
(syn) factor
(e.g.) The model operates under several syntactic **parameters**.

descriptive 기술적인

[dɪˈskrɪptɪv]

describing how language is actually used
(syn) analytic, explanatory
(e.g.) Modern linguistics adopts a **descriptive** rather than prescriptive view.

quantitative 양적인

[ˈkwɑːntɪteɪtɪv]

relating to measurable quantities
(syn) numerical, statistical
(e.g.) **Quantitative** data supported the study's hypothesis.

qualitative 질적인

[ˈkwɑːlɪteɪtɪv]

relating to descriptive or non-numerical data
(syn) interpretive, descriptive
(e.g.) **Qualitative** analysis explored learners' emotional responses.

substantive 실질적인

[ˈsʌbstəntɪv]

having a firm basis in reality or importance
(syn) significant, essential
(e.g.) The report offers **substantive** evidence for the claim.

DAY
18

dialectical 변증법적인

[ˌdaɪəˈlektɪkl]

relating to logical discussion of ideas and contradictions
(e.g.) The author adopted a **dialectical** approach to language change.

wane 약해지다, 쇠퇴하다

[weɪn]

to decrease in strength or intensity
(syn) decline, diminish, fade
(opp) wax, grow
(e.g.) Interest in the topic began to **wane** after the seminar.

withstand
견디다, 버티다

[wɪðstǽnd]

to resist or endure successfully
(syn) resist, endure, weather
(opp) succumb, yield
(e.g.) The structure can **withstand** high winds and heavy snow.

uphold
지지하다, 유지하나

[ʌ́phoʊld]

to support or maintain a decision, law, or principle
(syn) support, sustain, endorse
(opp) reject, oppose
(e.g.) The court **upheld** the decision despite strong opposition.

streamline
능률적으로 하다, 간소화하다

[stríːmlaɪn]

to make a process simpler or more efficient
(syn) simplify, optimize, rationalize
(e.g.) The company **streamlined** its workflow to improve productivity.

vigilance
경계, 주의

[vídʒɪləns]

careful attention to avoid danger or errors
(syn) alertness, watchfulness, caution
(e.g.) Constant **vigilance** is required to prevent data breaches.

lineage
혈통, 가계

[línɪɪdʒ]

the line of descent from an ancestor; heritage
(syn) ancestry, descent, pedigree
(e.g.) The artist came from a long **lineage** of musicians.

attest
증명하다, 입증하다

[ətést]

to prove or confirm that something is true or genuine
(syn) verify, confirm, prove, validate
(opp) deny, disprove, refute
(e.g.) Several studies **attest** to the benefits of a balanced diet.

confer

[kənfə́ːr]

상의하다, (권위·자격을) 부여하다

to discuss something or to grant a title, degree, or benefit
- (syn) consult, discuss, bestow, grant
- (opp) ignore, revoke, withdraw
- (e.g.) The committee will **confer** with experts before making a decision.

elude

[ɪlúːd]

피하다, (이해를) 회피하다

to avoid or escape from something by cleverness or skill
- (syn) evade, escape, dodge, avoid
- (opp) confront, face, pursue
- (e.g.) The meaning of the poem **eluded** many students at first.

benign

[bɪnáɪn]

상냥한, 온화한, 양성의

gentle and kind; not harmful or malignant
- (syn) gentle, kind, harmless, benevolent
- (opp) malignant, hostile, harmful
- (e.g.) The doctor assured him that the tumor was **benign**.

overt

[ouvə́ːrt]

공공연한, 명백한

done or shown openly; not secret or hidden
- (syn) open, explicit, obvious, clear
- (opp) covert, hidden, concealed
- (e.g.) The government made an **overt** attempt to negotiate peace.

fabricate

[fǽbrɪkèɪt]

조작하다, 제조하다

to invent or produce something, often in order to deceive
- (syn) fake, forge, manufacture, produce
- (opp) disprove, destroy, demolish
- (e.g.) The witness was accused of **fabricating** evidence.

ardent

[áːrdnt]

열렬한, 정열적인

showing strong enthusiasm or passion
- (syn) passionate, fervent, zealous, eager
- (opp) apathetic, indifferent, cold
- (e.g.) She is an **ardent** supporter of environmental reform.

DAY
18

2019

DAY

19

vast majority	○○○	shed	○○○
questionnaire	○○○	plague	○○○
preference	○○○	maturation	○○○
sermon	○○○	cross	○○○
charade	○○○	awkward	○○○
maximize	○○○	appreciable	○○○
colloquy	○○○	scorch	○○○
prompt	○○○	ebb and flow	○○○
reformulate	○○○	reassuringly	○○○
obligatory	○○○	keen	○○○
indiscriminately	○○○	patrolman	○○○
criterion	○○○	exclaim	○○○
duration	○○○	situational irony	○○○
paraphrase	○○○	compensate	○○○
attain	○○○	coinage	○○○
sentimentally	○○○	prefabricated	○○○
self-delusion	○○○	inanimate	○○○
apprehension	○○○	cunning	○○○
amusement	○○○	irritability	○○○
subtlety	○○○	transit	○○○
atomistic	○○○	conceal	○○○
liberty	○○○	invariably	○○○
grieve	○○○	hostile	○○○
fret	○○○	illumination	○○○
interference	○○○	antibacterial	○○○
tap into	○○○	obnoxious	○○○
rejoice	○○○	pineal gland	○○○
therapy	○○○	melatonin	○○○
serial	○○○	mismatch	○○○
remission	○○○	realign	○○○

vast majority | 대부분, 대다수

[ˌvæst məˈdʒɔːrəti]

an overwhelming number or amount
(syn) bulk, preponderance, lion's share
(e.g.) The **vast majority** of adjectives can appear in both positions.

questionnaire | 설문지

[ˌkwɛstʃəˈnɛər]

a set of questions designed to gather information
(syn) survey, form, poll
(e.g.) This **questionnaire** is designed to identify students' learning styles.

preference | 선호

[ˈprɛfərəns]

a greater liking for one alternative over others
(syn) liking, choice, inclination
(e.g.) Students are asked to check their **preferences** for study methods.

sermon | 강론, 훈계

[ˈsɜːrmən]

a long talk for instruction or moral teaching
(syn) homily, discourse, address
(e.g.) I remember information better when I listen to **sermons** (lectures).

charade | 몸짓 놀이

[ʃəˈreɪd]

a game where words are guessed from pantomimed actions
(syn) mime, pantomime, guessing game
(e.g.) I'm planning to do an animal **charade** activity in class.

maximize | 극대화하다

[ˈmæksɪmaɪz]

to increase something to the highest possible level
(syn) optimize, increase, make the most of
(e.g.) I want to **maximize** students' learning outcomes in my class.

colloquy
대화, 대담

[ˈkɑːləkwi]

a formal or scholarly conversation or discussion
(syn) conversation, discussion, exchange
(e.g.) In the above **colloquy**, the two teachers are talking about tasks.

prompt
유도하다

[prɑːmpt]

to bring about or cause an action or reaction
(syn) induce, cause, bring about
(e.g.) Her question **prompted** a long discussion in class.

reformulate
재구성하다, 다시 말하다

[ˌriːˈfɔːrmjəleɪt]

to express something again in a different, clearer way
(syn) rephrase, restate, reword
(e.g.) The technique is to induce the correct form by prompting the learner to **reformulate** the error.

obligatory
의무적인, 필수의

[əˈblɪɡəˌtɔːri]

required by rule or duty; not optional
(syn) mandatory, compulsory, required
(e.g.) Attendance at the safety meeting is **obligatory** for all staff.

indiscriminately
무분별하게

[ˌɪndɪˈskrɪmɪnətli]

without careful choice or distinction
(syn) randomly, aimlessly, arbitrarily
(opp) selectively, deliberately
(e.g.) The chemicals were sprayed **indiscriminately** across the farmland.

DAY

19

criterion
기준, 척도

[kraɪˈtɪəriən]

a standard used for comparison or judgment
(syn) standard, benchmark, measure
(e.g.) The phonetically based **criterion** focuses on duration.

duration
기간, 지속 시간

[dʊˈreɪʃən]

the length of time that something continues or lasts
(syn) span, time, length
(e.g.) A tense vowel has greater **duration** than its lax counterpart.

paraphrase
우회적 표현, 에둘러 말하기

[pəˈrɪfrəsɪs]

the use of indirect or roundabout expressions
(syn) circumlocution, rephrasing, verbosity
(e.g.) Sentences are of different types, as suggested in their **paraphrasing**.

attain
달성하다, 얻다

[əˈteɪn]

to succeed in achieving a goal after effort
(syn) achieve, reach, accomplish
(e.g.) It isn't often that men **attain** the true goal of their heart's desire.

sentimentally
감상적으로

[ˌsɛntrɪˈmɛntəli]

in a way that is influenced by, or appeals to, feelings and nostalgia
(syn) emotionally, nostalgically, wistfully
(e.g.) They **sentimentally** reminisce about their glory days while loafing around.

self-delusion
자기기만

[ˌsɛlf dɪˈluːʒən]

the act of deceiving oneself into believing something that is untrue
(syn) self-deception, illusion, fantasy
(e.g.) It is **self-delusion** rather than self-knowledge that sustains them.

apprehension
불안, 염려

[ˌæprɪˈhɛnʃən]

fear or anxiety that something bad will happen
(syn) fear, anxiety, dread
(e.g.) The greater my **apprehensions** were, the more I feared.

amusement

재미, 즐거움

[əˈmjuːzmənt]

the state or experience of finding something funny or entertaining
(syn) entertainment, diversion, pastime
(e.g.) The children watched the magic show with great **amusement**.

subtlety

미묘함, 교활함

[ˈsʌtəlti]

a delicate or precise quality that is difficult to analyze or describe
(syn) nuance, cleverness, finesse
(e.g.) All the notions we usually entertain of the **subtlety** of the devil.

atomistic

원자론적인, 분자적인

[ˌætəˈmɪstɪk]

viewing things as separate, discrete, or individual elements
(syn) individualistic, separate, fragmented
(e.g.) For the Westerners, a company is an **atomistic**, modular place.

liberty

자유

[ˈlɪbərti]

the state of being free within society from oppressive restrictions
(syn) freedom, independence, autonomy
(e.g.) Keep we both our **liberties**, never false and never true.

grieve

몹시 슬퍼하다, 한탄하다

[griːv]

to suffer great sorrow, especially over a death or loss
(syn) mourn, lament, sorrow
(e.g.) If you promised, you might **grieve** for lost liberty again.

fret

초조해하다, 안달하다

[frɛt]

to worry or be agitated, especially about trivial things
(syn) worry, bother, anguish
(e.g.) If I promised, I believe I should **fret** to break the chain.

DAY
19

interference

(언어학) 간섭

[ˌɪntərˈfɪərəns]

the negative influence of a first language on the learning of a second language
(syn) disruption, hindrance, obstruction
(e.g.) Negative transfer can be further divided into two types: overgeneralization and **interference**.

tap into

~을 이용하다, ~에 접근하다

[tæp ˈɪntuː]

to make use of a resource or situation
(syn) utilize, draw on, exploit
(e.g.) I decided to **tap into** the errors and explained them to students.

rejoice

기뻐하다

[rɪˈdʒɔɪs]

to feel or show great joy or delight
(syn) celebrate, cheer, delight
(e.g.) Instead of **rejoicing** at the possibility of rescue, the narrator reacts with fear.

therapy

치료

[ˈθɛrəpi]

a treatment intended to heal or relieve a disorder or disability
(syn) treatment, cure, remediation
(e.g.) There's no shortage of **therapies** for autism.

serial

연속적인, 하나씩 순서대로 처리되는

[ˈsɪəriəl]

happening in sequence rather than simultaneously
(syn) consecutive, sequential
(e.g.) Phonics assumes reading is a **serial** process.

remission

(병의) 완화

[rɪˈmɪʃən]

a temporary diminution or disappearance of the symptoms of a disease
(syn) abatement, recovery, relief
(e.g.) There have been hints that this kind of **remission** might be possible in autism.

shed

(증상을) 벗어나다

[ʃɛd]

to discard or get rid of something (e.g., symptoms or skin)
(syn) discard, lose, drop
(e.g.) Previous studies were plagued with questions about whether the children who had apparently **shed** their autism were properly diagnosed.

plague

괴롭히다, 문제를 일으키다

[pleɪg]

to cause continual trouble or distress to
(syn) trouble, afflict, beset
(e.g.) Previous studies were **plagued** with questions about whether the children were properly diagnosed.

maturation

성숙, 완성

[ˌmætʃəˈreɪʃən]

the process of becoming fully developed or mature
(syn) development, ripening, maturity
(e.g.) Something had to account for that, and **maturation**, in this research at least, is the best answer.

cross

건너다, 어떤 경계를 넘다

[krɒs]

to go over from one side to another
(syn) traverse
(e.g.) They **crossed** the river at dawn.

awkward

어색한, 서투른

[ˈɔːkwərd]

difficult to use or handle; clumsy or uncomfortable
(syn) clumsy, ungainly, unnatural
(e.g.) I wanted to use "make" but then the sentence looked a bit **awkward**.

appreciable

상당한, 쉽게 알아볼 수 있는

[əˈpriːʃəbəl]

sufficiently great or important to be recognized or estimated
(syn) considerable, noticeable, significant
(e.g.) The alveolar lateral approximant /l/ presents **appreciable** differences.

DAY
19

scorch
그슬리다, 타는 듯하다

['skɔːrtʃ]

to burn the surface of something
(syn) sear, burn
(e.g.) The paper **scorched** when it got too close to the candle.

ebb and flow
성쇠, 밀물과 썰물

[ɛb ənd floʊ]

a recurrent or rhythmical pattern of change, decline, and rise
(syn) fluctuation, undulation, tide
(e.g.) Nature, with the **ebb and flow** of its continuous cycles, once again provided.

reassuringly
안심시키듯이

[ˌriːəˈʃʊrɪŋli]

in a way that restores confidence or calms fears
(syn) comfortingly, consolingly, soothingly
(e.g.) "It's all right, officer," he said, **reassuringly**.

keen
날카로운, 예리한

[kiːn]

having or showing an eagerness or intense interest; (of eyes) sharp and perceptive
(syn) sharp, perceptive, astute
(e.g.) The light showed a pale, square-jawed face with **keen** eyes.

patrolman
순찰 경찰관

['pætroʊlmən]

a police officer assigned to patrol a specific area
(syn) officer, beat cop, constable
(e.g.) It's from **Patrolman** Wells.

exclaim
외치다, 소리치다

[ɪkˈskleɪm]

to cry out suddenly in surprise, pain, or excitement
(syn) shout, yell, cry out
(e.g.) "Bless my heart!" **exclaimed** the new arrival.

situational irony

상황적인 아이러니

[ˌsɪtʃuˈeɪʃənəl ˈaɪrəni]

a literary device where the outcome is contrary to what was expected
(syn) irony of fate, cosmic irony
(e.g.) **Situational irony** occurs when expected outcomes do not happen.

compensate

보충하다, 상쇄하다

[ˈkɑːmpənseɪt]

to provide something good to balance or make up for something bad
(syn) make up for, counterbalance, offset
(e.g.) Strategies can **compensate** for their lack of knowledge.

coinage

(새로운 단어의) 창조, 조어

[ˈkɔɪnɪdʒ]

the invention or creation of a new word or phrase
(syn) neologism, invention, creation
(e.g.) Strategies employed include avoidance, code switching, word **coinage**.

prefabricated

사전에 만들어진, 조립식의

[ˌpriːˈfæbrɪkeɪtɪd]

manufactured in advance in sections ready for quick assembly
(syn) ready-made, modular, pre-built
(e.g.) Strategies employed include using **prefabricated** patterns.

inanimate

무생물의

[ɪnˈænɪmət]

not alive; showing no sign of life
(syn) lifeless, non-living, inert
(e.g.) **Inanimate** objects are classified scientifically into three major categories.

DAY
19

cunning

교활함, 간계

[ˈkʌnɪŋ]

skills in achieving one's ends by deceit or evasion
(syn) slyness, craftiness, trickery
(e.g.) He admired the general's **cunning** in handling the crisis.

irritability
과민성, 짜증

[ˌɪrɪtəˈbɪləti]

the state of being easily annoyed or provoked

(syn) touchiness, peevishness, petulance

(e.g.) Thus it creates maximum inconvenience, frustration and **irritability** among its human cargo.

transit
이동, 운송

[ˈtrænzɪt]

the movement of people or goods from one place to another

(syn) passage, movement, transportation

(e.g.) The most plausible theory is that they have developed a secret method of **transit** (locomotion).

conceal
숨기다

[kənˈsiːl]

to keep from sight; to hide

(syn) hide, cover, keep secret

(e.g.) They are able to **conceal** the instant a human eye falls upon them.

invariably
변함없이, 언제나

[ɪnˈveəriəbli]

always; without exception

(syn) always, consistently, perpetually

(e.g.) A furnace will **invariably** break down at the depth of the first winter cold wave.

hostile
적대적인

[ˈhɑːstl]

unfriendly; opposed or aggressive

(syn) antagonistic, unfriendly, aggressive

(e.g.) Inanimate objects are not entirely **hostile** to man.

illumination
조명, 비추기

[ɪˌluːməˈneɪʃən]

light or the action of lighting up

(syn) light, brightness, radiance

(e.g.) He does not expect his flashlight to **illumination** (illuminate).

antibacterial
항균의, 박테리아 억제의

[ˌæntibɑːkˈtɪəriəl]

able to prevent or reduce the growth of bacteria
(syn) germ-killing, disinfecting
(e.g.) The government restricted **antibacterial** products that offered no proven benefit.

obnoxious
불쾌한, 아주 싫은

[əbˈnɑːkʃəs]

extremely unpleasant or offensive
(syn) offensive, repulsive, detestable
(e.g.) John reported Sue to be **obnoxious**.

pineal gland
솔방울샘

[ˈpɪniəl ɡlænd]

a small endocrine gland in the brain that produces melatonin
(syn) epiphysis, conarium
(e.g.) Melatonin is a hormone naturally produced by the **pineal gland**.

melatonin
멜라토닌

[ˌmɛləˈtoʊnɪn]

a hormone that regulates sleep-wake cycles
(syn) sleep hormone
(e.g.) **Melatonin** is released when darkness falls.

mismatch
불일치

[ˌmɪsˈmætʃ]

a failure to correspond or be compatible
(syn) discrepancy, incompatibility, disparity
(e.g.) Seasonal affective disorder is thought to be the effect of a **mismatch** between sleep cycles and the light-dark cycle.

realign
재조정하다

[ˌriːəˈlaɪn]

to adjust or restore to a new or straight position
(syn) readjust, restore, correct
(e.g.) Bright light therapy can **realign** the sleep-wake cycle.

DAY
19

2019

DAY
20

유희태 일반영어
⑤ 기출 VOCA 30days

cognitive	○○○	hardly	○○○
impairment	○○○	realization	○○○
toxic	○○○	shade	○○○
offset	○○○	vocalization	○○○
counter	○○○	delete	○○○
autonomy	○○○	environment	○○○
periodic	○○○	midway	○○○
contention	○○○	hardware store	○○○
attributive	○○○	lean	○○○
predicative	○○○	unlighted	○○○
modify	○○○	appointment	○○○
head noun	○○○	make certain	○○○
in contrast	○○○	tear down	○○○
function	○○○	strike a match	○○○
adjective of degree	○○○	pale	○○○
quantifying adjective	○○○	square-jawed	○○○
frequency	○○○	scar	○○○
associative adjective	○○○	scarfpin	○○○
entity	○○○	twirl	○○○
associate	○○○	club	○○○
humid	○○○	beat (policeman's)	○○○
crisp	○○○	overcoat	○○○
breeze	○○○	collar	○○○
relief	○○○	hurry	○○○
piercing	○○○	opposite	○○○
humidity	○○○	doubtfully	○○○
urban planner	○○○	grasping	○○○
varieties	○○○	sure as fate	○○○
ridge	○○○	in existence	○○○
velum	○○○	last	○○○

cognitive 인지적인

['kɑːgnətɪv]

relating to the mental processes of perception, memory, judgment, and reasoning

(syn) mental, intellectual, reasoning

(e.g.) Melatonin works by slowing the **cognitive** impairment associated with age-related diseases.

impairment 손상, 장애

[ɪm'pɛərmənt]

the state of being damaged or weakened

(syn) deterioration, damage, disability

(e.g.) Melatonin works by slowing the cognitive **impairment**.

toxic 유독한

['tɑːksɪk]

poisonous or capable of causing harm

(syn) poisonous, harmful, detrimental

(e.g.) Amyloid beta and tau proteins are **toxic** and they build up in patients.

offset 상쇄하다

['ɔːf,sɛt]

to counterbalance, counteract, or compensate for something

(syn) counterbalance, neutralize, compensate

(e.g.) Melatonin helps to **offset** the toxic effects of these proteins.

counter 반박하다, 대응하다

['kaʊntər]

to oppose or to act against something

(syn) oppose, resist

(e.g.) Melatonin supplements can improve cognitive function by **countering** the toxic influence.

autonomy 자율성

[ɔː'tɑːnəmi]

the right or condition of self-government or independence

(syn) independence, self-governance, freedom

(e.g.) Teachers should offer students a variety of strategies to develop learner **autonomy**.

periodic
주기적인, 정기적인

[ˌpɪəri'ɑːdɪk]

occurring or recurring at regular intervals
(syn) regular, recurring
(e.g.) I carried out **periodic** assessment over the whole course period.

contention
논쟁, 주장

[kən'tɛnʃən]

heated disagreement; an assertion made in an argument
(syn) dispute, argument, controversy
(e.g.) Students were expected to develop **contention** (debating) skills in English.

attributive
한정적인

[ə'trɪbjuːtɪv]

(of an adjective) preceding the noun it modifies
(syn) qualifying, modifying
(e.g.) **Attributive** adjectives modify the head noun in an NP.

predicative
서술적인

['prɛdɪkətɪv]

(of an adjective) following a verb, acting as a complement
(syn) descriptive, complementary
(e.g.) **Predicative** adjectives appear after a verb, not in an NP.

modify
수식하다

['mɑːdɪfaɪ]

to describe or limit the meaning of a word, especially a noun
(syn) qualify, describe, limit
(e.g.) Attributive adjectives **modify** the head noun in an NP.

head noun
핵심 명사

[hɛd naʊn]

the main noun in a noun phrase
(syn) nucleus, main noun, core
(e.g.) Attributive adjectives modify the **head noun** in an NP.

DAY
20

in contrast | 대조적으로

[ɪn ˈkɑːntræst]

when compared to something else, noting a striking difference
(syn) conversely, on the other hand
(e.g.) **In contrast**, predicative adjectives appear after a verb.

function | 기능하다

[ˈfʌŋkʃən]

to work or operate in a particular way or for a specific purpose
(syn) operate, serve, act as
(e.g.) Predicative adjectives **function** as a predicate.

adjective of degree | 정도 형용사

[ˌædʒɪktɪv əv dɪˈgriː]

an adjective that describes the intensity of a property
(syn) intensifier, degree modifiers
(e.g.) **Adjectives of Degree** describe the degree of the property.

quantifying adjective | 수량 형용사

[ˈkwɑːntɪfaɪɪŋ ˌædʒɪktɪv]

an adjective that indicates the amount, number, or frequency of a noun
(syn) numerical adjective, measure adjective
(e.g.) **Quantifying Adjectives** indicate the amount, quantity, or frequency.

frequency | 빈도

[ˈfriːkwənsi]

the rate at which something occurs or is repeated over a particular period of time
(syn) occurrence, rate, recurrence
(e.g.) Quantifying Adjectives indicate the amount, quantity, or **frequency**.

associative adjective

연관 형용사

[ə'soʊʃɪətɪv ˌædʒɪktɪv]

an adjective that describes a noun based on an associated entity rather than a literal property
(syn) relational adjective, connected modifier
(e.g.) **Associative Adjectives** describe a head noun in terms of some entity that is associated with it.

entity

개체, 실체

['ɛntɪti]

a thing with distinct and independent existence
(syn) being, object, item
(e.g.) Associative Adjectives describe a head noun in terms of some **entity** that is associated with it.

associate

연관짓다, 결부하다

[ə'soʊʃɪeɪt]

to connect with something else
(syn) connect, relate, link
(e.g.) Many **associate** classical music only with concert music.

humid

습한

['hjuːmɪd]

marked by a high level of water vapor in the air
(syn) damp, moist, muggy
(e.g.) It was a hot and **humid** day.

crisp

상쾌한, 바삭한

[krɪsp]

(of weather) cool, fresh, and invigorating
(syn) bracing, fresh, invigorating
(e.g.) A cool, **crisp** breeze came over the mountain.

breeze

산들바람

[briːz]

a gentle wind
(syn) zephyr
(e.g.) A cool, crisp **breeze** came over the mountain.

DAY
20

relief
안도, 구원

[rɪˈliːf]

a feeling of reassurance and relaxation following distress
(syn) comfort, solace, ease
(e.g.) The wind brought sweet **relief**.

piercing
꿰뚫는, 날카로운

[ˈpɪərsɪŋ]

very intense or sharp
(syn) penetrating, sharp, acute
(e.g.) The wind was **piercing** the scorching humidity.

humidity
습도

[hjuːˈmɪdəti]

the amount of water vapor in the air
(syn) moisture, dampness
(e.g.) The high **humidity** made the air feel hot and sticky all day.

urban planner
도시 계획가

[ˌɜːrbən ˈplænər]

a professional who develops designs and programs for the future of cities
(syn) city designer, development specialist
(e.g.) I'm so thankful to our **urban planners** for keeping this park.

varieties
변이, 종류

[vəˈraɪətiz]

different forms or types of the same thing
(syn) forms, types, kinds
(e.g.) The alveolar lateral approximant /l/ presents appreciable differences among different **varieties**.

ridge
능선, 융기

[rɪdʒ]

a long, narrow raised section of a surface
(syn) crest, bank, elevation
(e.g.) The clear 'l' is articulated with the tongue tip in contact with the alveolar **ridge**.

velum
연구개

['viːləm]

the soft palate at the back of the roof of the mouth
(syn) soft palate, palatal curtain
(e.g.) The back of the tongue is raising toward the **velum**.

hardly
거의 ~하지 않는

['hɑːrdli]

scarcely; barely
(syn) scarcely, barely, rarely
(e.g.) The clear 'l' may **hardly** be found in some varieties of AE.

realization
실현형

[ˌriːələˈzeɪʃən]

the actual phonetic form of a phoneme
(syn) allophones, phonetic forms
(e.g.) The **realizations** differ in terms of shades of the dark 'l'.

shade
농도, 미묘한 차이

[ʃeɪd]

slight variation or degree
(syn) tint, nuance, variations
(e.g.) The realizations differ in terms of **shades** of the dark 'l'.

vocalization
모음화

[ˌvoʊkələˈzeɪʃən]

a phonological change where a consonant is replaced by a vowel or semivowel
(syn) vowelization, softening
(e.g.) **Vocalization** of /l/ to [o] as in (2a).

DAY
20

delete
삭제하다

[dɪˈliːt]

to remove or leave out
(syn) omit, remove, erase
(e.g.) /l/ may be **deleted** as in (2b).

environment
(음운) 인접 환경

[ɪnˈvaɪrənmənt]

the surrounding sounds that affect the pronunciation of a phoneme
(syn) context, surrounding, setting
(e.g.) State the **environment** for dark 'l' and darker 'l', respectively.

midway
중간에

[ˈmɪdweɪ]

in the middle of the way or distance
(syn) halfway, centrally, in the middle
(e.g.) When about **midway** of a certain block, the policeman slowed his walk.

hardware store
철물점

[ˈhɑːrdwɛr stɔːr]

a shop that sells tools, materials, and domestic fittings
(syn) ironmonger's, home improvement store
(e.g.) In the doorway of a darkened **hardware store** a man leaned.

lean
기대다

[liːn]

to incline or rest the body against something
(syn) rest, prop, recline
(e.g.) In the doorway of a darkened hardware store a man **leaned**.

unlighted
불이 켜지지 않은

[ʌnˈlaɪtɪd]

not illuminated or lit
(syn) dark, unlit, extinguished
(e.g.) A man leaned, with an **unlighted** cigar in his mouth.

appointment
약속

[əˈpɔɪntmənt]

a formal arrangement to meet or visit at a particular time
(syn) engagement, meeting, date
(e.g.) It's an **appointment** made twenty years ago.

make certain — 확실히 하다

[meɪk 'sɜːrtən]

to ensure or verify that something is true or definite
(syn) ensure, verify, confirm
(e.g.) I'll explain if you'd like to **make certain** it's all straight.

tear down — 철거하다

[tɛər daʊn]

to demolish or dismantle
(syn) demolish, raze, level
(e.g.) The construction workers **tore down** the building.

strike a match — 성냥을 켜다

[straɪk ə mætʃ]

to ignite a match by rubbing it against a surface
(syn) to light a match
(e.g.) The man in the doorway **struck a match** and lit his cigar.

pale — 창백한

[peɪl]

(of a person's face) having less color than usual, typically from illness or fear
(syn) wan, ashen, ghostly
(e.g.) The light showed a **pale**, square-jawed face.

square-jawed — 네모난 턱의

[ˌskwɛr 'dʒɔːd]

having a distinctively square, firm jawline
(syn) chiseled-jawed, firm-jawed
(e.g.) The light showed a pale, **square-jawed** face.

scar — 흉터

[skɑːr]

a mark left on the skin after a wound or injury has healed
(syn) blemish, mark, cicatrix
(e.g.) A little white **scar** near his right eyebrow.

DAY
20

scarfpin
스카프 핀

['skɑːrfˌpɪn]

a decorative pin used to secure a scarf or tie
(syn) tie pin, brooch, lapel pin
(e.g.) His **scarfpin** was a large diamond.

twirl
빙빙 돌리다

[twɜːrl]

to spin or rotate something quickly and lightly
(syn) spin, rotate, whirl
(e.g.) The policeman **twirled** his club and took a step or two.

club
경찰봉

[klʌb]

a heavy stick used as a weapon by a police officer
(syn) baton, truncheon, nightstick
(e.g.) The policeman twirled his **club** and took a step or two.

beat (policeman's)
(경찰관의) 순찰 구역

[biːt]

a route or area assigned to a police officer for patrol
(syn) route, territory, precinct
(e.g.) The policeman, passing on along his **beat**, trying doors as he went.

overcoat
외투, 오버코트

['oʊvərkoʊt]

a long, warm coat worn over other clothing
(syn) greatcoat, topcoat, trench coat
(e.g.) A tall man in a long **overcoat**, with collar turned up to his ears.

collar
옷깃

['kɑːlər]

the part of a shirt, coat, or dress that fastens around the neck
(syn) neckline, lapel, ruff
(e.g.) With **collar** turned up to his ears.

hurry
서두르다

[ˈhɜːri]

to move or act with great speed
(syn) rush, hasten
(e.g.) He **hurried** across from the opposite side of the street.

opposite
반대편의

[ˈɑːpəzɪt]

facing or situated at the other side
(syn) facing, contrary, reverse
(e.g.) He hurried across from the **opposite** side of the street.

doubtfully
의심스럽게

[ˈdaʊtfəli]

in a hesitant or uncertain manner
(syn) skeptically, hesitantly, uncertainly
(e.g.) "Is that you, Bob?" he asked, **doubtfully**.

grasping
꽉 잡는

[ˈɡræspɪŋ]

seizing and holding firmly
(syn) clutching, seizing, holding
(e.g.) **Grasping** both the other's hands with his own.

sure as fate
운명처럼 확실한

[ʃʊr æz feɪt]

definitely, inevitably
(syn) definitely, certainly, inevitably
(e.g.) "It's Bob, **sure as fate**."

in existence
존재하는

[ɪn ɪɡˈzɪstəns]

still living or present in the world
(syn) alive, present, surviving
(e.g.) I was certain I'd find you here if you were still **in existence**.

last
지속하다

[ˈlæst]

to continue for a specified period of time
(syn) endure, continue, persist
(e.g.) I wish it had **lasted**, so we could have had another dinner there.

DAY
20

bully	○○○	
glare	○○○	
gaze upon	○○○	
release	○○○	
snapped	○○○	
Roman (nose)	○○○	
under arrest	○○○	
sensible	○○○	
unfold	○○○	
tremble	○○○	
wanted (by police)	○○○	
plain clothes man	○○○	
expected outcomes	○○○	
opposite(of what's expected)	○○○	
limited command	○○○	
target language	○○○	
avoidance	○○○	
code switching	○○○	
appeal to authority	○○○	
strategic competence	○○○	
promoting	○○○	
communicative competence	○○○	
quadricycle	○○○	
persevere	○○○	
defeat	○○○	
extraposition	○○○	
clausal modifier	○○○	
adjoined	○○○	
phrasal constituent	○○○	
VP preposing	○○○	

pronominal NP	○○○
postulated	○○○
morpheme boundary	○○○
coincidence	○○○
defy	○○○
solemn	○○○
reverie	○○○
bilabial	○○○
alveolar	○○○
velar	○○○
tense vowel	○○○
muscular effort	○○○
open syllable	○○○
stress	○○○
distributionally	○○○
conflict	○○○
loaf around	○○○
retreat	○○○
occasion	○○○
dismal	○○○
supposition	○○○
vessel	○○○
defaced	○○○
surge	○○○
footstep	○○○
continuous	○○○
discrete	○○○
organism	○○○
unwilling	○○○
committed	○○○

bully	(n) 괴롭히는 사람, (v) 협박하다, (a) *아주 좋은, 멋진
['buli]	someone who often hurts or frightens others (syn) terrorize, victimize, tease; (a) *great (e.g.) My son is being **bullied** at school.

glare	눈부신 빛
[glɛər]	a fierce or dazzling light (syn) brilliance, flash, beam (e.g.) When they came into this **glare** each of them turned.

gaze upon	~을 응시하다
[geɪz ə'pɑːn]	to look steadily and intently at something (syn) stare at, look fixedly at, contemplate (e.g.) They turned simultaneously to **gaze upon** the other's face.

release	놓아 주다
[rɪ'liːs]	to let go of (syn) let go, free (e.g.) The man from the West stopped suddenly and **released** his arm.

snapped	쏘아붙였다
[snæpt]	said something quickly and sharply (syn) retorted, barked, spoke sharply (e.g.) "You're not Jimmy Wells," he **snapped**.

Roman (nose)	매부리코
['roʊmən]	a nose with a prominent bridge, often hooked (syn) aquiline nose, hooked nose (e.g.) Change a man's nose from a **Roman** to a pug.

under arrest	체포된
['ʌndər ə'rɛst]	seized by police and held in custody (syn) apprehended, detained, captured (e.g.) "You've been **under arrest** for ten minutes, 'Silky' Bob."

sensible

현명한, 분별 있는

['sɛnsəbəl]

done or chosen in accordance with wisdom or prudence
(syn) reasonable, wise, prudent
(e.g.) "Going quietly, are you? That's **sensible**."

unfold

펴지다

[ʌnˈfoʊld]

to open or spread out from a folded state
(syn) open, spread out, straighten
(e.g.) The man from the West **unfolded** the little piece of paper.

tremble

떨리다

['trɛmbəl]

to shake involuntarily, typically as a result of anxiety, fear, or frailty
(syn) shiver, quiver
(e.g.) His hand was steady when he began to read, but it
trembled a little.

wanted (by police)

수배 중인

['wɑːntɪd]

sought by police in connection with a crime
(syn) sought, pursued, hunted
(e.g.) It was the face of the man **wanted** in Chicago.

plain clothes man

사복 경찰관

[ˌpleɪn kloʊz mæn]

a police detective who wears ordinary clothes rather than a
uniform
(syn) detective, undercover officer, civilian police
(e.g.) I went around and got a **plain clothes man** to do the job.

expected outcomes

예상된 결과

[ɪkˈspɛktɪd
ˈaʊtˌkʌmz]

the results or consequences that are anticipated or predicted
(syn) anticipated results, projected consequences
(e.g.) Situational irony occurs when **expected outcomes** do not
happen.

opposite (of what's expected)
반대

['ɑːpəzɪt]

a person or thing that is completely different from or contrary to another
(syn) reverse, contrary, antithesis
(e.g.) They are the **opposite** of what is expected.

limited command
제한된 구사력

[ˌlɪmɪtɪd kəˈmænd]

a low level of proficiency or mastery in a language
(syn) poor fluency, restricted mastery
(e.g.) Learners who have **limited command** of the second language may have to use a variety of strategies.

target language
목표 언어

['tɑːrgɪt 'læŋgwɪdʒ]

the language that a person is trying to learn or to which something is being translated
(syn) L2, foreign language
(e.g.) Their lack of knowledge of the **target language** grammar and vocabulary.

avoidance
회피

[əˈvɔɪdəns]

a strategy of refraining from using a difficult language structure or word
(syn) evasion, sidestepping, dodging
(e.g.) Strategies employed include **avoidance**, code switching, word coinage.

code switching
언어 전환

['koʊd ˌswɪtʃɪŋ]

the practice of alternating between two or more languages in a conversation
(syn) language mixing, cross-language communication
(e.g.) Strategies employed include avoidance, **code switching**, word coinage.

appeal to authority
권위에 호소

[ə'piːl tuː ə'θɔːrəti]

a strategy of seeking assistance from a more knowledgeable source
(syn) seeking help, consulting a source
(e.g.) Strategies employed include avoidance, code switching, word coinage, **appeal to authority**.

strategic competence
전략적인 능력

[strə'tiːdʒɪk 'kɑːmpətəns]

the ability to use communication strategies to compensate for imperfect language knowledge
(syn) coping skills, tactical ability
(e.g.) As these strategies constitute a significant part of **strategic competence**.

promoting
촉진하는, 장려하는

[prə'moʊtɪŋ]

supporting or actively encouraging the development of something
(syn) fostering, encouraging, furthering
(e.g.) Advances in the learners' ability play a considerable role in **promoting** their communicative competence.

communicative competence
의사소통 능력

[kə,mjuːnɪkətɪv 'kɑːmpətəns]

the ability to use language effectively and appropriately
(syn) overall language skill, functional ability
(e.g.) Promoting their **communicative competence**.

quadricycle
사륜 자전거

['kwɑːdrɪ,saɪkəl]

a four-wheeled vehicle powered by pedals
(syn) four-wheeled bicycle, four-cycle
(e.g.) Oh, it is called "**quadricycle**."

persevere
끈기 있게 계속하다, 인내하다

[pɔ̀ːrsəvíər]

to persist steadily in a course of action despite difficulties
(syn) persist, endure, continue
(e.g.) She **persevered** through hardship to achieve her dream.

defeat
패배시키다

[dɪˈfiːt]

to win a victory over someone in a battle, contest, or election
(syn) conquer, overcome, vanquish
(e.g.) The goal is to resist man and ultimately to **defeat** him.

extraposition
외치

[ˌɛkstrəpəˈzɪʃən]

a syntactic phenomenon where a clause or phrase is moved to the end of the sentence
(syn) displacement, postponement, rightward movement
(e.g.) Clausal modifiers can move to the end of the sentence, which is called '**extraposition**'.

clausal modifier
절 수식어

[ˌklɔːzəl ˈmɑːdɪfaɪər]

a clause that modifies a noun
(syn) modifying clause
(e.g.) **Clausal modifiers** of NPs can move to the end of the sentence.

adjoined
인접한, 추가된

[əˈdʒɔːnd]

attached or connected to something
(syn) attached, connected, appended
(e.g.) The extraposed CP can be **adjoined** to VP or TP.

phrasal constituent
구의 구성 성분

[ˌfreɪzəl kənˈstɪtʃuənt]

the element that makes up a phrase
(syn) phrase unit, grammatical part
(e.g.) Only a **phrasal constituent** can move.

VP preposing
VP 선행 이동

[viː piː ˈpriːˌpoʊzɪŋ]

the syntactic movement of a Verb Phrase to the front of the sentence
(syn) VP fronting, verb phrase movement
(e.g.) **VP preposing** can be further applied to (2b).

pronominal NP　대명사 명사구

[prouˌnɑːmɪnəl ɛn piː]

a Noun Phrase consisting of a pronoun
(syn) pronoun phrase, proform NP
(e.g.) An empty **pronominal NP** PRO is postulated in control constructions.

postulated　가정된, 상정된

[ˈpɑːstʃʊleɪtɪd]

suggested or assumed to be true as the basis for reasoning
(syn) hypothesized, assumed, supposed
(e.g.) An empty pronominal NP PRO is **postulated** in control constructions.

morpheme boundary　형태소 경계

[ˈmɔːrfiːm ˈbaʊndəri]

the point at which morpheme joins
(syn) morphological border, morpheme division
(e.g.) Across **morpheme boundaries**, obligatory nasal assimilation applies.

coincidence　우연의 일치, 관련 없어 보이는 사건들이 동시에 발생하는 상황

[koʊˈɪnsɪdəns]

a remarkable occurrence of events or circumstances at the same time by chance
(syn) concurrence, happenstance
(e.g.) Meeting her again in Paris was a strange **coincidence**.

defy　거역하다, 반항하다

[dɪˈfaɪ]

to resist openly or refuse to obey authority
(syn) resist, oppose, challenge, disobey
(opp) submit, obey, comply
(e.g.) The artist **defied** tradition with his bold new style.

solemn　엄숙한, 진지한

[sάləm]

formal and serious in manner or appearance
(syn) serious, grave, dignified, earnest
(opp) cheerful, frivolous, playful
(e.g.) The ceremony was a **solemn** tribute to the fallen heroes.

reverie
공상, 몽상

[révəri]

a state of being pleasantly lost in one's thoughts; a daydream
(syn) daydream, fantasy, contemplation, trance
(opp) reality, awareness, consciousness
(e.g.) The poet often slipped into **reverie** while watching the sunset.

bilabial
양순음

[baɪˈleɪbiəl]

consonants articulated with both lips
(syn) lip sounds, labial consonants
(e.g.) English **bilabials** include /p/, /b/, and /m/.

alveolar
차조음

[ælˈviːəlr]

consonants articulated with the tongue near or on the alveolar ridge
(syn) tongue-tip sounds, coronal consonants
(e.g.) Common **alveolars** are /t/, /d/, and /n/.

velar
연구개음

[ˈviːlər]

consonants articulated with the back of the tongue against the velum
(syn) back consonants, dorsal consonants
(e.g.) **Velars** like /k/ and /g/ are found in many languages.

tense vowel
긴장모음

[tɛns ˈvaʊəl]

a vowel pronounced with greater muscular effort and tongue tension
(syn) high vowel, effortful vowel
(e.g.) The vowel in "seat" is a **tense vowel**.

muscular effort
근육의 노력

[ˈmʌskjələr ˈɛfərt]

the tension or contraction of muscles required for an action
(syn) physical exertion, muscle tension
(e.g.) A tense vowel requires a greater **muscular effort** in production.

open syllable 개방 음절

[ˌoʊpən ˈsɪləbəl]

a syllable that ends with a vowel
(syn) vowel-final syllable, free syllable
(e.g.) A tense vowel can appear in an **open syllable** with stress.

stress 강세

[strɛs]

emphasis given to a specific syllable or word in speech
(syn) emphasis, accent, prominence
(e.g.) Tense vowels can appear in open syllables with **stress**.

distributionally 분포적으로

[ˌdɪstrɪˈbjuːʃənəli]

in terms of where a phoneme can occur
(syn) contextually, environmentally, locationally
(e.g.) The **distributionally** based phonological classification comes into conflict.

conflict 충돌, 상충

[ˈkɑːnflɪkt]

a serious disagreement or incompatibility
(syn) contradiction, clash, disagreement
(e.g.) The phonological classification comes into **conflict** with the phonetic classification.

loaf around 빈둥거리다

[ˈloʊf əˈraʊnd]

to spend time in an idle or lazy way
(syn) idle, lounge, waste time
(e.g.) They sentimentally reminisce about their glory days while **loafing around** doing nothing.

retreat 피난처, 은신처

[rɪˈtriːt]

a place of refuge, privacy, or safety
(syn) refuge, shelter, sanctuary
(e.g.) More terror of mind than I to this **retreat**.

occasion

원인, 이유

[əˈkeɪʒən]

a particular event or circumstance; a reason
(syn) cause, reason, grounds
(e.g.) The farther I was from the **occasion** of my fright, the greater my apprehensions were.

dismal

음울한, 비참한

[ˈdɪzməl]

depressing, dreary, or gloomy
(syn) gloomy, dreary, miserable
(e.g.) I form'd nothing but **dismal** imaginations to my self.

supposition

가정, 추정

[ˌsʌpəˈzɪʃən]

an assumption or hypothesis
(syn) assumption, hypothesis, conjecture
(e.g.) Reason joyn'd in with me upon this **supposition**.

vessel

배, 선박

[ˈvɛsəl]

a ship or large boat
(syn) ship, boat, craft
(e.g.) Where was the **vessel** that brought them?

defaced

훼손된, 손상된

[dɪˈfeɪst]

spoil the surface or appearance of (something)
(syn) spoiled, ruined, obliterated
(e.g.) The first surge of the sea... would have **defaced** entirely.

surge

파도, 밀려옴

[sɜːrdʒ]

a sudden powerful forward or upward movement
(syn) wave, swell, rush
(e.g.) The first **surge** of the sea upon a high wind would have defac'd entirely.

footstep 발자국

['fʊt,stɛp]

the sound of a step or the mark of a foot or shoe
(syn) print, track
(e.g.) What marks was there of any other **footsteps**!

continuous 연속적인

[kən'tɪnjuəs]

forming an unbroken whole; uninterrupted
(syn) uninterrupted, ongoing, ceaseless
(e.g.) Ancient Easterners saw the world as consisting of **continuous** substances.

discrete 개별적인, 분리된

[dɪ'skriːt]

individually separate and distinct
(syn) separate, distinct, unconnected
(e.g.) Ancient Westerners tended to see the world as being composed of **discrete** objects or separate atoms.

organism 유기체, 조직체

['ɔːrgənɪzəm]

a complex structure of interdependent elements
(syn) living thing, entity, structure
(e.g.) Easterners view a company as an **organism** coordinating people working together.

unwilling 꺼리는

[ʌn'wɪlɪŋ]

not ready, eager, or prepared to do something
(syn) reluctant, hesitant, averse
(e.g.) She is **unwilling** to be committed to the man.

committed 헌신하는, 약속하는

[kə'mɪtɪd]

pledged or bound to a certain course or relationship
(syn) devoted, pledged, dedicated
(e.g.) She is unwilling to be **committed** to the man.

ascend	○○○	oblivion	○○○
beseech	○○○	refine	○○○
candor	○○○	legitimate	○○○
devout	○○○	enlist	○○○
falter	○○○	abstract	○○○
immerse	○○○	contemplate	○○○
rebuke	○○○	spurt	○○○
serene	○○○	stammer	○○○
initial course goal	○○○	manuscript	○○○
change the goal set earlier	○○○	inscription	○○○
one-shot assessment	○○○	ultimate	○○○
self-assessment	○○○	anatomy	○○○
subjective	○○○	frivolous	○○○
objective	○○○	mediate	○○○
strictly following	○○○	adjacent	○○○
challenging	○○○	dormant	○○○
over-generalization	○○○	imminent	○○○
negative transfer	○○○	conspicuous	○○○
positive transfer	○○○	frigid	○○○
subsequent	○○○	futile	○○○
analytic	○○○	succumb	○○○
global rating	○○○	deteriorate	○○○
recorded test	○○○	constrain	○○○
social-skill training	○○○	ponder	○○○
one-on-one assistance	○○○	inborn	○○○
ill-formed expression	○○○	replicate	○○○
pre-writing activity	○○○	squander	○○○
meaning-focused feedback	○○○	stealthy	○○○
reflective journal	○○○	morbid	○○○
relinquish	○○○	austere	○○○

ascend	오르다, 상승하다
[əsénd]	to move upward; to rise to a higher position or level (syn) climb, rise, mount, soar (opp) descend, fall, drop (e.g.) The balloon slowly **ascended** into the morning sky.

beseech	간청하다, 애원하다
[bɪsíːtʃ]	to ask someone urgently and fervently to do something (syn) implore, beg, plead, entreat (opp) refuse, deny, reject (e.g.) The villagers **beseeched** the king for mercy.

candor	솔직함, 정직함
[kǽndər]	the quality of being open and honest in expression (syn) frankness, honesty, sincerity, openness (opp) deceit, dishonesty, guile (e.g.) Her **candor** during the interview impressed everyone.

devout	독실한, 열렬한
[dɪváut]	having or showing deep religious feeling or commitment (syn) pious, sincere, reverent, faithful (opp) irreligious, indifferent, skeptical (e.g.) He was a **devout** follower of his faith.

falter	비틀거리다, 주저하다
[fɔ́ːltər]	to lose strength or confidence; to hesitate or stumble (syn) hesitate, waver, stumble, flounder (opp) persist, continue, advance (e.g.) His voice **faltered** as he delivered the bad news.

immerse	몰입하다, 담그다
[ɪmə́ːrs]	to involve deeply; to submerge in liquid (syn) involve, engage, absorb, submerge (opp) detach, withdraw, disengage (e.g.) She **immersed** herself in her research for months.

rebuke
꾸짖다, 비난하다

[rɪbjúːk]

to express sharp disapproval or criticism of someone's actions
(syn) scold, reproach, reprimand, criticize
(opp) praise, commend, approve
(e.g.) The teacher **rebuked** the student for cheating.

serene
고요한, 평온한

[səríːn]

calm, peaceful, and untroubled
(syn) tranquil, placid, composed, undisturbed
(opp) agitated, disturbed, turbulent
(e.g.) The lake looked **serene** under the pale moonlight.

initial course goal
초기 과정 목표

[ɪ́nɪʃəl kɔːrs goʊl]

the original aim or objective set for a lesson or program
(syn) preliminary objective, starting aim
(e.g.) I should change the **initial course goal** after assessing my
students.

change the goal set earlier
이전에 설정된 목표를 변경하다

[tʃeɪndʒ ðə goʊl set ˈɜːrliər]

to revise or alter a previously established objective
(syn) revise the objective, alter the initial plan
(e.g.) I **change the goal set earlier** and include essays.

one-shot assessment
일회성 평가

[wʌn ʃɑːt əˈsɛsmənt]

an evaluation conducted only once at a single point in time
(syn) single-test evaluation, non-periodic exam
(e.g.) **One-shot assessment** at the end of the course is not
effective.

self-assessment
자기 평가

[sɛlf əˈsɛsmənt]

an evaluation of one's own work or performance
(syn) self-evaluation, personal reviews
(e.g.) A students' **self-assessment** is rather subjective in some ways.

subjective
주관적인

[səbˈdʒɛktɪv]

based on or influenced by personal feelings, tastes, or opinions
(syn) personal, biased, arbitrary
(e.g.) Students' self-assessments are rather **subjective** in some ways.

objective
객관적인

[əbˈdʒɛktɪv]

not influenced by personal feelings or opinions; based on facts
(syn) unbiased, factual, impartial
(e.g.) I also believe assessment should be **objective**.

strictly following
엄격하게 따르는

[ˈstrɪktli ˈfɑːloʊɪŋ]

adhering precisely and rigidly to a procedure or rule
(syn) rigidly adhering to, precisely conforming to
(e.g.) **Strictly following** the lesson procedure was rather challenging to my students.

challenging
어려운, 힘든

[ˈtʃælɪndʒɪŋ]

demanding, difficult, or testing one's abilities
(syn) demanding, tough, formidable
(e.g.) Strictly following the lesson procedure was rather **challenging** to my students.

over-generalization

과잉 일반화

[ˌoʊvər, dʒɛnərəlaɪˈzeɪʃən]

the extension of a rule of grammar to cases in which it does not apply

(syn) misapplication of a rule, extended use

(e.g.) Negative transfer can be further divided into two types: **overgeneralization** and interference.

negative transfer

부정적 전이

[ˈnɛɡətɪv ˈtrænsfər]

prior learning hindering new learning

(syn) interference, detrimental influence

(e.g.) **Negative transfer** can be further divided into two types.

positive transfer

긍정적 전이

[ˈpɑːzətɪv ˈtrænsfər]

prior learning facilitating new learning

(syn) facilitation, helpful influence

(e.g.) Transfer can be categorized into **positive transfer** and negative transfer.

subsequent

다음의, 이어진

[ˈsʌbsɪkwənt]

coming after something in time

(syn) following, later, ensuing

(e.g.) The effects of the learner's previous language knowledge on **subsequent** language learning.

analytic

분석적인

[ˌænəˈlɪtɪk]

relating to or using analysis or logical reasoning

(syn) detailed, criterion-referenced

(e.g.) **Analytic** scoring method.

global rating · 총체적 평점

[ˌɡloʊbəl ˈreɪtɪŋ]

an overall assessment or score based on general impressions
(syn) holistic score, overall assessment
(e.g.) Providing a **global rating** with overall impressions.

recorded test · 녹화된 시험

[rɪˈkɔːrdɪd tɛst]

an examination preserved on audio or video
(syn) archived examination, video-taped assessment
(e.g.) Examiners discuss rating disagreements based on the **recorded test**.

social-skill training · 사회성 기술 훈련

[ˌsoʊʃəl skɪl ˈtreɪnɪŋ]

an instruction designed to improve interpersonal and social interaction abilities
(syn) social etiquette instruction, interpersonal skill development
(e.g.) She needed no further **social-skill training**.

one-on-one assistance · 일대일 보조

[ˌwʌn ɑːn wʌn əˈsɪstəns]

direct, individualized help from one person to another
(syn) individualized help, dedicated support
(e.g.) We were able to attend school without **one-on-one assistance**.

ill-formed expression · 문법적으로 틀린 표현

[ˌɪl fɔːrmd ɪkˈsprɛʃən]

a phrase or sentence that violates grammatical rules
(syn) ungrammatical phrase, incorrect language
(e.g.) Corrective feedback that reformulates an **ill-formed expression**.

pre-writing activity · 쓰기 전 활동

[ˌpriː raɪtɪŋ ækˈtɪvəti]

an activity like brainstorming or outlining done before drafting a text
(syn) brainstorming, planning phase, outline creation
(e.g.) Start with **pre-writing activities** with little emphasis on ungrammaticalities.

meaning-focused feedback

['miːnɪŋ fookəst 'fiːdbæk]

의미 중심 피드백

correction that prioritizes the message and content over grammatical accuracy
- (syn) content-based correction, semantic feedback
- (e.g.) Provide **meaning-focused** feedback.

reflective journal

[rɪ'flɛktɪv 'dʒɜːrnəl]

성찰 일지

written record of one's thoughts and feelings about their learning experiences
- (syn) self-analysis log, introspection record
- (e.g.) Tasks Ss to write **reflective journals** about their writing.

relinquish

[rɪlíŋkwɪʃ]

포기하다, 양도하다

to voluntarily give up or surrender something
- (syn) surrender, renounce, abandon, yield
- (opp) retain, keep, hold
- (e.g.) The general refused to **relinquish** command of his army.

oblivion

[əblívɪən]

망각, 잊혀짐

the state of being forgotten or unaware of what is happening
- (syn) forgetfulness, obscurity, unconsciousness
- (opp) remembrance, awareness, fame
- (e.g.) The old town has faded into **oblivion** over the years.

refine

[rɪfáin]

정제하다, 세련되게 하다

to make something pure or improve it by removing impurities
- (syn) purify, polish, improve, perfect
- (opp) worsen, coarsen
- (e.g.) The artist continued to **refine** his technique over many years.

legitimate
합법적인, 정당한

[lɪdʒítəmət]

conforming to law or accepted rules and standards
- (syn) lawful, valid, authorized
- (opp) illegal, false, fake
- (e.g.) The company's actions were ruled **legitimate** by the court.

enlist
참여하다, 모집하다

[ɪnlíst]

to join or recruit for a cause or organization
- (syn) recruit, engage, sign up
- (opp) exclude, dismiss
- (e.g.) He **enlisted** several experts to work on the research project.

abstract
추상적인, 구체적 사물이나 경험에서 분리되어 관념적으로 존재하는

['æbstrækt]

an idea existing in thought rather than in physical or concrete form
- (syn) conceptual, theoretical
- (e.g.) The concept was too **abstract** for beginners to grasp easily.

contemplate
심사숙고하다, 곰곰이 생각하다

[kántəmplèɪt]

to think deeply or carefully about something
- (syn) ponder, meditate, reflect, consider
- (opp) disregard, ignore
- (e.g.) She sat quietly, **contemplating** the meaning of the painting.

spurt
(액체·감정 등의) 분출, 급증

[spɜːrt]

a sudden and brief burst or increase of activity, effort, or emotion
- (syn) surge, burst, gush, flare-up
- (opp) stagnation, calm
- (e.g.) She finished the race with a final **spurt** of energy.

stammer

[stǽmər]

(v) 말을 더듬다, (n) 말 더듬기

to speak with involuntary pauses or repetitions of sounds
- (syn) falter, hesitate, splutter
- (opp) articulate, pronounce clearly
- (e.g.) The nervous student began to **stammer** during his presentation.

manuscript

[mǽnjuskrɪpt]

필사본, 원고

a handwritten or typed document, especially a writer's draft before publication
- (syn) document, text, draft
- (e.g.) The author submitted his **manuscript** to the editor for final review.

inscription

[ɪnskrípʃən]

비문, 새겨진 글

words carved or engraved on a surface
- (syn) engraving, carving, etching
- (opp) erasure
- (e.g.) The ancient coin bore a Latin **inscription** on its surface.

ultimate

[ʌ́ltəmət]

궁극적인, 최종의

final or eventual in a process or development
- (syn) final, terminal, conclusive
- (opp) initial, preliminary
- (e.g.) Her **ultimate** goal is to become a professor of linguistics.

anatomy

[ənǽtəmi]

해부학, 인체 구조

the scientific study of the structure of living organisms
- (syn) morphology, physiology, structure
- (e.g.) Medical students must master human **anatomy** before beginning surgery training.

frivolous
경솔한, 하찮은

[frívələs]

not having any serious purpose or value
- (syn) trivial, silly, flippant
- (opp) serious, important
- (e.g.) He spent his money on **frivolous** purchases.

mediate
중재하다, 조정하다

[míːdièit]

to try to end a dispute between two people or groups
- (syn) arbitrate, intervene, reconcile
- (opp) provoke, worsen
- (e.g.) She was asked to **mediate** between the two sides.

adjacent
인접한

[ədʒéisənt]

next to or very near something
- (syn) neighboring, adjoining
- (e.g.) The two **adjacent** rooms were converted into one large classroom.

dormant
휴면 중인, 잠재된

[dɔ́ːrmənt]

temporarily inactive
- (syn) inactive, latent, inert
- (opp) active, lively
- (e.g.) The volcano has been **dormant** for centuries.

imminent
임박한, 곧 일어날

[ímənənt]

likely to happen soon
- (syn) impending, forthcoming, approaching
- (opp) distant, unlikely
- (e.g.) Dark clouds suggested that a storm was **imminent**.

conspicuous
눈에 잘 띄는, 현저한

[kənspíkjuəs]

easily seen or noticed; attracting attention
- (syn) noticeable, prominent, distinct
- (opp) obscure, hidden
- (e.g.) Her red coat made her **conspicuous** in the crowd.

frigid

몹시 추운, 냉담한

[frídʒɪd]

very cold in temperature or lacking warmth in manner
(syn) icy, freezing, cold-hearted
(opp) warm, affectionate
(e.g.) His **frigid** response showed no trace of sympathy.

futile

쓸모없는, 헛된

[fjúːtl]

incapable of producing any useful result; pointless
(syn) vain, ineffective, fruitless
(opp) effective, productive
(e.g.) Their attempts to stop the flood were ultimately **futile**.

succumb

(유혹, 질병 등에) 굴복하다, 쓰러지다

[səkʌ́m]

to yield or give in to something stronger
(syn) yield, surrender, give in
(opp) resist, withstand
(e.g.) He finally **succumbed** to the pressure and resigned.

deteriorate

악화되다, 나빠지다

[dɪtíəriərèɪt]

to become progressively worse
(syn) worsen, decline, degenerate
(opp) improve, enhance
(e.g.) The patient's condition began to **deteriorate** rapidly.

constrain

강요하다, 제한하다

[kənstréɪn]

to compel or restrict; to limit freedom
(syn) compel, restrict, restrain
(opp) release, liberate
(e.g.) His financial situation **constrained** his choices.

ponder

숙고하다, 깊이 생각하다

[pándər]

to think about something carefully, especially before deciding
(syn) contemplate, reflect, consider
(opp) disregard, ignore
(e.g.) She **pondered** the question for a long time before answering.

inborn
타고난, 선천적인

['ɪnbɔːrn]

existing naturally from birth; not acquired through learning
(syn) innate, inherent, natural
(e.g.) **Inborn** talent alone does not guarantee effective teaching ability.

replicate
복제하다, 되풀이하다

[répləkèit]

to make an exact copy or reproduce something
(syn) duplicate, reproduce, copy
(e.g.) Scientists tried to **replicate** the experiment's results.

squander
낭비하다, 허비하다

[skwándər]

to waste something, especially money or time, in a reckless way
(syn) waste, fritter away, dissipate
(opp) save, conserve, accumulate
(e.g.) He **squandered** his inheritance on luxury cars and gambling.

stealthy
은밀한, 몰래 하는

[stélθi]

behaving or done in a secret and quiet way to avoid being noticed
(syn) secretive, furtive, sneaky
(opp) open, obvious, overt
(e.g.) The cat made a **stealthy** move toward the bird.

morbid
병적인, 소름끼치는

[mɔ́ːrbɪd]

having an abnormal interest in disturbing or unpleasant subjects
(syn) gruesome, gloomy, macabre
(opp) healthy, cheerful
(e.g.) He had a **morbid** fascination with crime stories.

austere
엄격한, 소박한

[ɔːstíər]

simple and strict in manner or appearance
(syn) stern, severe, plain
(opp) indulgent, luxurious
(e.g.) The room's **austere** design reflected his disciplined personality.

insertion	○○○	censored	○○○
non-permissible	○○○	satire	○○○
grasp	○○○	province	○○○
literally	○○○	euphemism	○○○
significance	○○○	conjoin	○○○
unbearable	○○○	constituent	○○○
domesticated	○○○	abstain	○○○
underscored	○○○	imbibe	○○○
pinion	○○○	flawed	○○○
figurative	○○○	random assignment	○○○
ascertain	○○○	teetotaling	○○○
prediction	○○○	slave's atmosphere	○○○
volitional	○○○	liberate	○○○
consolidation	○○○	hawk	○○○
closure	○○○	widening gyre	○○○
jot down	○○○	commentary	○○○
repository	○○○	vacant barn	○○○
reevaluated	○○○	double blind	○○○
reinventing	○○○	neutral	○○○
conform to	○○○	real communication	○○○
deviate from	○○○	under-represented	○○○
conducive	○○○	aloof	○○○
declarative	○○○	social construct	○○○
procedural	○○○	hallowed hall	○○○
outdated	○○○	vernacular	○○○
pace	○○○	global error	○○○
antecedent	○○○	communication strategy	○○○
ceremonial	○○○	intend	○○○
printable	○○○	giggle	○○○
groveling	○○○	nudge	○○○

insertion	삽입
[ɪnˈsɜːrʃən]	the action of putting something into something else (syn) inclusion, interpolation, introduction (e.g.) The rule governs the conditions for /j/ **insertion** and /w/ **insertion**.

non-permissible	허용되지 않는
[ˌnɑːn pərˈmɪsəbəl]	not allowed or permitted by rule or standard (syn) forbidden, disallowed, illegitimate (e.g.) The asterisk indicates a **non-permissible** form in phonology.

grasp	파악하다, 이해하다
[ɡræsp]	to fully comprehend or understand a difficult concept or message (syn) perceive, apprehend, comprehend (e.g.) Ashbury's mother might not immediately **grasp** the message of his letter.

literally	문자 그대로
[ˈlɪtərəli]	in a literal sense or manner; exactly as stated (syn) exactly, precisely, verbatim (e.g.) The room was **literally** freezing because the heater was broken.

significance	중요성, 의미
[sɪɡˈnɪfɪkəns]	the quality of being important or the hidden meaning of something (syn) importance, import, meaning (e.g.) It will take time for her to discover the **significance** of the long letter.

unbearable	참을 수 없는
[ʌnˈberəbəl]	not able to be endured or tolerated; extremely painful or unpleasant (syn) intolerable, agonizing, insufferable (e.g.) Writing the letter had sometimes been **unbearable** to him.

domesticated
길들여진, 사육된

[dəˈmestɪkeɪtɪd]

tamed and kept by humans as a pet or on a farm
(syn) tamed, cultivated, trained
(e.g.) His imagination was like a bird that had been **domesticated**, refusing to fly.

underscored
강조된, 밑줄이 그어진

[ˌʌndərˈskɔːrd]

emphasized or drawn attention to
(syn) emphasized, highlighted, underlined
(e.g.) The next words in his letter were **underscored** twice for emphasis.

pinion
(날개를) 묶다, 속박하다

[ˈpɪnjən]

to confine or restrain someone by binding their arms or wings
(syn) shackle, restrain, confine
(e.g.) Woman, why did you **pinion** me and prevent my flight?

figurative
비유적인

[ˈfɪgjərətɪv]

departing from a literal use of words; metaphorical
(syn) metaphorical, non-literal, symbolic
(e.g.) Ashbury employs **figurative** language to represent his imagination as an animal.

ascertain
확인하다, 알아내다

[ˌæsərˈteɪn]

to find out something for certain; to make sure of
(syn) discover, determine, confirm
(e.g.) The dowser was required to **ascertain** where the pipe with water was located.

prediction
예측

[prɪˈdɪkʃən]

a statement about what will happen or might happen in the future
(syn) forecast, prophecy, projection
(e.g.) The modal auxiliary will can express a neutral **prediction** of a future event.

volitional

의지의, 의도적인

[voʊˈlɪʃənəl]

relating to or resulting from the use of the will or intention
(syn) willful, deliberate, intentional
(e.g.) The modal will can have a **volitional** meaning for describing what one will do.

consolidation

통합, 강화

[kənˌsɑːləˈdeɪʃən]

the action or process of making something stronger or more solid
(syn) cementing, reinforcement, strengthening
(e.g.) The lesson plan includes a **Consolidation** stage to review the lesson.

closure

마무리, 종결

[ˈkloʊʒər]

the act or process of closing something, often referring to a lesson's ending
(syn) ending, conclusion, wrap-up
(e.g.) The **Closure** stage includes reviewing what students learned and assigning homework.

jot down

간단히 적다

[dʒɑːt daʊn]

to write something quickly or briefly
(syn) write down, note, transcribe
(e.g.) Students **jot down** the key words in the passage as the teacher reads.

repository

저장소, 보관소

[rɪˈpɑːzətɔːri]

a place where things are deposited or stored
(syn) archive, storehouse, collection
(e.g.) Museums were only seen as cultural **repositories** of great works.

reevaluated

재평가된

[ˌriːɪˈvæljueɪtɪd]

assessed or considered again
(syn) reassessed, reconsidered, revised
(e.g.) Museums have **reevaluated** the purpose of their collections in recent decades.

reinventing
재창조하는, 혁신하는

[ˌriːɪnˈventɪŋ]

changing something so much that it appears to be entirely new
(syn) redefining, redesigning, transforming
(e.g.) Modern museums are **reinventing** themselves as centers of contemporary culture.

conform to
~을 따르다, ~에 순응하다

[kənˈfɔːrm tuː]

to comply with rules, standards, or laws
(syn) comply with, adhere to, match
(e.g.) Identify suggestions that Ms. Shin's class **conforms to** and provide evidence.

deviate from
~에서 벗어나다, 이탈하다

[ˈdiːvieɪt frɑːm]

to depart from an established course, standard, or norm
(syn) depart from, diverge from, stray from
(e.g.) Explain how the identified step **deviates from** its corresponding suggestion.

conducive
도움이 되는, 어떤 결과를 가능하게 하거나 촉진하는

[kənˈduːsɪv]

making a certain situation or outcome likely or easier
(syn) favorable, beneficial
(e.g.) A quiet environment is **conducive** to focused study.

declarative
선언적인, 진술적인

[dɪˈklærətɪv]

relating to the nature of facts, knowledge, or information
(syn) explicit, informational, factual
(e.g.) The learning of skills starts with **declarative** knowledge.

procedural
절차적인, 과정적인

[prəˈsiːdʒərəl]

relating to or consisting of a series of steps or actions
(syn) operational, practical, skill-based
(e.g.) Declarative knowledge converts into **procedural** knowledge through practice.

outdated
시대에 뒤떨어진, 구식의

[ˌaʊtˈdeɪtɪd]

obsolete; no longer modern or useful
(syn) obsolete, archaic, old-fashioned
(e.g.) The classic mode of a teacher at the chalkboard is considered **outdated**.

pace
속도

[peɪs]

the rate of movement or activity
(syn) speed, rate, tempo
(e.g.) Students can study the lectures at home at their own **pace**.

antecedent
선행하는, 앞서는

[ˌæntəˈsiːdənt]

existing or happening before something else; the word a pronoun refers to
(syn) preceding, prior, former
(e.g.) The teacher adjusted the class according to the students' **antecedent** knowledge.

ceremonial
의식적인, 공식적인

[ˌserəˈmoʊniəl]

used for or relating to a formal, often religious or public, occasion
(syn) formal, ritual, official
(e.g.) The King demands a few **ceremonial** pieces on demand from the composer.

printable
인쇄 가능한, 출판 가능한

[ˈprɪntəbəl]

suitable for being printed
(syn) publishable, suitable for press, fit for print
(e.g.) The King wants a **printable** paragraph on his respect for art.

groveling
굽실거리는

[ˈɡrɑːvəlɪŋ]

acting in an overly subservient manner to obtain forgiveness or favor
(syn) subservience, fawning, cringing
(e.g.) The King wants some good **groveling** to make clear his position.

censored

검열된

['sensərd]

having had parts removed or suppressed because they are considered objectionable

(syn) edited, suppressed, controlled

(e.g.) The King demands a belief that the composer hasn't been **censored** in any way.

DAY

23

satire

풍자

['sætaɪər]

the use of humor, irony, exaggeration, or ridicule to expose and criticize people's stupidity or vices

(syn) parody, mockery, ridicule

(e.g.) **Satire** might sometime be a problem, but it's beyond serious music.

province

범위, 영역

['prɑːvɪns]

an area of activity or authority

(syn) domain, scope, sphere

(e.g.) Satire is beyond the **province** of serious music, in the King's view.

euphemism

완곡어법

['juːfəmɪzəm]

a mild or indirect word or expression substituted for one considered to be too harsh or blunt

(syn) polite term, circumlocution, understatement

(e.g.) Pass away is an example of a **euphemism** for die.

conjoin

결합하다, 연결하다

[kən'dʒɔɪn]

to join together; to link

(syn) combine, coordinate, link

(e.g.) Coordinate conjunctions can **conjoin** constituents of the same grammatical category.

constituent

(문법) 구성 요소

[kənˈstɪtʃuənt]

a word or group of words that functions as a single unit within a sentence
(syn) component, element, unit
(e.g.) Conjunctions cannot conjoin **constituents** of different grammatical categories.

abstain

삼가다, 금하다

[æbˈsteɪn]

to restrain oneself from doing or enjoying something
(syn) refrain, desist, avoid
(e.g.) People who imbibe alcohol have healthier hearts than those who **abstain** from drinking.

imbibe

(특히 술을) 마시다, 섭취하다

[ɪmˈbaɪb]

to drink (alcohol or another liquid)
(syn) consume, ingest
(e.g.) People who **imbibed** one alcoholic beverage per day showed better health.

flawed

결함이 있는

[flɔːd]

having a fundamental weakness or imperfection
(syn) defective, faulty, erroneous
(e.g.) The methods used in these studies may be **flawed** in design.

random assignment

무작위 배정

[ˈrændəm əˈsaɪnmənt]

the use of chance procedures in experiments to ensure unbiased grouping
(syn) random allocation, chance grouping
(e.g.) Most studies had not used **random assignment** to the drinking and non-drinking groups.

DAY
23

teetotaling
금주하는

[ˌtiːˈtoʊtəlɪŋ]

choosing or intending never to drink alcohol
(syn) abstaining, non-drinking
(e.g.) The studies compared moderate drinkers to people who were already **teetotaling**.

slave's atmosphere
(비유) 노예의 분위기

[sleɪvz ˈætməsfɪr]

a figurative term for an environment that feels oppressive and restricts one's freedom
(syn) oppressive environment, subjugated feeling
(e.g.) He came here to escape the **slave's atmosphere** of home.

liberate
해방시키다, 자유롭게 하다

[ˈlɪbəreɪt]

to set free from a situation or state of imprisonment or bondage
(syn) free, emancipate, release
(e.g.) He wanted to **liberate** his imagination and set it free.

hawk
매 (맹금류)

[hɔːk]

a bird of prey known for its sharp vision and speed, often used to symbolize freedom
(syn) raptor, bird of prey
(e.g.) He wanted to take his imagination like a **hawk** and set it whirling.

widening gyre
(문학적 비유) 넓어지는 소용돌이

[ˈwaɪdnɪŋ ˈdʒaɪər]

an expanding spiral motion, often symbolizing chaos or the collapse of order in literature
(syn) expanding spiral, vortex, chaotic rotation
(e.g.) He wanted to set his imagination 'whirling off into the **widening gyre**'.

commentary
해설, 논평

['kɑːmənteri]

an expression of opinions or an explanation about an event or text

(syn) analysis, critique, annotation

(e.g.) Complete the **commentary** below by filling in the blank.

vacant barn
비어있는 헛간

['veɪkənt bɑːrn]

an empty agricultural building, usually used for storage

(syn) empty shed, deserted outbuilding

(e.g.) The experiment was set up on the ground floor of a **vacant barn**.

double blind
이중 맹검법

[ˌdʌbəl 'blaɪnd]

a study design where neither the participants nor the researchers know who is receiving a particular treatment

(syn) masked experiment, blinded trial

(e.g.) The experiment was "**double blind**" to prevent bias.

neutral
중립적인

['nuːtrəl]

not supporting or helping either side in a conflict or disagreement

(syn) impartial, objective, unbiased

(e.g.) Will can be used to express a **neutral** prediction of a future event.

real communication
실제 의사소통

[riːəl kəˌmjuːnɪ'keɪʃən]

genuine and meaningful interaction aimed at conveying information or achieving understanding

(syn) authentic interaction, meaningful exchange

(e.g.) Activities should involve students in **real communication**.

under-represented

불충분하게 대변되는

[ˌʌndərrəpriˈzentid]

not having a sufficient number or amount of people or things shown

(syn) marginalized, underserved, inadequately shown

(e.g.) Museums are showing relevance to people who were previously **underrepresented**.

aloof

냉담한, 거리를 두는

[əˈluːf]

conspicuously uninvolved and often distant; cool and distant

(syn) distant, detached, reserved

(e.g.) It is no longer an option for a museum to remain isolated and **aloof**.

social construct

사회적 구성물

[ˈsoʊʃəl ˈkɑːnstrʌkt]

a concept or idea that exists because society as a whole agrees that it exists

(syn) cultural artifact, societal creation

(e.g.) Museums are **social constructs** and have taken their place in contemporary life.

hallowed hall

(비유) 신성한 홀

[ˈhæloʊd hɔːl]

figurative term for a place that is greatly respected, often due to its history or importance

(syn) sacred place, venerable building, revered institution

(e.g.) The institutions that once were just **hallowed halls** of important objects are now adapting.

vernacular

(특정 지역이나 집단 사람들이 일상적으로 사용하는) 일상어, 방언

[vərˈnækjələr]

the everyday language spoken by ordinary people in a particular region

(syn) local language, colloquial speech

(e.g.) The author wrote dialogue in the local **vernacular** to enhance realism.

global error	전역 오류

['gloʊbəl 'erər]

an error that significantly impedes the overall comprehensibility or meaning of a message
(syn) meaning-impeding error, severe mistake
(e.g.) Error correction should focus only on **global errors** that hinder communication.

communication strategy	의사소통 전략

[kəˌmjuːnɪˈkeɪʃən ˈstrætədʒi]

a technique used to overcome language problems in order to express meaning
(syn) compensatory technique, conversational tactic
(e.g.) Encourage the use of **communication strategies** like using similar words or gestures.

intend	의도하다

[ɪnˈtend]

to have a course of action as one's purpose or objective
(syn) mean, aim, plan
(e.g.) If you can't come up with the exact words to express the meaning you **intend**, use similar words.

giggle	낄낄거리다

['gɪgəl]

to laugh lightly and repeatedly in a silly or nervous way
(syn) titter, snicker, smirk
(e.g.) Perhaps some children will just **giggle**, or nudge each other, when a child makes a mistake.

nudge	(팔꿈치로) 쿡 찌르다

[nʌdʒ]

to push gently, typically with the elbow, to attract attention
(syn) prod, elbow, poke
(e.g.) Children may **nudge** each other when a classmate makes an error.

2018

DAY

24

hum	○○○	turret	○○○
stalwart	○○○	speck	○○○
scaffolded help	○○○	nutmeg	○○○
sociocultural perspective	○○○	keel	○○○
Zone of Proximal Development	○○○	balsa	○○○
matrix	○○○	Generals	○○○
theta role	○○○	rite of passage	○○○
anaphor	○○○	conversion	○○○
sewer	○○○	revere	○○○
dowsing	○○○	subvert	○○○
emanate	○○○	compunction	○○○
radiation	○○○	pejorative	○○○
hazardous	○○○	illusionism	○○○
c-command	○○○	fatalism	○○○
preliminary	○○○	materialism	○○○
fraudulent	○○○	nihilism	○○○
perpendicular	○○○	tavern	○○○
random	○○○	pipe dream	○○○
decimeter	○○○	plot	○○○
well-formed	○○○	climax	○○○
projection	○○○	resolution	○○○
impart	○○○	stanza	○○○
supervise	○○○	verse	○○○
voiceless	○○○	simile	○○○
voiced	○○○	irony	○○○
gossamer	○○○	allegory	○○○
jostling	○○○	motif	○○○
jockey for place	○○○	elicitation	○○○
clear their throat	○○○	pedagogical task	○○○
small bankers	○○○	contextual cue	○○○

hum

흥얼거리다

[hʌm]

to sing with closed lips, without articulating words
(syn) murmur, croon, chant
(e.g.) The King asks for ceremonial pieces that people can follow and **hum**, meaning easy to sing.

stalwart

굳센, 충직한

[ˈstɔːlwərt]

loyal, reliable, and hardworking; sturdily resolute
(syn) steadfast, staunch, trusty
(e.g.) She was a **stalwart** advocate of open-access publication.

scaffolded help

비계 도움

[ˈskæfəldɪd help]

structured and temporary support given to a learner to help them achieve a task
(syn) structured support, guided assistance
(e.g.) Effective learning occurs with **scaffolded help** from more knowledgeable others.

sociocultural perspective

사회문화적 관점

[ˌsoʊʃiˌoʊˈkʌltʃərəl pərˈspektɪv]

the view that learning occurs through social and cultural interaction (Vygotsky's theory)
(syn) Vygotskian view, social learning theory
(e.g.) From a **sociocultural perspective**, effective learning is situated within interaction.

Zone of Proximal Development

근접 발달 영역

[zoʊn əv ˈprɑːksɪməl dɪˈveləpmənt]

the space between what a learner can do without help and what they can do with guidance
(syn) ZPD, potential developmental space
(e.g.) Effective learning takes place when what a student attempts to learn is within his or her **Zone of Proximal Development**.

matrix
주절

['meɪtrɪks]

the main clause within a complex sentence that contains another clauses

(syn) main clause, governing clause

(e.g.) The **matrix** subject Tom has no theta role in the ungrammatical sentence.

theta role
세타 역할

['θeɪtə roʊl]

the semantic role that a verb assigns to its arguments (e.g., agent, theme)

(syn) semantic role, thematic role

(e.g.) The matrix subject Tom has no **theta role** in this construction.

anaphor
대용어

['ænəfɔːr]

a word (like a reflexive pronoun) that refers back to an earlier word or phrase (antecedent)

(syn) reflexive pronoun, reciprocal pronoun

(e.g.) Consider sentences containing an **anaphor**, such as herself or himself.

sewer
하수구, 오수관

['suːər]

an underground channel for conveying liquid waste

(syn) drain, conduit, culvert

(e.g.) The word **sewer** is provided as an example of /w/ insertion.

dowsing
수맥 찾기

['daʊzɪŋ]

the practice of searching for underground water or minerals using a divining rod

(syn) water witching, divining

(e.g.) The act of searching for water using a rod is commonly known as **dowsing**.

emanate
발산하다, 나오다

['emənent]

to issue or spread out from (a source)
(syn) issue, radiate, originate
(e.g.) German dowsers claim they respond to "earthrays" that **emanate** from water.

radiation
방사선

[ˌreɪdiˈeɪʃən]

the emission of energy as electromagnetic waves or moving subatomic particles
(syn) ray, emission, wave
(e.g.) Earthrays are described as a subtle form of **radiation** that is potentially hazardous.

hazardous
위험한, 유해한

['hæzərdəs]

risky; dangerous
(syn) dangerous, perilous, risky
(e.g.) This subtle form of radiation is potentially **hazardous** to human health.

c-command
c-지배, 구문 구조에서 한 노드가 다른 노드를 지배하는 관계

['siː kəˌmænd]

a hierarchical relation where one node dominates its sister's nodes
(syn) syntactic dominance (approx.)
(e.g.) An anaphor must be **c-commanded** by its antecedent.

preliminary
예비의, 사전의

[prɪˈlɪmɪneri]

denoting an action or event preceding or done in preparation for something more important
(syn) introductory, initial, preparatory
(e.g.) Candidates participated in **preliminary** tests of their skill.

fraudulent
사기를 치는, 부정직한

['frɔːdʒələnt]

deceitful or dishonest; obtained or done by deception
(syn) deceptive, dishonest, spurious
(e.g.) To avoid **fraudulent** claims, the most successful individuals were selected for the final experiment.

perpendicular 수직의, 직각의

[ˌpɜːrpənˈdɪkjələr]

at an angle of 90 degrees to a given line, plane, or surface
(syn) upright, vertical, at right angles
(e.g.) A short length of pipe was placed **perpendicular** to the test line.

random 무작위의

[ˈrændəm]

made, done, or chosen without method or conscious decision; haphazard
(syn) arbitrary, haphazard, unsystematic
(e.g.) The position for each trial was assigned using a computer-generated **random** number.

DAY
24

decimeter 데시미터

[ˈdesɪmiːtər]

a metric unit of length equal to one tenth of a meter
(syn) one-tenth of a meter
(e.g.) The actual pipe's location was recorded in **decimeters** from the beginning of the line.

well-formed 적절한 형태를 갖춘

[wel ˈfɔːrmd]

conforming to the rules of grammar; acceptable
(syn) correct, grammatical, acceptable
(opp) ill-formed
(e.g.) Determine if sentence (5) is **well-formed** or ill-formed.

projection 예측, 투영

[prəˈdʒekʃən]

an estimate or forecast of a future situation based on a study of present trends
(syn) forecast, prediction, estimation
(e.g.) The company's sales **projection** shows a strong increase next year.

impart

전하다, 주다

[ɪmˈpɑːrt]

to make (information) known; to communicate
(syn) convey, transmit, communicate
(e.g.) The test is given to **impart** individual attention for any strong and weak points.

supervise

감독하다

[ˈsuːpərvaɪz]

to observe and direct the execution of a task or activity
(syn) oversee, monitor, manage
(e.g.) Collaborative work is **supervised** by the teacher.

voiceless

무성음의

[ˈvɔɪsləs]

(in phonetics) produced without vibration of the vocal cords
(syn) unvoiced, surd
(e.g.) The examples show consonant clusters where the sounds are not both **voiceless**.

voiced

유성음의

[vɔɪst]

(in phonetics) produced with vibration of the vocal cords
(syn) sonant, vibrating
(e.g.) The examples show consonant clusters where the sounds are not both **voiced**.

gossamer

거미줄처럼 가벼운

[ˈgɑːsəmər]

used to refer to something very light, thin, and delicate
(syn) sheer, delicate, fine
(e.g.) The composer's music is compared to **gossamer** wings.

jostling

부딪히며 밀치는

[ˈdʒɑːslɪŋ]

pushing, elbowing, or bumping against someone roughly
(syn) shoving, pushing, elbowing
(e.g.) The short men stand around **jostling**, jockeying for place.

jockey for place
위치 다툼을 하는

['dʒɑːkiɪ fɔːr pleɪs]

to compete to gain a better position or advantage
(syn) compete for position, maneuver
(e.g.) The boys stand around jostling, **jockeying for place** to establish dominance.

clear their throat
목청을 가다듬다

[klɪər ðeɪr θroʊt]

to make a slight cough to clear mucus from the throat (often signaling nervousness or seriousness)
(syn) cough, hawk
(e.g.) They **clear their throats** a lot, like small bankers.

DAY
24

small bankers
(비유) 작은 은행가들

[smɔːl 'bæŋkərz]

figurative expression for boys acting with forced seriousness and authority
(syn) serious boys, miniature professionals
(e.g.) The guests are described as a room of **small bankers**.

turret
(성벽의) 작은 탑

['tɜːrɪt]

a small tower on a large building, often a castle
(syn) tower, bastion, gun carriage
(e.g.) The dark cake is round and heavy as a **turret**, suggesting a link to war.

speck
작은 조각, 얼룩

[spek]

a tiny spot or piece
(syn) spot, dot, fleck
(e.g.) His son has freckles like **specks** of nutmeg on his cheeks.

nutmeg
육두구 (향신료)

['nʌtmeg]

a spice made from the seed of an evergreen tree
(syn) spice, seasoning
(e.g.) The freckles are compared to **nutmeg** on his cheeks.

keel	(배의) 용골
[ki:l]	the longitudinal structure along the center line at the bottom of a boat's hull (syn) spine, base, bottom (e.g.) His son's chest is narrow as the balsa **keel** of a model boat.

balsa	발사 나무
['bɔ:lsə]	a lightweight, strong wood from a tropical American tree, often used for model making (syn) light wood, tropical tree wood (e.g.) The narrow chest is compared to the **balsa** keel of a model boat.

Generals	장군들 (비유)
['dʒenərəlz]	high-ranking military officers (figuratively representing authority) (syn) commanders, leaders, high-ranking officers (e.g.) The other men agree and clear their throats like **Generals**.

rite of passage	통과 의례
[raɪt əv 'pæsɪdʒ]	a ceremony or ritual marking the transition from one social status to another (syn) initiation ceremony, transition ritual (e.g.) The poem is titled **Rite of Passage**, suggesting a significant transition in the boys' lives.

conversion	전환, 변환
[kən'vɜ:rʒən]	the process of changing or causing something to change from one form to another (syn) change, transformation, shift (e.g.) Learning entails the **conversion** of declarative knowledge into procedural knowledge.

revere

존경하다, 숭배하다

[rɪvíər]

to feel deep respect or admiration for someone or something
(syn) admire, venerate, honor
(opp) despise, disrespect
(e.g.) Many students **revere** their teacher for her wisdom and patience.

subvert

전복시키다, 약화시키다

[səbvə́ːrt]

to undermine the power or authority of something
(syn) overthrow, destabilize, undermine
(opp) strengthen, support, uphold
(e.g.) The rebels attempted to **subvert** the government's authority.

compunction

양심의 가책, 후회

[kəmˈpʌŋkʃən]

a feeling of guilt or moral scruple that prevents or follows the doing of something bad
(syn) remorse, guilt, repentance, scruple
(opp) indifference, callousness
(e.g.) He donated anonymously out of **compunction** for his earlier remarks.

pejorative

경멸적인, 비난조의

[pɪˈdʒɔːrətɪv]

expressing contempt or disapproval
(syn) derogatory, disparaging, belittling
(opp) laudatory, complimentary
(e.g.) The article avoided **pejorative** labels and focused on facts.

illusionism

진짜 같은 환영법, 착시법

[ɪˈluːʒəˌnɪzəm]

the artistic or literary technique of creating an illusion of reality
(syn) optical illusion art, verisimilitude
(e.g.) The painter's **illusionism** made the figures appear almost alive.

fatalism 운명론

['feɪtəlɪzəm]

the belief that all events are predetermined and inevitable
(syn) determinism, predestination
(e.g.) His **fatalism** led him to accept every hardship without complaint.

materialism 유물론, 물질주의

[mə'tɪəriəlɪzəm]

the tendency to consider material possessions more important than spiritual values
(syn) consumerism, worldliness
(e.g.) The novel criticizes modern society's growing **materialism**.

nihilism 허무주의

['naɪɪlɪzəm]

the rejection of all religious and moral principles, often in the belief that life is meaningless
(syn) cynicism, skepticism
(e.g.) The character's **nihilism** reflects his loss of faith in human goodness.

tavern 선술집, 여인숙

['tævərn]

an old-fashioned pub or inn where food and drink are served
(syn) inn, pub
(e.g.) The men gathered in the dim **tavern** to share their stories.

pipe dream 허황된 꿈

[paɪp driːm]

an unattainable or fanciful hope
(syn) fantasy, illusion
(e.g.) His plan to become rich overnight was dismissed as a **pipe dream**.

plot 줄거리, 구성

[plɑːt]

the main sequence of events in a play, novel, or film
(syn) storyline, narrative
(e.g.) The **plot** unfolds as the hero struggles against his fate.

climax
['klaɪmæks]

절정, 최고조

the most intense or important point in a story
(syn) peak, culmination
(e.g.) The play reaches its **climax** when the truth is finally revealed.

resolution
[ˌrezə'luːʃn]

해결, 결말

the conclusion of a literary work where conflicts are resolved
(syn) conclusion, denouement
(e.g.) The **resolution** provides a sense of closure for the audience.

DAY

24

stanza
['stænzə]

연 (시(詩)의 단락)

a grouped set of lines in a poem
(syn) verse, section
(e.g.) The poet repeats the same rhythm in each **stanza**.

verse
[vɜːrs]

시, 연, 운문

a writing arranged with rhythm and sometimes rhyme
(syn) poetry, line
(e.g.) The first **verse** of the poem sets the tone for the rest of the work.

simile
['sɪmɪli]

직유

a figure of speech comparing one thing with another using "like" or "as"
(syn) comparison, analogy
(e.g.) The poet uses a **simile** to describe her eyes as bright as stars.

irony
['aɪrəni]

아이러니, 반어

the expression of meaning by using language that normally signifies the opposite
(syn) sarcasm, paradox
(e.g.) There is a deep **irony** in the hero's success leading to his downfall.

allegory
우의, 풍유

[ˈæləgɔːri]

a story, poem, or picture that can be interpreted to reveal a hidden moral or political meaning

(syn) parable, symbolism

(e.g.) *Animal Farm* is an **allegory** of political power and corruption.

motif
모티프, 주제의 반복

[moʊˈtiːf]

a recurring element or theme that has symbolic significance in a story

(syn) theme, symbol

(e.g.) The **motif** of light and darkness runs throughout the novel.

elicitation
유도, 유발

[ɪˌlɪsɪˈteɪʃən]

the technique of drawing out information, language, or responses from learners

(syn) extraction, prompting

(e.g.) The teacher used **elicitation** to encourage students to form their own sentences.

pedagogical task
교수학습 과제

[ˌpedəˈgɑːdʒɪkl tæsk]

a learning activity designed to promote language use in meaningful contexts

(syn) teaching activity, instructional task

(e.g.) Role-playing activities are common examples of a **pedagogical task** in communicative classrooms.

contextual cue
맥락 단서

[kənˈtekstʃuəl kjuː]

a piece pf information in the surrounding context that helps infer meaning or response

(syn) situational clue, contextual signal

(e.g.) Learners rely on **contextual cues** to guess the meaning of unfamiliar words.

유희태 일반영어

⑤ 기출 VOCA 30days

enumerate	○○○	empathetic	○○○
detract	○○○	validate	○○○
equitable	○○○	simulation	○○○
implausible	○○○	unyielding	○○○
dispel	○○○	superficial	○○○
artifact	○○○	assign	○○○
artistry	○○○	mislabelling	○○○
insightful	○○○	proviso	○○○
magnitude	○○○	fanciful	○○○
overwhelmed	○○○	imitation	○○○
foresee	○○○	doze off	○○○
specimen	○○○	ephemeral	○○○
judiciously	○○○	conundrum	○○○
inundated	○○○	verisimilitude	○○○
consecutive	○○○	inchoate	○○○
exemplified	○○○	empiricism	○○○
preceding	○○○	pallid	○○○
deceptively	○○○	poignant	○○○
imply	○○○	esoteric	○○○
steadfast	○○○	laconic	○○○
loathsome	○○○	bellicose	○○○
inhibition	○○○	trenchant	○○○
profane	○○○	fastidious	○○○
bustle	○○○	impecunious	○○○
agitation	○○○	nascent	○○○
pressing	○○○	tacit	○○○
multitasking	○○○	oscillate	○○○
output	○○○	prodigious	○○○
allege	○○○	disseminate	○○○
expeditious	○○○	surreptitious	○○○

enumerate
열거하다, 하나하나 세다

[ɪˈnuːməreɪt]

to list things one by one; to count
(syn) list, itemize, detail, recite
(opp) generalize, overlook
(e.g.) The witness calmly **enumerated** the events of that evening.

detract
(가치·명성 등을) 떨어뜨리다, 손상시키다

[dɪtrǽkt]

to reduce the value or importance of something
(syn) diminish, reduce, lessen
(e.g.) The poor design **detracted** from the building's beauty.

equitable
공정한, 공평한

[ékwɪtəbl]

fair and impartial
(syn) fair, just, impartial
(e.g.) The decision was both **equitable** and reasonable.

implausible
믿기 어려운, 그럴듯하지 않은

[ɪmplɔ́ːzəbl]

not seeming reasonable or probable
(syn) unlikely, improbable, doubtful
(e.g.) His excuse sounded **implausible** to everyone.

dispel
(의심·불안 등을) 없애다, 떨쳐 버리다

[dɪspél]

to make a doubt or feeling disappear
(syn) dismiss, eliminate, banish
(e.g.) The new evidence **dispelled** any lingering suspicion.

artifact
인공물, 유물

[ɑ́ːrtɪfækt]

a human-made object of cultural or historical interest
(syn) relic, creation
(e.g.) The museum displayed ancient **artifacts** from the Bronze Age.

artistry
예술성, 기교

[ɑ́ːrtɪstri]

creative skill or craftsmanship
(syn) creativity, mastery
(e.g.) The dancer's **artistry** captivated the audience.

insightful
통찰력 있는

[ɪnsáɪtfəl]

showing deep understanding or perception
(syn) perceptive, astute
(e.g.) She wrote an **insightful** essay on human behavior.

magnitude
규모, 중요성

[mǽgnɪtùːd]

great size, extent, or importance
(syn) scale, significance
(e.g.) Scientists were surprised by the **magnitude** of the earthquake.

DAY

25

overwhelmed
압도된, 감당할 수 없는

[ˌoʊvərˈwɛlmd]

buried or drowned beneath a huge mass of something
(syn) swamped, inundated, burdened
(e.g.) Students often feel **overwhelmed** by the number of grammatical structures.

foresee
예견하다, 내다보다

[fɔːrˈsiː]

to be aware of beforehand; to predict
(syn) predict, anticipate, envision
(e.g.) He **foresees** celebrity status for himself upon the appearance of the article.

specimen
표본, 견본

[ˈspɛsɪmɪn]

an individual animal, plant, or piece of a mineral used as an example of its species or type
(syn) sample, example, model
(e.g.) What we think of as me is, in fact, just the **specimen** jar.

judiciously
신중하게, 현명하게

[dʒuːˈdɪʃəsli]

with good judgement or sense
(syn) wisely, sensibly, prudently
(e.g.) The funds were spent **judiciously** to maximize their impact.

inundated
감당 못 할 정도로 많은

[ˈɪnəndeɪtɪd]

overwhelmed with things or people to be dealt with
(syn) overwhelmed, flooded, swamped
(e.g.) The office was **inundated** with requests after the announcement.

consecutive
연속적인, 계속되는

[kənˈsɛkjətɪv]

following continuously one after the other
(syn) successive, continuous, sequential
(e.g.) Do NOT copy more than four **consecutive** words from the passage.

exemplified
예시된, 좋은 예가 되는

[ɪgˈzɛmplɪfaɪd]

to be a typical example of
(syn) illustrated, demonstrated, shown
(e.g.) Identify the type of instruction **exemplified** in each teaching journal.

preceding
이전의, 앞선

[priːˈsiːdɪŋ]

existing or coming before in time or order
(syn) previous, former, prior
(e.g.) She requests assistance in understanding the other's **preceding** utterance.

deceptively
속이는 듯이, 겉보기와 달리

[dɪˈsɛptɪvli]

in a misleading way
(syn) misleadingly, falsely, seemingly
(e.g.) The English article system seems **deceptively** simple.

imply

암시하다, 내포하다

[ɪmˈplaɪ]

to strongly suggest the truth or existence of something not expressly stated

(syn) suggest, hint, indicate

(e.g.) As the research on multitasking **implies**, it is time to challenge the assumption.

steadfast

확고한, 변함없는

[ˈstɛdfæst]

resolutely or dutifully firm and unwavering

(syn) resolute, unwavering, loyal

(e.g.) In everything I have done, I have been **steadfast**.

loathsome

혐오스러운, 역겨운

[ˈloʊðsəm]

causing hatred or disgust; repulsive

(syn) repulsive, detestable, abominable

(e.g.) There was nothing more **loathsome** in the way of food than sausages.

DAY

25

inhibition

억제, 금지

[ˌɪnhɪˈbɪʃən]

a feeling that makes one self-conscious and unable to act in a relaxed and natural way

(syn) restraint, suppression, constraint

(e.g.) He regretted the time drawing near to go back to his lecture-room and his **inhibition**.

profane

불경스러운, 세속적인

[prəˈfeɪn]

relating or devoted to that which is not sacred or religious

(syn) secular, irreverent, vulgar

(e.g.) The comedian's routine included some rather **profane** language.

bustle

부산함, 분주함

[ˈbʌsəl]

move in an energetic and busy manner

(syn) flurry, commotion, hustle

(e.g.) Hurry, **bustle**, and agitation have become a regular way of life.

agitation
동요, 불안

[ˌædʒɪˈteɪʃən]

a state of anxiety or nervous excitement
(syn) anxiety, turmoil, unrest
(e.g.) Make sure your life is not under the control of **agitation**.

pressing
긴급한, 중요한

[ˈprɛsɪŋ]

requiring immediate attention
(syn) urgent, crucial, demanding
(e.g.) We respond to the many **pressing** demands of our time.

multitasking
멀티태스킹, 다중 작업

[ˈmʌltiˌtæskɪŋ]

the simultaneous execution of multiple tasks
(syn) parallel processing, simultaneous work
(e.g.) **Multitasking** became shorthand for the human attempt to do as many things as possible.

output
결과, 산출량

[ˈaʊtpʊt]

the amount of something produced by a person, machine, or industry
(syn) production, yield, outcome
(e.g.) Their **output** reached only 186 units.

allege
주장하다, 혐의를 제기하다

[əˈlɛdʒ]

to claim or assert that someone has done something illegal or wrong, typically without proof
(syn) claim, assert, declare
(e.g.) The witness **alleged** that he saw the suspect near the scene of the crime.

expeditious
신속한, 효율적인

[ˌɛkspəˈdɪʃəs]

done with speed and efficiency
(syn) fast, quick, rapid
(e.g.) Identify the two kinds of **expeditious** reading that the teacher instructs students to use.

empathetic
공감하는

[ˌɛmpəˈθɛtɪk]

showing an ability to understand and share the feelings of another
(syn) compassionate, understanding, sympathetic
(e.g.) Eyes can provide signals as to one's mood, such as being interested, bored, **empathetic**, or annoyed.

validate
입증하다, 확인하다

[ˈvælɪdeɪt]

to check or prove the validity or accuracy of
(syn) confirm, prove, justify
(e.g.) Mr. Lee wants to **validate** how well the scores from the College Entrance Exam predict academic success.

simulation
모방, 흉내

[ˌsɪmjuˈleɪʃən]

imitation of a situation or process
(syn) imitation, pretense, acting
(e.g.) At first he had been merely a good actor, but as time went on, **simulation** became second nature.

unyielding
굽히지 않는, 단호한

[ʌnˈjiːldɪŋ]

not giving way to pressure; immovably firm
(syn) inflexible, adamant, rigid
(e.g.) She took an **unyielding** stance on transparency standards.

superficial
표면적인, 외견상의

[ˌsuːpərˈfɪʃəl]

existing or occurring at or on the surface
(syn) surface, external, apparent
(e.g.) In the sentence, the **superficial** subject originates in the complement position.

assign
할당하다, 부여하다

[əˈsaɪn]

to allocate a job or duty to someone
(syn) allocate, give, attribute
(e.g.) It would be impossible to **assign** a value to it until one knew the whole word.

DAY
25

mislabelling
오표기, 잘못된 라벨링

[ˌmɪsˈleɪbəlɪŋ]

the action of wrongly describing or classifying something
(syn) misrepresentation, false tagging
(e.g.) The legislation stopped outright **mislabelling**.

proviso
단서, 조건

[prəˈvaɪzoʊ]

a condition attached to an agreement
(syn) condition, stipulation, clause
(e.g.) A "distinctive name" **proviso** was inserted into the law that allowed clever names.

fanciful
상상 속의, 기발한

[ˈfænsɪfəl]

overimaginative and unrealistic
(syn) imaginative, whimsical, creative
(e.g.) The 1938 Act mandated that products could still bear **fanciful** names.

imitation
모조품, 흉내

[ˌɪmɪˈteɪʃən]

a thing intended to simulate or copy something else
(syn) copy, fake, simulacrum
(e.g.) Manufacturers of cheap **imitation** food came up with a way around the new rules.

doze off
잠들다, 졸다

[ˈdoʊz ɔːf]

to fall asleep lightly or briefly
(syn) fall asleep, nod off, slumber
(e.g.) Some students **dozed off** after ten minutes.

ephemeral
단명하는, 덧없는

[ɪˈfɛmərəl]

lasting for a very short time
(syn) transient, fleeting, short-lived
(e.g.) Fashion trends are **ephemeral**, changing with the seasons.

conundrum
수수께끼, 난제

[kə'nʌndrəm]

a confusing and difficult problem or question
(syn) puzzle, enigma, mystery
(e.g.) The decision presents a philosophical **conundrum** for the government.

verisimilitude
진실성, 사실 같음

[ˌvɛrəsɪ'mɪlɪˌtuːd]

the appearance of being true or real
(syn) realism, authenticity, plausibility
(e.g.) The novel's dialogue has a high degree of **verisimilitude**.

inchoate
초기의, 불완전한

['ɪnkoʊət]

just begun and so not fully formed or developed; rudimentary
(syn) rudimentary, incipient, undeveloped
(e.g.) The project is still in its **inchoate** stages.

empiricism
경험주의, 지식은 경험에서 온다는 철학

[ɛm'pɪrɪsɪzəm]

the view that knowledge comes from experience
(syn) experiential philosophy
(e.g.) Modern science is rooted in **empiricism**.

pallid
창백한, 핼쑥한

['pælɪd]

pale, typically because of poor health
(syn) pale, ashen, wan
(e.g.) His usually ruddy complexion was **pallid** and sickly.

poignant
가슴 아픈, 신랄한

['pɔɪnjənt]

evoking a keen sense of sadness or regret
(syn) moving, touching, pathetic
(e.g.) It was a **poignant** reminder of the passing of time.

esoteric
난해한, 비밀의

[ˌɛsəˈtɛrɪk]
intended for or likely to be understood by only a small number of people with a specialized knowledge
(syn) obscure, arcane, abstruse
(e.g.) The poem was full of **esoteric** references.

laconic
말수가 적은, 간결한

[ləˈkɒnɪk]
using very few words
(syn) brief, concise, terse
(e.g.) His **laconic** reply suggested a lack of interest.

bellicose
호전적인, 싸움을 좋아하는

[ˈbɛlɪkoʊs]
demonstrating aggression and willingness to fight
(syn) belligerent, warlike, aggressive
(e.g.) The nation's **bellicose** stance threatened regional peace.

trenchant
정곡을 찌르는, 날카로운

[ˈtrɛntʃənt]
vigorous or incisive in expression or style
(syn) cutting, sharp, perceptive
(e.g.) Her commentary was **trenchant** and insightful.

fastidious
까다로운, 세심한

[fæˈstɪdiəs]
very attentive to and concerned about accuracy and detail
(syn) meticulous, scrupulous, punctilious
(e.g.) He was **fastidious** about his appearance.

impecunious
가난한, 무일푼의

[ˌɪmpɪˈkjuːniəs]
having little or no money
(syn) penniless, poor, destitute
(e.g.) He was once a wealthy man, but died **impecunious**.

nascent
초기의, 발생기의

['næsənt]

just coming into existence and beginning to display signs of future potential
(syn) emerging, budding, incipient
(e.g.) The **nascent** art movement quickly gained traction.

tacit
암묵적인, 무언의

['tæsɪt]

understood or implied without being stated
(syn) implicit, unstated, inferred
(e.g.) Their agreement was **tacit**, signaled by a simple nod.

oscillate
진동하다, 흔들리다

['ɒsɪleɪt]

to move or swing back and forth in a regular rhythm
(syn) swing, waver, fluctuate
(e.g.) His moods **oscillate** between euphoria and despair.

DAY
25

prodigious
엄청난, 거대한

[prə'dɪdʒəs]

remarkably or impressively great in extent, size, or degree
(syn) colossal, enormous, immense
(e.g.) He had a **prodigious** appetite for knowledge.

disseminate
흩뿌리다, 전파하다

[dɪ'sɛmɪneɪt]

to spread or disperse something, especially information, widely
(syn) spread, circulate, propagate
(e.g.) The organization **disseminates** information about health risks.

surreptitious
비밀의, 몰래 하는

[ˌsɜːrəp'tɪʃəs]

kept secret, especially because it would not be approved of
(syn) secret, furtive, clandestine
(e.g.) He took a **surreptitious** glance at his watch.

2017

DAY

26

유희태 일반영어

5 기출 VOCA 30days

pernicious	○○○	parity	○○○
deleterious	○○○	quiescent	○○○
abrogate	○○○	reticent	○○○
demur	○○○	solicitous	○○○
ebullient	○○○	tantamount	○○○
fortuitous	○○○	zealous	○○○
meticulous	○○○	circumvent	○○○
plethora	○○○	harbinger	○○○
spurious	○○○	metamorphosis	○○○
wistful	○○○	perfunctory	○○○
zenith	○○○	tenuous	○○○
nadir	○○○	bolster	○○○
capricious	○○○	cryptic	○○○
dogmatic	○○○	fervid	○○○
effusive	○○○	probity	○○○
magnanimous	○○○	somber	○○○
obdurate	○○○	torpid	○○○
ascetic	○○○	atrophy	○○○
chide	○○○	burgeoning	○○○
contrite	○○○	clandestine	○○○
confrontation	○○○	dearth	○○○
garrulous	○○○	protégé	○○○
gravitate	○○○	extol	○○○
immutable	○○○	fatigue	○○○
jocular	○○○	germane	○○○
kudos	○○○	nuance	○○○
languid	○○○	obliterate	○○○
mellifluous	○○○	panacea	○○○
noxious	○○○	querulous	○○○
ostracize	○○○	respite	○○○

pernicious
치명적인, 해로운

[pər'nɪʃəs]

having a harmful effect, especially in a gradual or subtle way
(syn) destructive, harmful, ruinous
(e.g.) The **pernicious** effects of envy are often underestimated.

deleterious
해로운, 유해한

[ˌdɛlɪ'tɪrɪəs]

causing harm or damage
(syn) detrimental, harmful, injurious
(e.g.) The drug has a proven **deleterious** effect on the liver.

abrogate
폐지하다, 철회하다

['æbrəˌgeɪt]

to repeal or do away with a law, right, or formal agreement
(syn) repeal, revoke, annul
(e.g.) The committee voted to **abrogate** the treaty.

demur
이의를 제기하다, 반대하다

[dɪ'mɜːr]

to raise doubts or objections or show reluctance
(syn) protest, object, hesitate
(e.g.) They accepted the proposal without **demur**.

ebullient
활기 넘치는, 열광적인

[ɪ'bʊljənt]

cheerful and full of energy
(syn) exuberant, buoyant, cheerful
(e.g.) The **ebullient** host welcomed the guests warmly.

fortuitous
우연한, 행운의

[fɔːr'tuːɪtəs]

happening by accident or chance, rather than design
(syn) accidental, chance, serendipitous
(e.g.) The discovery was a **fortuitous** event.

meticulous
꼼꼼한, 세심한

[mə'tɪkjələs]

showing great attention to detail; very careful and precise
(syn) diligent, scrupulous, painstaking
(e.g.) The architect was **meticulous** in his design.

plethora
과잉, 다량

[ˈplɛθərə]

a large or excessive amount of something
(syn) excess, surplus, abundance
(e.g.) There is a **plethora** of advice on the subject.

spurious
가짜의, 위조의

[ˈspjʊriəs]

not being what it purports to be; false or fake
(syn) false, fake, bogus
(e.g.) They dismissed the claim as **spurious**.

wistful
애석해하는, 그리워하는

[ˈwɪstfəl]

having or showing a feeling of vague or regretful longing
(syn) longing, mournful, yearning
(e.g.) She had a **wistful** look on her face.

DAY

26

zenith
정점, 절정

[ˈziːnɪθ]

the time at which something is most powerful or successful
(syn) apex, peak, summit
(e.g.) The singer reached the **zenith** of her career in the 1990s.

nadir
최저점, 밑바닥

[ˈneɪdɪr]

the lowest point in the fortunes of a person or organization
(syn) lowest point, bottom, rock bottom
(e.g.) The relationship reached its **nadir** during the final argument.

capricious
변덕스러운, 예측 불가능한

[kəˈprɪʃəs]

given to sudden and unaccountable changes of mood or behavior
(syn) fickle, arbitrary, unpredictable
(e.g.) Her **capricious** nature made her difficult to deal with.

dogmatic
독단적인, 교조적인

[dɔːɡˈmætɪk]

inclined to lay down principles as incontrovertibly true
(syn) opinionated, prejudiced, doctrinaire
(e.g.) She was not **dogmatic** in her views.

effusive
감정을 넘치게 표현하는

[ɪˈfjuːsɪv]

expressing feelings of gratitude, pleasure, or approval in an unrestrained or heartfelt manner
(syn) gushy, emotional, unrestrained
(e.g.) The couple received **effusive** praise for their wedding.

magnanimous
관대한, 도량이 넓은

[mæɡˈnænɪməs]

generous or forgiving, especially toward a rival or less powerful person
(syn) generous, charitable, benevolent
(e.g.) He was **magnanimous** in defeat, praising the winner.

obdurate
고집이 센, 완고한

[ˈɒbdʊrət]

stubbornly refusing to change one's opinion or course of action
(syn) stubborn, unyielding, inflexible
(e.g.) The child remained **obdurate** and refused to apologize.

ascetic
금욕적인

[əˈsɛtɪk]

characterized by severe self-discipline and abstention from all forms of indulgence
(syn) austere, self-denying, abstinent
(e.g.) He lived an **ascetic** life of prayer and contemplation.

chide
꾸짖다, 잔소리하다

[tʃaɪd]

to scold or rebuke
(syn) reprimand, rebuke, admonish
(e.g.) She **chided** him for his reckless spending.

contrite
깊이 뉘우치는

[kənˈtraɪt]

feeling or expressing remorse or penitence
(syn) remorseful, penitent, regretful
(e.g.) The **contrite** criminal apologized to his victims.

confrontation
(의견·이해관계의 충돌로 인한) 대립, 대면

[ˌkɑːnfrənˈteɪʃən]

a situation in which people or groups face conflict or strong disagreement
(syn) conflict, clash, dispute
(e.g.) The policy change led to a **confrontation** between teachers and administrators.

garrulous
말이 많은, 수다스러운

[ˈgærələs]

excessively talkative, especially on trivial matters
(syn) talkative, loquacious, voluble
(e.g.) The **garrulous** passenger monopolized the conversation.

gravitate
끌리다, 자연스럽게 향하다, 저절로 움직이거나 관심이 가다

[ˈgrævɪˌteɪt]

to be naturally drawn or attracted to something
(syn) drift toward, be attracted to, lean toward
(e.g.) Students often **gravitate** toward teachers who explain concepts clearly.

immutable
불변의, 바꿀 수 없는

[ɪˈmjuːtəbəl]

unchanging over time or unable to be changed
(syn) fixed, permanent, unalterable
(e.g.) The laws of physics are **immutable**.

jocular
익살맞은, 농담하는

[ˈdʒɒkjələr]

fond of or characterized by joking; playful
(syn) humorous, witty, playful
(e.g.) The **jocular** mood of the meeting lightened the atmosphere.

DAY
26

kudos
영광, 찬사

['kjuːdoʊs]

praise and honor received for an achievement
(syn) praise, acclaim, glory
(e.g.) She was given **kudos** for her exceptional performance.

languid
나른한, 활기 없는

['læŋgwɪd]

displaying or having a disinclination for physical exertion or effort; slow and relaxed
(syn) relaxed, unhurried, listless
(e.g.) They enjoyed a **languid** afternoon in the sun.

mellifluous
감미로운, 듣기 좋은

[mɛˈlɪfluəs]

pleasant to hear
(syn) sweet-sounding, harmonious, resonant
(e.g.) Her **mellifluous** voice captivated the audience.

noxious
유독한, 해로운

['nɒkʃəs]

harmful, poisonous, or very unpleasant
(syn) poisonous, toxic, dangerous
(e.g.) The factory emitted **noxious** fumes into the air.

ostracize
배척하다, 추방하다

['ɒstrəsaɪz]

to exclude someone from a society or group
(syn) shun, exclude, exile
(e.g.) She was **ostracized** by her colleagues for questioning the decision.

parity
동등, 일치

['pærəti]

the state or condition of being equal, especially regarding status or pay
(syn) equality, equivalence, uniformity
(e.g.) The workers demanded **parity** with their counterparts.

quiescent
정지한, 활동이 없는

[kwɪˈɛsənt]

in a state or period of inactivity or dormancy
(syn) dormant, inactive, resting
(e.g.) For the time being, the volcano is **quiescent**.

reticent
과묵한, 말이 없는

[ˈrɛtɪsənt]

not revealing one's thoughts or feelings readily
(syn) reserved, taciturn, silent
(e.g.) He was extremely **reticent** about his personal life.

solicitous
염려하는, 걱정하는

[səˈlɪsɪtəs]

characterized by or showing interest or concern
(syn) concerned, caring, anxious
(e.g.) He was always **solicitous** about the welfare of his students.

tantamount
~와 마찬가지의, 동등한

[ˈtæntəˌmaʊnt]

equivalent in seriousness to; virtually the same as
(syn) equivalent, parallel, commensurate
(e.g.) His silence was **tantamount** to an admission of guilt.

zealous
열정적인, 열심인

[ˈzɛləs]

having or showing great energy or enthusiasm in pursuit of a cause or objective
(syn) fervent, passionate, devoted
(e.g.) He was a **zealous** advocate for reform.

circumvent
피해가다, 우회하다

[ˌsɜːrkəmˈvɛnt]

to find a way around an obstacle
(syn) avoid, bypass, evade
(e.g.) He tried to **circumvent** the rules.

DAY

26

harbinger
선구자, 징조

['hɑːrbɪndʒər]

a person or thing that announces or signals the approach of another

(syn) precursor, omen, sign

(e.g.) The robin is a **harbinger** of spring.

metamorphosis
변태, 변형

[ˌmɛtəˈmɔːrfəsɪs]

a change of the form or nature of a thing or person into a completely different one

(syn) transformation, change, evolution

(e.g.) The caterpillar undergoes **metamorphosis** into a butterfly.

perfunctory
형식적인, 의무적인

[pərˈfʌŋktəri]

carried out with a minimum of effort or reflection

(syn) cursory, superficial, automatic

(e.g.) He gave a **perfunctory** nod of greeting.

tenuous
미약한, 보잘것없는

['tɛnjuəs]

very weak or slight

(syn) flimsy, fragile, weak

(e.g.) The **tenuous** link between the two events was hard to prove.

bolster
강화하다, 지지하다

['boʊlstər]

to support or strengthen

(syn) reinforce, strengthen, prop up

(e.g.) He needed to **bolster** his confidence before the presentation.

cryptic
수수께끼 같은, 암호 같은

['krɪptɪk]

having a meaning that is mysterious or obscure

(syn) enigmatic, obscure, puzzling

(e.g.) The message was written in **cryptic** code.

fervid
열렬한, 열정적인

[ˈfɜːrvɪd]

intensely enthusiastic or passionate
(syn) ardent, passionate, zealous
(e.g.) The speaker delivered a **fervid** appeal for unity.

probity
정직, 청렴

[ˈproʊbɪti]

the quality of having strong moral principles; honesty and decency
(syn) integrity, honesty, rectitude
(e.g.) The public demanded greater **probity** from their leaders.

somber
어두침침한, 우울한

[ˈsɒmbər]

dark or dull in color or tone; gloomy
(syn) gloomy, solemn, melancholic
(e.g.) The funeral was a **somber** affair.

DAY

26

torpid
무기력한, 둔한

[ˈtɔːrpɪd]

mentally or physically inactive; lethargic
(syn) sluggish, lethargic, inert
(e.g.) The bear remained **torpid** throughout the winter.

atrophy
위축되다, 퇴화하다

[ˈætrəfi]

to waste away, typically due to the degeneration of cells
(syn) decay, degenerate, waste away
(e.g.) Muscles can **atrophy** from lack of use.

burgeoning
급증하는, 발전하는

[ˈbɜːrdʒənɪŋ]

beginning to grow or increase rapidly; flourishing
(syn) expanding, thriving, escalating
(e.g.) The **burgeoning** population created housing problems.

clandestine 은밀한, 비밀의

[klænˈdɛstɪn]

kept secret or done secretively, especially because illicit

(syn) secret, covert, surreptitious

(e.g.) The couple held a **clandestine** meeting.

dearth 부족, 결핍

[dɜːrθ]

a scarcity or lack of something

(syn) scarcity, shortage, deficiency

(e.g.) There was a **dearth** of fresh water during the drought.

protégé 제자, 선배의 보호·지도 아래 있는 사람

[ˈproʊtəʒeɪ]

a person guided or supported by a more experienced mentor

(syn) pupil, apprentice

(e.g.) Einstein's **protégé** later became a leading physicist.

extol 극찬하다, 칭찬하다

[ɪkˈstoʊl]

to praise enthusiastically

(syn) praise, laud, acclaim

(e.g.) He **extolled** the virtues of the new system.

fatigue (육체·정신적 활동으로 인한) 피로, 기진

[fəˈtiːg]

extreme tiredness resulting from mental or physical exertion

(syn) exhaustion, weariness, burnout

(e.g.) Listening **fatigue** often reduces students' comprehension during long tasks.

germane 관련된, 적절한

[dʒɜːrˈmeɪn]

relevant to a subject under consideration

(syn) relevant, applicable, pertinent

(e.g.) The details are not **germane** to this discussion.

nuance
미묘한 차이, 뉘앙스

['nuːɑːns]

a subtle difference in or shade of meaning, expression, or sound

(syn) subtlety, shade, distinction

(e.g.) The painter was able to capture every **nuance** of the human face.

obliterate
지우다, 제거하다

[əˈblɪtəreɪt]

to destroy utterly; to wipe out

(syn) destroy, erase, annihilate

(e.g.) The town was **obliterated** by the earthquake.

panacea
만병통치약

[ˌpænəˈsiːə]

a solution or remedy for all difficulties or diseases

(syn) cure-all, remedy, solution

(e.g.) Technology is not a **panacea** for all educational problems.

DAY
26

querulous
불평이 많은, 툴툴거리는

[ˈkwɛrələs]

complaining in a petulant or whining manner

(syn) petulant, whining, complaining

(e.g.) He became **querulous** and difficult in his old age.

respite
휴식, 유예

[ˈrɛspɪt]

a short period of rest or relief from something difficult or unpleasant

(syn) break, recess, intermission

(e.g.) The rain provided a brief **respite** from the heat.

veracity	○○○	anomaly	○○○
corpulent	○○○	credence	○○○
fathom	○○○	exigent	○○○
guile	○○○	impunity	○○○
impervious	○○○	resentful	○○○
kindle	○○○	dishonest	○○○
lethargy	○○○	blur	○○○
myriad	○○○	disloyal	○○○
obstinate	○○○	sardonic	○○○
propensity	○○○	impassive	○○○
redundant	○○○	haughty	○○○
sanguine	○○○	bulky	○○○
trepidation	○○○	venerate	○○○
uncanny	○○○	whimsical	○○○
vehement	○○○	zany	○○○
wanton	○○○	impute	○○○
yoke	○○○	haptics	○○○
aberration	○○○	nonchalant	○○○
acrimonious	○○○	reprobate	○○○
activate	○○○	serendipity	○○○
deride	○○○	surfeit	○○○
galvanize	○○○	unremitting	○○○
hiatus	○○○	vicarious	○○○
idiosyncrasy	○○○	vociferous	○○○
languish	○○○	wry	○○○
maverick	○○○	abject	○○○
paucity	○○○	concord	○○○
quixotic	○○○	decry	○○○
replete	○○○	misanthrope	○○○
sophistry	○○○	notwithstanding	○○○

veracity
진실성, 정확성

[vəˈræsɪti]
conformity to facts; accuracy
(syn) truthfulness, accuracy, credibility
(e.g.) The jury questioned the **veracity** of the witness's statement.

corpulent
뚱뚱한, 살찐

[ˈkɔːrpjələnt]
fat
(syn) fat, obese, portly
(e.g.) The **corpulent** man struggled to climb the stairs.

fathom
헤아리다, 이해하다

[ˈfæðəm]
to understand a difficult problem or an enigmatic person after much thought
(syn) comprehend, grasp, understand
(e.g.) He struggled to **fathom** the depths of her despair.

guile
교활함, 간계

[gaɪl]
sly or cunning intelligence
(syn) cunning, craftiness, deceit
(e.g.) The politician used his charm and **guile** to win the election.

impervious
통과할 수 없는, 영향을 받지 않는

[ɪmˈpɜːrviəs]
not allowing fluid to pass through
(syn) impenetrable, resistant, immune
(e.g.) He seemed **impervious** to criticism.

kindle
불을 붙이다, 자극하다

[ˈkɪndəl]
to light or set on fire
(syn) ignite, arouse, inspire
(e.g.) The teacher's enthusiasm **kindled** the students' interest.

lethargy
무기력, 혼수

[ˈlɛθərdʒi]
a lack of energy and enthusiasm
(syn) sluggishness, inertia, torpor
(e.g.) A feeling of **lethargy** overcame him after lunch.

myriad

무수히 많은

['mɪriəd]

a countless or extremely great number
(syn) countless, infinite, numerous
(e.g.) There are a **myriad** of options to choose from.

obstinate

완고한, 고집이 센

['ɒbstɪnət]

stubbornly refusing to change one's opinion or chosen course of action
(syn) stubborn, pigheaded, tenacious
(e.g.) The child was **obstinate** and refused to eat his vegetables.

propensity

성향, 경향

[prə'pɛnsəti]

an inclination or natural tendency to behave in a particular way
(syn) tendency, inclination, proclivity
(e.g.) He has a **propensity** for exaggeration.

redundant

불필요한, 장황한

[rɪ'dʌndənt]

not or no longer needed or useful
(syn) unnecessary, superfluous, excessive
(e.g.) The phrase "I personally" is often **redundant**.

DAY
27

sanguine

낙관적인, 쾌활한

['sæŋgwɪn]

optimistic or positive, especially in an apparently bad or difficult situation
(syn) optimistic, hopeful, cheerful
(e.g.) He remained **sanguine** about the company's future.

trepidation

두려움, 떨림

[ˌtrɛpɪ'deɪʃən]

a feeling of fear or agitation about something that may happen
(syn) fear, apprehension, anxiety
(e.g.) He approached the examination with some **trepidation**.

uncanny | 이상한, 묘한

[ʌnˈkæni]
strange or mysterious, especially in an unsettling way
(syn) strange, eerie, bizarre
(e.g.) She had an **uncanny** ability to predict the weather.

vehement | 격렬한, 열정적인

[ˈviːəmənt]
showing strong feeling; forceful, passionate, or intense
(syn) passionate, forceful, ardent
(e.g.) He issued a **vehement** denial of the accusations.

wanton | 마음대로의, 무자비한

[ˈwɒntən]
deliberate and unprovoked
(syn) arbitrary, malicious, cruel
(e.g.) The invaders were accused of **wanton** destruction.

yoke | 멍에, 구속

[joʊk]
a wooden crosspiece that is fastened over the necks of two animals and attached to the plow or cart that they are to pull
(syn) bond, burden, subjugation
(e.g.) The peasants were freed from the **yoke** of serfdom.

aberration | 일탈, 비정상

[ˌæbəˈreɪʃən]
a departure from what is normal, usual, or expected
(syn) deviation, anomaly, irregularity
(e.g.) The lapse in judgment was an **aberration**.

acrimonious | 앙심을 품은, 신랄한

[ˌækrɪˈmoʊniəs]
(typically of speech or a debate) angry and bitter
(syn) bitter, rancorous, caustic
(e.g.) The couple had an **acrimonious** divorce.

activate

[ˈæktɪˌveɪt]

(어떤 기능이나 과정을) 활성화하다

to make a process, device, or system start working or become active

(syn) trigger, stimulate, initiate

(e.g.) The teacher **activated** students' background knowledge before reading.

deride

[dɪˈraɪd]

조롱하다, 비웃다

to express contempt for; to ridicule

(syn) ridicule, mock, scoff

(e.g.) Critics **derided** the film as a predictable failure.

galvanize

[ˈgælvənaɪz]

자극하다, 활성화시키다

to shock or excite someone into taking action

(syn) stimulate, stir, motivate

(e.g.) The speech **galvanized** the audience into action.

hiatus

[haɪˈeɪtəs]

중단, 공백

a pause or gap in a sequence, series, or process

(syn) pause, break, gap

(e.g.) There was a brief **hiatus** in the band's career.

DAY
27

idiosyncrasy

[ˌɪdioʊˈsɪŋkrəsi]

특이성, 기이함

a mode of behavior or way of thought peculiar to an individual

(syn) peculiarity, oddity, quirk

(e.g.) His biggest **idiosyncrasy** was his hatred of tomatoes.

languish

[ˈlæŋgwɪʃ]

쇠약해지다, 시들다

to suffer from being forced to remain in an unpleasant place or situation

(syn) suffer, decline, waste away

(e.g.) The prisoners continue to **languish** in jail.

maverick	독불장군, 개성이 강한 사람
['mævərık]	an unorthodox or independent-minded person syn nonconformist, rebel, individualist e.g. He was a political **maverick** who often voted against his own party.

paucity	부족, 소량
['pɔːsɪti]	the presence of something only in small or insufficient quantities or amounts syn scarcity, shortage, lack e.g. There was a **paucity** of evidence to support the claim.

quixotic	돈키호테 식의, 비현실적인
[kwɪk'sɒtɪk]	extremely idealistic; unrealistic and impractical syn impractical, idealistic, utopian e.g. His **quixotic** pursuit of justice often led to trouble.

replete	가득한, 충분한
[rɪ'pliːt]	filled or well-supplied with something syn full, brimming, stuffed e.g. The book is **replete** with humor and witty anecdotes.

sophistry	궤변
['sɒfistri]	the use of subtle but false arguments, especially with the intention of deceiving syn fallacy, specious reasoning, casuistry e.g. He saw through the politician's charming **sophistry**.

anomaly	변칙, 이례
[ə'nɒməli]	something that deviates from what is standard, normal, or expected syn oddity, abnormality, exception e.g. The low reading was considered an **anomaly**.

credence

신임, 신뢰

['kri:dəns]

belief in or acceptance of something as true
(syn) belief, trust, faith
(e.g.) The theory has gained little **credence** in the scientific community.

exigent

위급한, 절박한

['ɛksɪdʒənt]

pressing; demanding
(syn) urgent, critical, imperative
(e.g.) The **exigent** needs of the refugees required immediate aid.

impunity

처벌을 면함

[ɪm'pju:nəti]

exemption from punishment or freedom from the injurious consequences of an action
(syn) immunity, exemption, freedom
(e.g.) Criminals often act with **impunity** in failed states.

resentful

분개한, 원망하는

[rɪ'zentfl]

feeling angry or bitter because of unfair treatment
(syn) bitter, indignant, aggrieved
(e.g.) The promotion created a **resentful** atmosphere among the staff who felt overlooked.

dishonest

부정직한, 거짓의

[dɪs'ɒnɪst]

not truthful; likely to lie or cheat
(syn) untruthful, deceitful, false
(e.g.) The **dishonest** report contained several misleading statements.

blur

흐리게 하다, 모호하게 만들다

[blɜ:r]

to make something unclear or difficult to see or understand
(syn) obscure, cloud, confuse
(e.g.) The speaker tried to **blur** the issue with unnecessary technical details.

DAY
27

disloyal
불성실한, 배신하는

[dɪsˈlɔɪəl]
not faithful or trustworthy; betraying trust
(syn) unfaithful, untrustworthy, untrue
(e.g.) The King was betrayed by his **disloyal** advisor.

sardonic
냉소적인, 비꼬는

[saːrˈdɒnɪk]
grimly mocking or cynical
(syn) cynical, mocking, satirical
(e.g.) A **sardonic** smile played on his lips.

impassive
무표정한, 감정을 드러내지 않는

[ɪmˈpæsɪv]
not showing or feeling any emotion
(syn) expressionless, unemotional, calm
(e.g.) The guard remained **impassive** even when insulted by the crowd.

haughty
거만한, 오만한

[ˈhɔːti]
proud and unfriendly; thinking you are better than others
(syn) arrogant, disdainful, snobbish
(e.g.) Her **haughty** tone made it clear she thought little of his opinion.

bulky
부피가 큰, 다루기 힘든

[ˈbʌlki]
large and difficult to move or handle
(syn) unwieldy, cumbersome, heavy
(e.g.) The **bulky** suitcase would not fit into the overhead compartment.

venerate
존경하다, 숭배하다

[ˈvɛnəreɪt]
to show deep respect or admiration for someone or something
(syn) respect, honor, revere
(e.g.) The students **venerated** their teacher for her lifelong dedication to education.

whimsical
변덕스러운, 기발한

['wɪmzɪkəl]

playfully quaint or fanciful, especially in an appealing and amusing way
(syn) fanciful, capricious, quaint
(e.g.) The **whimsical** decor made the cafe charming.

zany
우스꽝스러운, 별난

['zeɪni]

amusingly unconventional and idiosyncratic
(syn) eccentric, oddball, peculiar
(e.g.) The comedian's **zany** antics entertained the crowd.

impute
(죄·불명예 등을) ~에게 돌리다

[ɪm'pjuːt]

to attribute to (typically, blame or fault)
(syn) attribute, ascribe, charge
(e.g.) The failures were **imputed** to the lack of funding.

haptics
촉각학(신체 접촉과 감각을 연구하거나 설명하는 분야), 접촉 행동

['hæptɪks]

the study of touch and physical contact as a form of communication
(syn) touch behavior, tactile communication
(e.g.) In intercultural communication, **haptics** varies greatly across cultures.

DAY
27

nonchalant
무관심한, 태연한

[ˌnɒnʃəˈlɑːnt]

feeling or appearing casually calm and relaxed; not displaying anxiety, interest, or enthusiasm
(syn) indifferent, unconcerned, casual
(e.g.) He gave a **nonchalant** shrug when questioned.

reprobate
(n) 타락한 사람, (a) 무뢰한

['rɛprəˌbeɪt]

an unprincipled person
(syn) scoundrel, rogue, villain
(e.g.) He was a charming **reprobate** who lived life to the full.

serendipity

뜻밖의 행운

[ˌsɛrənˈdɪpɪti]

the occurrence and development of events by chance in a happy or beneficial way

(syn) chance, fluke, happy accident

(e.g.) It was a case of pure **serendipity** that I found the old photograph.

surfeit

과다, 과식

[ˈsɜːrfɪt]

an excessive amount of something

(syn) excess, superfluity, glut

(e.g.) A **surfeit** of food and drink made the guests sleepy.

unremitting

끊임없는, 쉼 없는

[ˌʌnrɪˈmɪtɪŋ]

never relaxing or slackening; incessant

(syn) constant, relentless, ceaseless

(e.g.) The heat was an **unremitting** burden.

vicarious

대리 만족의, 간접적인

[vaɪˈkɛəriəs]

experienced in the imagination through the feelings or actions of another person

(syn) proxy, indirect, secondhand

(e.g.) He felt a **vicarious** thrill watching the race.

vociferous

소리 높여 외치는, 떠들썩한

[voʊˈsɪfərəs]

(especially of a person or speech) vehement or clamorous

(syn) loud, vehement, clamorous

(e.g.) The town council meeting was marked by **vociferous** arguments.

wry

비꼬는, 씁쓸한

[raɪ]

using or expressing dry, especially mocking, humor

(syn) ironic, sardonic, dry

(e.g.) He gave a **wry** smile at the unexpected outcome.

abject

비참한, 절망적인

['æbdʒɛkt]

(of a situation or condition) extremely bad, unpleasant, and degrading
(syn) miserable, wretched, pathetic
(e.g.) The family lived in **abject** poverty.

concord

화합, 일치

['kɒŋkɔːrd]

agreement or harmony between people or groups
(syn) agreement, harmony, unity
(e.g.) The meeting ended in a spirit of **concord**.

decry

비난하다, 헐뜯다

[dɪ'kraɪ]

to publicly denounce
(syn) criticize, condemn, denounce
(e.g.) He **decried** the terrible conditions of the factory.

DAY
27

misanthrope

인간 혐오자

['mɪsənˌθroʊp]

a person who dislikes humankind and avoids human society
(syn) cynic, recluse, hater
(e.g.) The old man was a grumpy **misanthrope** who kept to himself.

notwithstanding

~에도 불구하고

[ˌnɒtwɪθ'stændɪŋ]

in spite of
(syn) despite, although, nevertheless
(e.g.) **Notwithstanding** his inexperience, he got the job.

covet	○○○	complacent	○○○
notoriety	○○○	concur	○○○
endow	○○○	condone	○○○
almshouse	○○○	conflate	○○○
dreadnought	○○○	conspicuity	○○○
totter	○○○	contend	○○○
thrust	○○○	culminate	○○○
aberrant	○○○	debunk	○○○
abstruse	○○○	deferential	○○○
accretion	○○○	delineate	○○○
adherent	○○○	demarcate	○○○
adversary	○○○	denote	○○○
altruistic	○○○	desist	○○○
ameliorate	○○○	configure	○○○
anachronism	○○○	diffident	○○○
apportion	○○○	dilute	○○○
arbitrary	○○○	disparate	○○○
assertive	○○○	dissent	○○○
attuned	○○○	eclectic	○○○
augmentation	○○○	emulate	○○○
belittle	○○○	endemic	○○○
brevity	○○○	erratic	○○○
buoyant	○○○	espouse	○○○
catalyst	○○○	exacerbate	○○○
circumspect	○○○	exemplify	○○○
coalesce	○○○	fallacious	○○○
cognition	○○○	fluctuate	○○○
collate	○○○	formidable	○○○
commensurate	○○○	fortify	○○○
communal	○○○	gregarious	○○○

covet
몹시 탐내다

['kʌvɪt]

to yearn to possess or have something, especially something belonging to another
(syn) desire, crave, yearn
(e.g.) He **coveted** the ancient, leather-bound volume more than gold.

notoriety
악명, 평판

[ˌnoʊtəˈraɪəti]

the state of being famous or well known for some bad quality or deed
(syn) infamy, disrepute
(e.g.) His eccentric behavior earned him unwelcome **notoriety** in the small town.

endow
기부하다, 부여하다

[ɪnˈdaʊ]

to give an income or property to, or provide with a quality, ability, or asset
(syn) bestow, grant, fund
(e.g.) Nature had seen fit to **endow** her with an exceptional singing voice.

almshouse
구빈원 (고어적 표현)

['ɑːmzˌhaʊs]

a historical house founded by charity for poor people
(syn) poorhouse, hospice, shelter
(e.g.) The old gentleman's will included a generous sum to support the local **almshouse**.

dreadnought
거대한 전함 (특이적 표현)

['drɛdnɔːt]

a type of battleship, especially an early 20th-century one with all big guns
(syn) battleship, man-of-war
(e.g.) The colossal **dreadnought** loomed large on the horizon, a symbol of naval power.

totter

비틀거리다, 흔들리다

['tɒtər]

to move in a feeble or unsteady way, especially from age or weakness
(syn) stagger, wobble, sway
(e.g.) The old regime began to **totter** under the weight of popular discontent.

thrust

세게 밀치다, 찔러 넣다

[θrʌst]

to push suddenly or violently in a specified direction.
(syn) shove, propel, jab
(e.g.) He delivered a powerful **thrust** in defense of his honor.

aberrant

비정상적인, 일탈한

[ə'bɛrənt]

deviating from what is normal or expected
(syn) deviant, abnormal
(e.g.) His **aberrant** behavior shocked even his closest friends.

abstruse

난해한

[æb'struːs]

difficult to understand; obscure
(syn) obscure, complex
(e.g.) The professor's **abstruse** theory left many students puzzled.

accretion

축적, 증가

[ə'kriːʃn]

the process of growth by gradual accumulation
(syn) accumulation, buildup
(e.g.) Coral reefs are formed by the slow **accretion** of calcium carbonate.

adherent

지지자, 추종자

[əd'hɪərənt]

a person who supports a particular idea or party
(syn) follower, supporter
(e.g.) He is a loyal **adherent** of environmental causes.

DAY
28

adversary
적, 상대

['ædvərsəri]

one's opponent in a contest, conflict, or dispute
(syn) opponent, rival
(e.g.) The two political **adversaries** debated fiercely on live television.

altruistic
이타적인

[,æltru'ɪstɪk]

showing selfless concern for others' well-being
(syn) selfless, charitable
(e.g.) Her altruistic actions inspired the whole community.

ameliorate
개선하다

[ə'miːliəreɪt]

to make something better or more tolerable
(syn) improve, enhance
(e.g.) The reforms were intended to **ameliorate** living conditions for the poor.

anachronism
시대착오

[ə'nækrənɪzəm]

something belonging to a period other than the one being portrayed
(syn) misplacement, chronological error
(e.g.) The film was full of historical **anachronisms**.

apportion
배분하다

[ə'pɔːrʃn]

to divide and allocate proportionally
(syn) allocate, distribute
(e.g.) The committee will **apportion** the funds based on project size.

arbitrary
임의의, 독단적인

['ɑːrbɪtreri]

based on random choice rather than reason
(syn) capricious, subjective
(e.g.) The manager's arbitrary decisions frustrated his employees.

assertive
단호한, 적극적인

[əˈsɜːrtɪv]

confident and direct in stating one's opinions
(syn) confident, forceful
(e.g.) She became more **assertive** after the leadership workshop.

attuned
조화된, 잘 맞는

[əˈtuːnd]

familiar with and responsive to
(syn) harmonious, aligned
(e.g.) Teachers must be **attuned** to their students' emotional needs.

augmentation
(크기·양·효과 등의) 증가, 확대

[ˌɔːɡmɛnˈteɪʃən]

the act of increasing or enhancing something, especially by adding to it
(syn) expansion, enhancement, amplification
(e.g.) Technological **augmentation** of learning materials improved student engagement.

belittle
폄하하다

[bɪˈlɪtl]

to make someone or something seem less important
(syn) disparage, devalue
(e.g.) It's unfair to **belittle** others' efforts.

DAY
28

brevity
간결함

[ˈbrevəti]

concise and exact use of words
(syn) conciseness, succinctness
(e.g.) The report's strength lay in its clarity and brevity.

buoyant
쾌활한, 활기찬

[ˈbɔɪənt]

cheerful and optimistic; able to float
(syn) cheerful, resilient
(e.g.) Despite setbacks, she remained **buoyant** and positive.

catalyst
촉매, 계기

['kætəlɪst]

something that causes or accelerates change
syn stimulus, trigger
e.g. The protest acted as a **catalyst** for political reform.

circumspect
신중한

['sɜːrkəmspekt]

careful to consider all circumstances and consequences
syn cautious, prudent
e.g. He was **circumspect** in revealing personal information.

coalesce
합쳐지다

[ˌkoʊəˈles]

to come together to form one mass or whole
syn merge, unite
e.g. The groups **coalesced** to form a powerful alliance.

cognition
인지, 인식

[kɒɡˈnɪʃən]

the mental process of acquiring knowledge
syn perception, understanding
e.g. Language and **cognition** are deeply interconnected.

collate
대조하다, 맞추다

[kəˈleɪt]

to collect and arrange information in proper order
syn compare, assemble
e.g. The researcher **collated** the survey responses for analysis.

commensurate
상응하는, 비례한

[kəˈmenʃərət]

corresponding in size, degree, or extent
syn proportionate, equivalent
e.g. Salary should be **commensurate** with experience.

communal
공동의, 공유의

[kəˈmjuːnl]

shared by all members of a community
(syn) shared, collective
(e.g.) The residents built a **communal** garden behind their apartments.

complacent
자기만족의, 안주하는

[kəmˈpleɪsnt]

showing smug or uncritical satisfaction with oneself
(syn) self-satisfied, unconcerned
(e.g.) The company became **complacent** after its initial success.

concur
동의하다, 일치하다

[kənˈkɜːr]

to agree or have the same opinion
(syn) agree, coincide
(e.g.) Most critics **concur** that this was his finest work.

condone
묵인하다, 용납하다

[kənˈdoʊn]

to accept or allow behavior that is morally wrong
(syn) overlook, tolerate
(e.g.) The teacher could not **condone** cheating under any circumstance.

conflate
혼합하다, 합치다

[kənˈfleɪt]

to combine two or more ideas into one
(syn) merge, blend
(e.g.) The article **conflated** two unrelated theories.

conspicuity
뚜렷함, 눈에 띔

[ˌkɒnspɪˈkjuːɪti]

the state of being clearly visible or noticeable
(syn) prominence, distinctness
(e.g.) High **conspicuity** clothing improves safety for cyclists.

DAY
28

contend
주장하다, 다투다

[kən'tend]

to assert something as a position; to struggle against
(syn) argue, compete
(e.g.) The lawyer **contended** that the evidence was insufficient.

culminate
정점에 달하다, 끝나다

['kʌlmɪneɪt]

to reach the highest point or final stage
(syn) climax, conclude
(e.g.) The negotiations **culminated** in a historic peace treaty.

debunk
정체를 밝히다, (틀렸음을) 드러내다

[diː'bʌŋk]

to expose the falseness of an idea or belief
(syn) expose, disprove
(e.g.) The scientist **debunked** the myth with solid evidence.

deferential
공손한, 경의를 표하는

[ˌdefə'renʃl]

showing respect and submission to others
(syn) respectful, polite
(e.g.) He was always **deferential** toward his elders.

delineate
묘사하다, 윤곽을 그리다

[dɪ'lɪnieɪt]

to describe or portray something precisely
(syn) depict, outline
(e.g.) The map **delineates** the boundaries of each district.

demarcate
구분하다, 경계를 정하다

['diːmɑːrkeɪt]

to set the limits or boundaries of
(syn) separate, define
(e.g.) The river **demarcates** the border between the two countries.

denote

[dɪ'noʊt]

나타내다, 의미하다

to indicate or signify
(syn) signify, represent
(e.g.) A red light **denotes** danger or prohibition.

desist

[dɪ'sɪst]

그만두다, 중지하다

to stop doing something; to cease
(syn) cease, refrain
(e.g.) Protesters were ordered to **desist** from blocking traffic.

configure

[kən'fɪgjər]

구성하다, 설정하다, 특정 목적에 맞게 배치하거나 조정하다

to arrange or set up for a purpose
(syn) set up, arrange
(e.g.) The software is **configured** for faster processing.

diffident

['dɪfɪdənt]

소심한, 자신감 없는

lacking self-confidence; shy and reserved
(syn) timid, hesitant
(e.g.) He was too **diffident** to voice his opinion during the meeting.

dilute

[daɪ'luːt]

희석하다, 약화시키다

to make a liquid thinner or weaken the strength of something
(syn) weaken, water down
(e.g.) The report's impact was **diluted** by unnecessary details.

disparate

['dɪspərət]

이질적인, 본질적으로 다른

essentially different in kind
(syn) distinct, divergent
(e.g.) The study compared two **disparate** approaches to language learning.

DAY
28

dissent

반대, 이의

[dɪˈsent]

the expression or holding of opinions that differ from those previously held
(syn) disagreement, opposition
(e.g.) A few members voiced their **dissent** against the new policy.

eclectic

절충적인, 다양한

[ɪˈklektɪk]

deriving ideas, style, or taste from a broad range of sources
(syn) varied, diverse
(e.g.) Her teaching style was **eclectic**, combining traditional and modern methods.

emulate

모방하다, 능가하다

[ˈemjuleɪt]

to imitate with the intent of matching or surpassing
(syn) imitate, rival
(e.g.) Many young artists **emulate** the techniques of the masters.

endemic

고유한, 풍토적인

[ɛnˈdɛmɪk]

native or restricted to a certain region
(syn) native, indigenous
(e.g.) The disease is **endemic** to tropical climates.

erratic

불규칙한, 변덕스러운

[ɪˈrætɪk]

inconsistent or unpredictable
(syn) irregular, unstable
(e.g.) His attendance at class was **erratic** throughout the semester.

espouse

지지하다, 신봉하다

[ɪˈspaʊz]

to adopt or support a cause or belief
(syn) advocate, embrace
(e.g.) The professor **espoused** a new theory of social change.

exacerbate
악화시키다

[ɪɡˈzæsərbeɪt]

to make a problem or situation worse
(syn) worsen, aggravate
(e.g.) The new tax policy only **exacerbated** inequality.

exemplify
전형적으로 보여주다

[ɪɡˈzemplɪfaɪ]

to be a typical example of something
(syn) illustrate, typify
(e.g.) Her dedication **exemplifies** the spirit of the organization.

fallacious
잘못된, 허위의

[fəˈleɪʃəs]

based on a mistaken belief or unsound reasoning
(syn) erroneous, misleading
(e.g.) The argument was built on **fallacious** assumptions.

fluctuate
변동하다

[ˈflʌktʃueɪt]

to rise and fall irregularly in number or amount
(syn) vary, oscillate
(e.g.) Prices tend to **fluctuate** with changes in demand.

formidable
어마어마한, 위압적인

[ˈfɔːrmɪdəbl]

inspiring fear or respect due to size, strength, or ability
(syn) intimidating, impressive
(e.g.) The team faced a **formidable** opponent in the finals.

DAY
28

fortify
강화하다, 보강하다

[ˈfɔːrtɪfaɪ]

to strengthen physically or mentally
(syn) reinforce, strengthen
(e.g.) Regular exercise **fortifies** the body and mind.

gregarious
사교적인

[ɡrɪˈɡeəriəs]

fond of company; sociable
(syn) outgoing, convivial
(e.g.) She was a **gregarious** host who loved lively gatherings.

유희태 일반영어

⑤ 기출 VOCA 30days

gratuitous	○○○	pertinent	○○○
hindrance	○○○	augment	○○○
illicit	○○○	temporal	○○○
impediment	○○○	judicious	○○○
imperative	○○○	precursor	○○○
implicate	○○○	procrastinate	○○○
improvised	○○○	adjutant	○○○
inadvertent	• ○○○	rucksack	○○○
incessant	○○○	conspiracy	○○○
incipient	○○○	obscene	○○○
incriminate	○○○	skeptical	○○○
incumbent	○○○	perspire	○○○
indigenous	○○○	fragile	○○○
indolent	○○○	eventuate	○○○
inept	○○○	slender	○○○
inferential	○○○	abnormal	○○○
insidious	○○○	destitute	○○○
instigate	○○○	tedious	○○○
intrepid	○○○	spot-on	○○○
intricate	○○○	devious	○○○
invigorate	○○○	proficient	○○○
juncture	○○○	hoodwink	○○○
latent	○○○	residue	○○○
lenient	○○○	bulge	○○○
malevolent	○○○	decipher	○○○
mundane	○○○	tentative	○○○
nefarious	○○○	robust	○○○
onerous	○○○	curtail	○○○
peripheral	○○○	sublime	○○○
permeate	○○○	paragon	○○○

gratuitous
불필요한, 쓸데없는

[grəˈtuːɪtəs]
uncalled for; lacking good reason
(syn) unnecessary, unwarranted
(e.g.) The film was filled with **gratuitous** violence that added nothing to the story.

hindrance
방해, 장애

[ˈhɪndrəns]
something that impedes progress or movement
(syn) obstacle, barrier
(e.g.) Bureaucratic red tape is a major **hindrance** to innovation.

illicit
불법의, 부정한

[ɪˈlɪsɪt]
forbidden by law, rules, or custom
(syn) illegal, unlawful
(e.g.) The gang was arrested for trafficking in **illicit** goods.

impediment
방해물, 장애

[ɪmˈpɛdɪmənt]
an obstruction or hindrance
(syn) barrier, obstruction
(e.g.) Poor internet connection is an **impediment** to remote work.

imperative
필수적인, 긴요한

[ɪmˈpɛrətɪv]
of vital importance; crucial
(syn) essential, urgent
(e.g.) It is **imperative** that we act before the deadline passes.

implicate
연루시키다, 관련시키다

[ˈɪmplɪkeɪt]
to show someone to be involved in a crime or wrongdoing
(syn) involve, entangle
(e.g.) The evidence **implicated** several officials in the scandal.

improvised
즉흥적인, 임시의

['ɪmprəvaɪzd]

created or performed without preparation
(syn) spontaneous, makeshift
(e.g.) The speaker gave an **improvised** but powerful response.

inadvertent
부주의한, 의도하지 않은

[ˌɪnəd'vɜːrtnt]

not deliberate; unintentional
(syn) unintentional, careless
(e.g.) The error was the result of an **inadvertent** oversight.

incessant
끊임없는

[ɪn'sesnt]

continuing without pause or interruption
(syn) constant, relentless
(e.g.) The **incessant** noise from the construction site disturbed the residents.

incipient
초기의, 막 시작된

[ɪn'sɪpiənt]

in an initial stage; beginning to develop
(syn) nascent, emerging
(e.g.) The project is still in its **incipient** phase.

incriminate
죄를 씌우다

[ɪn'krɪmɪneɪt]

to make someone appear guilty of a crime or wrongdoing
(syn) accuse, implicate
(e.g.) The documents could **incriminate** several senior officials.

DAY
29

incumbent
의무로서 요구되는, 재임 중인

[ɪn'kʌmbənt]

necessary as a duty; currently holding office
(syn) obligatory, current
(e.g.) It is **incumbent** upon educators to ensure equality of opportunity.

indigenous
토착의

[ɪnˈdɪdʒənəs]

originating or occurring naturally in a particular region
(syn) native, aboriginal
(e.g.) The museum houses artifacts made by **indigenous** peoples of the Amazon.

indolent
게으른, 나태한

[ˈɪndələnt]

habitually lazy or avoiding activity
(syn) lazy, idle
(e.g.) His **indolent** attitude frustrated his coworkers.

inept
서투른, 무능한

[ɪˈnept]

having or showing no skill; clumsy
(syn) incompetent, awkward
(e.g.) The company suffered from **inept** management.

inferential
추론의, 추정에 의한

[ˌɪnfəˈrɛnʃəl]

based on reasoning or inference
(syn) deductive, reasoned
(e.g.) The study relied on **inferential** statistics rather than direct observation.

insidious
서서히 퍼지는, 교묘한

[ɪnˈsɪdiəs]

proceeding in a gradual or subtle way but with harmful effects
(syn) stealthy, treacherous
(e.g.) The virus has an **insidious** course that makes early diagnosis difficult.

instigate
선동하다, 촉발하다

[ˈɪnstɪɡeɪt]

to bring about or initiate something bad or controversial
(syn) incite, provoke
(e.g.) His remarks **instigated** a heated debate among the audience.

intrepid
용감한, 대담한

[ɪnˈtrɛpɪd]

fearless and resolute, especially in the face of danger
(syn) brave, valiant
(e.g.) The **intrepid** journalist entered the war zone to report the truth.

intricate
복잡한, 정교한

[ˈɪntrɪkət]

very detailed and complicated in design or structure
(syn) complex, elaborate
(e.g.) The novel's intricate plot requires close attention.

invigorate
활기를 주다

[ɪnˈvɪɡəreɪt]

to energize or give fresh strength to something or someone
(syn) energize, stimulate
(e.g.) A morning run **invigorates** both body and mind.

juncture
중요한 시점, 연결점

[ˈdʒʌŋktʃər]

a particular moment of time or a critical turning point
(syn) crossroad, stage
(e.g.) The company faces a decisive **juncture** in its expansion strategy.

latent
잠재된, 숨은

[ˈleɪtənt]

existing but not yet visible or active
(syn) hidden, potential
(e.g.) The training program helped employees develop their **latent** talents.

DAY
29

lenient
관대한, 너그러운

[ˈliːniənt]

not strict or harsh in discipline or judgment
(syn) forgiving, tolerant
(e.g.) The teacher was **lenient** with students who made honest mistakes.

malevolent

악의적인, 해로운

[mə'levələnt]

having or showing a desire to cause harm
(syn) malicious, spiteful
(e.g.) The novel's malevolent antagonist was both charming and cruel.

mundane

세속적인, 평범한

[mʌn'deɪn]

ordinary or lacking interest; relating to daily life
(syn) prosaic, commonplace
(e.g.) He sought escape from **mundane** office routines.

nefarious

사악한, 범죄의

[nɪ'feərɪəs]

extremely wicked or criminal
(syn) evil, villainous
(e.g.) They were caught engaging in a **nefarious** scheme to defraud investors.

onerous

부담스러운, 고된

['oʊnərəs]

involving a great deal of difficulty or responsibility
(syn) burdensome, arduous
(e.g.) He found the task too **onerous** to complete alone.

peripheral

주변의, 부수적인

[pə'rɪfərəl]

marginal or secondary in importance
(syn) marginal, tangential
(e.g.) The issue was **peripheral** to the main discussion.

permeate

스며들다, 퍼지다

['pɜːrmieɪt]

to spread through or be present in every part
(syn) penetrate, diffuse
(e.g.) Optimism **permeated** the atmosphere after the victory.

pertinent
적절한, 관련된

['pɜːrtɪnənt]

relevant and directly related to the matter at hand
(syn) applicable, appropriate
(e.g.) She raised several **pertinent** points during the meeting.

augment
확대하다, 증가시키다

[ɔːɡ'ment]

to increase the value, amount, or effect of something
(syn) expand, enhance
(e.g.) New technology can **augment** students' learning experiences.

temporal
시간의, 시간적 순서·범주·제약과 관련된

['tempərəl]

relating to time or the sequence of events
(syn) time-related, chronological
(e.g.) **Temporal** adverbials can create structural ambiguity in sentences.

judicious
현명한, 신중한

[dʒu'dɪʃəs]

having or showing good judgment and sense
(syn) wise, sensible
(e.g.) A **judicious** investment can yield long-term benefits.

precursor
선구자, 전조

[prikúːrsər]

a person or thing that comes before another
(syn) forerunner, harbinger
(e.g.) The audio-lingual method was a **precursor** to communicative language teaching.

DAY
29

procrastinate
게으름을 피우다, 일을 미루다

[proʊkrǽstɪnèɪt]

to delay doing something intentionally
(syn) delay, postpone, dawdle
(e.g.) Some students **procrastinate** when faced with challenging assignments.

adjutant
부하, 보좌관

['ædʒətənt]

a person under the authority or control of another
(syn) assistant, aide, deputy
(e.g.) The **adjutant** officers followed the commander's detailed instructions.

rucksack
배낭, 짐

['rʌksæk]

bags and suitcases used for traveling
(syn) baggage, pack
(e.g.) The travelers loaded their rucksack before boarding the bus.

conspiracy
음모, 계략

[kənspírəsi]

a secret plan by a group to do something unlawful
(syn) plot, scheme
(e.g.) The **conspiracy** was uncovered before it could be carried out.

obscene
음란한, 외설적인

[əbsíːn]

offensive or indecent in a sexual way
(syn) vulgar, indecent
(e.g.) The teacher warned students not to use **obscene** language.

skeptical
의심 많은

[sképtɪkəl]

having doubt or reservation
(syn) suspicious, doubtful
(e.g.) Some teachers are **skeptical** about the effectiveness of AI tools.

perspire
더위로 땀을 흘리다

[pəːrspáɪər]

to sweat due to heat or exertion
(syn) sweat, exude
(e.g.) The athletes **perspired** heavily under the summer sun.

fragile
연약한, 부서지기 쉬운

[frǽdʒəl]

easily broken or physically weak
(syn) delicate, weak
(e.g.) The **fragile** vase shattered when it fell from the table.

eventuate
결과로서 일어나다

[ɪˈventʃueɪt]

to happen as a consequence
(syn) happen, occur
(e.g.) Effective communication often **eventuates** in better cooperation.

slender
마르고 길쭉한

[sléndər]

thin and graceful in figure
(syn) slim, lean
(e.g.) The model's **slender** figure was ideal for the runway.

abnormal
비정상적인, 기이한

[æbnɔ́ːrməl]

deviating from what is normal or usual
(syn) unusual, strange
(e.g.) The **abnormal** weather patterns affected agricultural production.

destitute
가난한, 궁핍한

[déstɪtùːt]

extremely poor; lacking necessities
(syn) impoverished, needy
(e.g.) The **destitute** families relied on community support programs.

DAY
29

tedious
지루한, 짜증나는

[tíːdiəs]

too long, slow, or dull; tiresome
(syn) boring, monotonous
(e.g.) Repetitive grammar drills can be **tedious** for students.

spot-on
정확히 맞는, 아주 정확한

[spát-àn]

extremely accurate or correct; exactly right
(syn) accurate, precise, exact
(e.g.) Her prediction about the test questions was **spot-on**.

devious
정직하지 않은, 기만적인

[díːviəs]

using dishonest or indirect methods to achieve something; willing to trick people
(syn) dishonest, deceitful, sly
(e.g.) The politician was accused of **devious** tactics during the campaign.

proficient
능숙한, 숙련된

[prəfíʃənt]

skilled and able to do something well, especially through practice or training
(syn) skilled, adept, accomplished
(e.g.) She is **proficient** in both English and Chinese translation.

hoodwink
속이다, 현혹하다

[ˈhʊdwɪŋk]

to trick or deceive someone, especially by making something seem true when it is not
(syn) trick, mislead, delude
(e.g.) The con artist deceived investors with **hoodwink** schemes.

residue
찌꺼기, 잔여물

[rézədjùː]

what remains or is left behind after the main part has been removed or used
(syn) remains, debris, remnant
(e.g.) Only a small **residue** of ash was left after the fire burned out.

bulge
튀어나온 부분, 돌출부

[bʌldʒ]

a rounded swelling or part that sticks out from a surface
(syn) projection, bump, swelling
(e.g.) A **bulge** on the wall indicated a structural flaw behind the plaster.

decipher
해독하다, 판독하다

[dɪˈsaɪfər]

to succeed in understanding, interpreting, or identifying (something)
(syn) decode, interpret
(e.g.) He struggled to **decipher** the old manuscript.

tentative
잠정적인, 시험적인

[ˈtentətɪv]

not fully decided or confirmed; done as an experiment or showing hesitation and uncertainty
(syn) provisional, unconfirmed, hesitant
(e.g.) We have a **tentative** plan for the trip, but nothing is finalized.

robust
튼튼한, 강력한

[roʊˈbʌst]

strong and healthy; firm and reliable in structure, design, or logic
(syn) strong, vigorous, sturdy
(e.g.) The study's conclusions are supported by **robust** statistical analysis.

curtail
줄이다, 축소하다

[kɜːrtéɪl]

to reduce or limit something
(syn) reduce, cut back, restrict
(opp) expand, extend
(e.g.) Budget constraints **curtailed** the scope of the program.

sublime
숭고한, 탁월한

[səˈblaɪm]

of such excellence, grandeur, or beauty as to inspire great admiration or awe
(syn) magnificent, majestic, superb
(e.g.) He composed a piece of **sublime** music.

DAY
29

paragon
귀감, 완벽한 모범

[ˈpærəgɒn]

a person or thing regarded as a perfect example of a particular quality
(syn) model, ideal, archetype
(e.g.) He was a **paragon** of virtue and morality.

유희태 일반영어

⑤ 기출 VOCA 30days

abandonment	○○○	indexicality	○○○
annuity	○○○	presupposition	○○○
circumlocution	○○○	felicity	○○○
collaborative	○○○	performativity	○○○
consciousness	○○○	paratext	○○○
equanimity	○○○	focalization	○○○
executive	○○○	intertextual	○○○
expansion	○○○	narrativity	○○○
expression	○○○	liminality	○○○
glottal	○○○	commodification	○○○
evaluation	○○○	hegemony	○○○
interaction	○○○	reification	○○○
mutation	○○○	embodiment	○○○
nothingness	○○○	hybridity	○○○
perpetuity	○○○	transitivity	○○○
preverbal	○○○	allomorph	○○○
providence	○○○	polysemy	○○○
radical	○○○	dichotomization	○○○
reflexively	○○○	atmospheric	○○○
residual	○○○	automatization	○○○
synchronous	○○○	multimodality	○○○
metalinguistic	○○○	translanguaging	○○○
epistemic	○○○	acculturation	○○○
interlocutor	○○○	ethnography	○○○
prosodic	○○○	stratification	○○○
salience	○○○	diachronic	○○○
entailment	○○○	idiolect	○○○
nominalization	○○○	superordinate	○○○
gradience	○○○	prototypicality	○○○
schematicity	○○○	allegorical	○○○

abandonment 버림, 유기

[ə'bændənmənt]

the act of leaving something permanently
(syn) desertion, forsaking
(e.g.) The protagonist's decisions are shaped by early emotional **abandonment**.

annuity 연금

[ə'nuːəti]

a fixed yearly income paid to an individual
(syn) pension, allowance
(e.g.) She lived comfortably on an **annuity** left by her aunt.

circumlocution 우회적 표현

[ˌsɜːrkəmləˈkjuːʃən]

unnecessarily wordy, indirect expression
(syn) verbosity, evasion
(e.g.) His **circumlocution** obscured the core issue in the lesson.

collaborative 협력적인

[kəˈlæbəreɪtɪv]

involving joint effort between individuals
(syn) cooperative, shared
(e.g.) Students performed better through **collaborative** tasks.

consciousness 의식

[ˈkɑːnʃəsnəs]

the state of being aware
(syn) awareness, perception
(e.g.) The text probes the narrator's shifting **consciousness**.

equanimity 평정

[ˌekwəˈnɪməti]

calmness under stress
(syn) composure, serenity
(e.g.) She maintained **equanimity** despite intense pressure.

executive
임원 · 관리의

[ɪgˈzɛkjətɪv]

relating to decision-making authority
(syn) managerial, administrative
(e.g.) **Executive** decisions reflected the institution's priorities.

expansion
확장

[ɪkˈspænʃən]

the act of growing or increasing
(syn) growth, enlargement
(e.g.) The **expansion** of the program required new resources.

expression
표현

[ɪkˈsprɛʃən]

the communication of ideas or feelings
(syn) articulation, representation
(e.g.) Idiomatic **expression** often challenges EFL learners.

glottal
성문(의)

[ˈglɑːtəl]

relating to the glottis or vocal folds
(syn) phonatory, vocalic
(e.g.) A **glottal** stop frequently occurs before vowels in casual speech.

evaluation
평가

[ˌvæljuˈeɪʃən]

a systematic assessment
(syn) appraisal, assessment
(e.g.) Formative **evaluation** enhances classroom learning.

DAY
30

interaction
상호 작용

[ˌɪntərˈækʃən]

reciprocal action between individuals
(syn) engagement, communication
(e.g.) Negotiation of meaning arises during **interaction**.

mutation
돌연변이

[mjuːˈteɪʃən]

a structural change in genetic material
(syn) alteration, variation
(e.g.) The **mutation** alters protein expression.

nothingness
무, 공허

[ˈnʌθɪŋnəs]

the state of nonexistence
(syn) void, emptiness
(e.g.) The novel explores existential **nothingness**.

perpetuity
영속성

[ˌpɜːrpəˈtuːəti]

lasting forever
(syn) eternity, permanence
(e.g.) The land agreement was secured in **perpetuity**.

preverbal
동사 앞의

[ˌpriːˈvɜːrbəl]

placed before the verb
(syn) preposed, pre-verb
(e.g.) **Preverbal** adverbs may alter scope interpretation.

providence
섭리

[ˈprɑːvɪdəns]

divine or protective guidance
(syn) fate, divine will
(e.g.) The narrator attributes survival to **providence**.

radical
근본적인, 급진적인

[ˈrædɪkəl]

relating to fundamental change
(syn) revolutionary, profound
(e.g.) The theory sparked a **radical** shift in linguistic thought.

reflexively
반사적으로, 재귀적으로

[rɪˈflɛksɪvli]

in a reflexive manner
(syn) automatically
(e.g.) The pronoun refers **reflexively** to the subject.

residual
잔여의

[rɪˈzɪdʒuəl]

remaining after a process
(syn) leftover, remaining
(e.g.) Durable products produce less **residual** waste.

synchronous
동시 발생의

[ˈsɪŋkrənəs]

occurring at the same time
(syn) simultaneous, concurrent
(e.g.) **Synchronous** CMC allows real-time negotiation of meaning.

metalinguistic
메타언어적인

[ˌmɛtəlɪŋˈgwɪstɪk]

relating to reflection on language itself
(syn) analytic, reflective
(e.g.) **Metalinguistic** awareness helps learners notice form.

epistemic
인지적인, 지식에 관한

[ˌɛpɪˈstiːmɪk]

relating to knowledge or belief
(syn) cognitive, interpretive
(e.g.) **Epistemic** stance markers reveal speaker certainty.

interlocutor
대화 상대

[ˌɪntərˈlɒkjətər]

a participant in conversation
(syn) conversational partner
(e.g.) The **interlocutor**'s clarification request triggered uptake.

DAY
30

prosodic
운율적인

[prə'sɑːdɪk]

relating to rhythm, stress, intonation
(syn) rhythmic, intonational
(e.g.) **Prosodic** cues assist listeners in parsing structure.

salience
현저성

['seɪliəns]

prominence or noticeability
(syn) prominence, conspicuousness
(e.g.) Corrective feedback increases error **salience**.

entailment
함의

[ɛn'teɪlmənt]

logical relationship in which one proposition follows from another
(syn) implication, consequence
(e.g.) Semantic **entailment** determines truth conditions.

nominalization
명사화

[ˌnɑːmənələ'zeɪʃən]

converting a verb/adjective into a noun
(syn) noun-formation
(e.g.) Academic writing often uses heavy **nominalization**.

gradience
점진성, 연속성

['greɪdiəns]

presence of intermediate forms along a continuum
(syn) continuum, scalarity
(e.g.) Membership in word classes often shows **gradience**.

schematicity
도식성

[ˌskiːmə'tɪsəti]

degree to which a construction is abstract
(syn) abstraction
(e.g.) High **schematicity** characterizes productive patterns.

indexicality 지시성

[ˌɪndɛksɪˈkæləti]

linguistic pointing tied to context
(syn) deixis, contextual reference
(e.g.) Pronouns gain meaning through **indexicality**.

presupposition 전제

[ˌpriːsʌpəˈzɪʃən]

background assumption required for meaning
(syn) assumption, premise
(e.g.) **Presupposition** triggers operate regardless of negation.

felicity 적합조건

[fəˈlɪsəti]

appropriateness for successful speech acts
(syn) appropriateness, validity
(e.g.) The apology failed due to violated **felicity** conditions.

performativity 수행성

[pərˌfɔːrməˈtɪvəti]

language that enacts rather than describes
(syn) enactment
(e.g.) "I promise" demonstrates **performativity**.

paratext 주변텍스트

[ˈpærəˌtɛkst]

materials framing a main text
(syn) frame, supplement
(e.g.) Prefaces function as **paratext** guiding interpretation.

focalization 초점화

[ˌfoʊkələˈzeɪʃən]

the lens through which narrative events are perceived
(syn) perspective, viewpoint
(e.g.) Internal **focalization** restricts reader access to knowledge.

DAY
30

intertextual
상호텍스트적인

[ˌɪntərˈtɛkstʃuəl]
referencing or echoing other texts
(syn) cross-textual
(e.g.) The novel's **intertextual** references enrich its themes.

narrativity
서사성

[ˌnærəˈtɪvɪti]
the quality of having narrative features
(syn) storyness, narrativeness
(e.g.) Even casual anecdotes may display **narrativity**.

liminality
경계상태

[ˌlɪməˈnælɪti]
being on a threshold during transition
(syn) in-betweenness
(e.g.) Adolescence represents a state of **liminality**.

commodification
상품화

[kəˌmɑːdɪfɪˈkeɪʃən]
turning something into a marketable commodity
(syn) commercialization
(e.g.) Education faces increasing **commodification**.

hegemony
패권

[hɪˈdʒɛməni]
dominance over others
(syn) dominance, supremacy
(e.g.) Linguistic **hegemony** shapes global language norms.

reification
실체화

[ˌreɪəfəˈkeɪʃən]
treating an abstract concept as concrete
(syn) objectification
(e.g.) Ideologies often undergo **reification** in discourse.

embodiment 구체화

[ɪmˈbɑːdɪmənt]

a physical or concrete expression of an idea
(syn) incarnation, realization
(e.g.) Her teaching practice is the embodiment of empathy.

hybridity 혼종성

[haɪˈbrɪdəti]

mixing of cultural or linguistic elements
(syn) mixture, synthesis
(e.g.) Postcolonial texts reveal linguistic hybridity.

transitivity 타동성, 전이구조

[ˌtrænsɪˈtɪvəti]

system of expressing participants in an event
(syn) valency pattern
(e.g.) Transitivity choices reflect stance in discourse.

allomorph 이형태

[ˈæləˌmɔːrf]

a variant form of a morpheme
(syn) morphological variant
(e.g.) /s/, /z/, and /ɪz/ are allomorphs of the plural morpheme.

polysemy 다의성

[ˈpɑːləsɪmi]

one form having multiple related meanings
(syn) multiple meaning
(e.g.) "Head" exhibits clear polysemy.

dichotomization 이분화

[daɪˌkɑːtəmaɪˈzeɪʃən]

dividing into two mutually exclusive categories
(syn) binarization
(e.g.) Simplistic dichotomization obscures linguistic gradience.

DAY
30

atmospheric 분위기 있는

[ˌætməsˈfɪrɪk]

creating a distinct emotional or sensory mood

(syn) moody, evocative

(e.g.) The author's **atmospheric** descriptions intensify the sense of foreboding.

automatization 자동화

[ˌɔːtəmətaɪˈzeɪʃən]

making a process automatic

(syn) habituation, routinization

(e.g.) Repetition leads to **automatization** of forms.

multimodality 다중양식성

[ˌmʌltiˌmoʊˈdælɪti]

use of multiple semiotic modes

(syn) multisemiotic design

(e.g.) Digital texts rely heavily on **multimodality**.

trans-languaging 트랜스랭귀징

[ˌtrænsˈlæŋgwɪdʒɪŋ]

fluid use of multiple linguistic repertoires

(syn) flexible bilingualism

(e.g.) Students used **translanguaging** to co-construct meaning.

acculturation 문화적 적응

[əˌkʌltʃəˈreɪʃən]

adopting cultural traits through contact

(syn) assimilation, adaptation

(e.g.) Language learning accelerates **acculturation**.

ethnography 민족지 연구

[ɛθˈnɑːgrəfi]

qualitative study of cultural practices

(syn) field study, cultural analysis

(e.g.) Classroom **ethnography** reveals hidden power dynamics.

stratification 계층화

[ˌstrætɪfɪˈkeɪʃən]

hierarchical organization
(syn) layering, hierarchy
(e.g.) Language **stratification** reflects social inequality.

diachronic 통시적인

[ˌdaɪəˈkrɑːnɪk]

concerning linguistic change over time
(syn) historical, evolutionary
(e.g.) **Diachronic** analysis traces phonological shifts.

idiolect 개인 언어체

[ˈɪdioʊlɛkt]

linguistic habits unique to an individual
(syn) personal dialect
(e.g.) The writer's **idiolect** is distinct in rhythm and syntax.

superordinate 상위범주

[suːˈpɔːrdɪnət]

broader category containing subtypes
(syn) higher category
(e.g.) "Animal" is a **superordinate** of "dog."

prototypicality 원형성

[ˌproʊtoʊˌtɪpɪˈkælɪti]

a degree to which something represents central features of a category
(syn) typicality
(e.g.) Sparrows show high **prototypicality** for the category "bird."

allegorical 우의적인, 상징적인

[ˌælɪˈgɔːrɪkəl]

containing symbolic meaning beyond the literal level
(syn) symbolic, metaphorical
(e.g.) The story operates on an **allegorical** level, critiquing social inequality through symbolic characters.

DAY

30

Appendix
& Index

유희태 일반영어

⑤ 기출 VOCA 30days

Appendix

PHRASAL VERB

❶ Separable Transitive Phrasal Verbs

back up (=support)	뒷받침하다, 도와주다
bear out (=support)	지탱하다, 지원하다, 지지하다
beef up (=fortify)	보강하다, 강화하다
blow up (=inflate)	부풀리다, 날려버리다
break in (=make usable)	길들이다, 훈련시키다
break out (=unveil, make available)	달아나다, 벗어나다, 탈피하다
bring up (=broach)	꺼내다, 불러일으키다
bring off (=execute a task successfully)	해내다
brush off (=reject)	무시하다, 거절하다
call off (=abandon, cancel)	취소하다, 중지하다, 포기하다
call up (=telephone)	전화를 걸다
carry out (=execute)	수행하다, 이행하다
clean up (=make clean and tidy)	치우다, 청소하다, 정화하다
clean out (=remove all objects)	말끔히 씻어 내다, 깨끗이 치우다
clear up (=resolve)	해결하다, 설명하다
check out (=investigate)	조사하다, 확인하다
empty out (=remove something from a container)	텅 비게 하다, 몽땅 비워 내다, 텅 비다
figure out (=solve, find a solution)	이해하다, 알아내다, 계산해내다
fill in (=supply information)	정보를 주다, 자세히 알리다, 대신하다
fill out (=complete a form)	기입하다
get back (=reacquire)	되찾다
give back (=return)	돌려주다, 응수하다, 앙갚음하다
give up (=abandon)	그만두다, 포기하다, 단념하다
hand in (=submit)	제출하다, 내다, 인계하다
hand out (=distribute)	나누어주다
hand over (=give something to someone)	넘겨주다, 이양하다
hold up (=delay)	견디다, 지체되다
jot down (=write)	쓰다, 적다
keep out (=deny access)	억제하다, 억압하다
leave out (=omit)	빠뜨리다, 빼다, 배제시키다, 생략하다, 무시하다
line up (=form in a line)	줄을 서다, 줄을 이루다
lock in (=secure)	가두다, 감금하다
look over (=examine)	훑어보다, 살펴보다

look up (＝find information)	찾아보다, 방문하다
make out (＝discern, recognize)	알아보다, 알아듣다
make up (＝fabricate)	이루다, 형성하다
open up (＝unlock a door, show something hidden)	마음을 터놓다
pay back (＝settle debts, get revenge)	갚다, 상환하다
pick out (＝select)	고르다, 선발하다
pick up (＝acquire, obtain, fetch)	듣게 되다, 알게 되다, 익히게 되다
point out (＝indicate)	가리키다, 지적하다, 주목하다
put off (＝postpone)	취소하다, 미루다, 연기하다
put on (＝dress)	입다, 쓰다, 끼다, 걸치다
put out (＝place outside, extinguish)	내다 놓다
rule out (＝eliminate)	배제하다, 제외시키다
set up (＝arrange, erect)	세우다, 건립하다, 준비하다
sort out (＝separate, solve)	정리하다, 해결하다, 구분하다
spread out (＝move apart, unfold)	몸을 뻗다, 넓은 공간을 차지하다
take on (＝undertake)	착수하다, 떠맡다, 고용하다
try on (＝test for size)	입어보다
try out (＝test)	시험해보다
take off (＝undress)	벗다, 벗기다
take on (＝assume)	일을 맡다, 책임을 지다
talk over (＝discuss)	～에 대해 이야기를 나누다, 논의하다
track down (＝find, locate)	～을 찾아내다
turn down (＝refuse)	거절하다, 거부하다
turn off (＝deactivate)	신경을 끊다, 정지시키다
turn on (＝activate)	작동시키다, 활성화시키다, 관심을 갖게 하다
turn over (＝place with other side up)	뒤집다, 뒤집히다
use up (＝exhaust supply)	다 써버리다
work out (＝develop, solve)	계산하다, 이해하다
work over (＝beat badly)	두들겨 패다
wrap up (＝cover, finish)	마무리 짓다
zip up (＝close)	지퍼로 잠그다, 지퍼로 잠기다

❷ Ergative Phrasal Verbs

(1) unpaired

break down (=stop functioning)	고장나다
break up (=disintegrate)	부서지다
catch on (=become popular)	유행하다
come apart (=disintegrate)	부서지다
come up (=arise)	오르다, 올라가다
crop up (=appear)	갑자기 나타나다
die down (=abate)	점점 잦아들다
die out (=disappear)	멸종되다
doze off (=fall asleep)	잠이 들다
drag on (=continue too long)	질질 끌다
dry up (=end [supply of money, food, water, etc.])	고갈되다
end up (=finish)	끝내다
fall behind (=lose ground)	(~에) 뒤지다
fall out (=become loose and come out)	헐거워지다
grow up (=mature, increase)	성장하다
pass away (=die)	돌아가시다
pass out (=become unconscious)	의식을 잃다, 기절하다
show up (=appear)	나타나다
sink in (=become comprehensible)	충분히 이해되다
taper off (=decrease)	(수 · 양 · 정도가) 점점 줄어들다
wind down (=decrease)	(열의 · 활동 따위가) 약화되다

(2) paired

blow up	~을 폭파하다	heat up	~을 뜨겁게 데우다
break off	~을 분리시키다	open up	~을 열다, 개방하다
break up	~을 부수다	slow down	~을 늦추다
build up	~을 창조(개발)하다	thaw out	~를 녹이다
burn down	태워 없애다	wake up	~을 깨우다
burn up	~을 다 태워버리다	warm up	~을 데우다
cheer up	~을 응원하다	wear down	~을 닳아빠지게 하다
clear up	(날씨가) 개다 (=weather)	wear out	~을 써서 낡게 하다, 닳게 하다
close down	폐쇄(폐업)하다		

❸ Prepositional Verbs

abide by	~을 준수하다[지키다]	laugh at	~을 비웃다
account for	~을 해명하다, ~의 이유가 되다	lead to	~로 이어지다, ~을 초래하다
agree on	~에 동의하다	lie about	~에 대해 거짓말하다
allow for	~을 감안하다[참작하다]	listen to	~에 귀를 기울이다
apply for	~에 지원하다	look at	~을 보다
approve of	~을 승인하다	look for	~을 바라다, ~을 찾다
ask for	~에 대해 묻다[~를 찾다]	object to	~에 반대하다
bank on	~에 의지하다; ~을 기대하다	part with	~와 헤어지다
call for (=require)	~을 필요로 하다	reason with	~을 설득하다
call on (=visit)	~을 방문하다	refer to	~와 관련이 있다, ~에 대해 언급하다
comment on	~에 주석을 달다	resort to	~에 의지하다
conform to	~을 따르다, ~에 맞추다	result in	~을 야기하다
consent to	~에 동의하다, ~을 비준하다	see about (=attend to something)	~을 처리하다
consist of	~으로 이루어지다 [구성되다]	serve as	~의 역할을 하다
contribute to	~에 기여하다	smile at	~을 보고 미소짓다
decide on	~으로 결정하다	stand for (=represent)	~을 나타내다[상징하다]
depend on	~에 의존하다		
differ from	~와 다르다	stare at	~을 응시하다
enlarge on(=expand in greater detail)	더 상세히 말하다[쓰다]	tamper with	~을 간섭하다
go through(=search, pass through)	~을 살펴보다[조사하다]	wait for	~을 기다리다
		wait on	~의 시중을 들다
hint at	~을 암시하다[내비치다]	watch for	(~이 나타나기·발생하기를) 기다리다
hope for	~을 기대하다		
insist on	~을 주장[요구]하다	worry about	~에 대해 걱정하다

❹ Phrasal Prepositional Verbs

break in on (=interrupt)	(갑자기) ~에 침입하다, 끼어들다
bring (someone /something) in on (=enlist the help of someone/something)	도움을 요청하다
cash in on (=take advantage of)	~을 이용하다

come in for (=be due or receive criticism/praise, etc.)	(특히 좋지 않은 것을) 받다
come up with (=produce, devise)	생산하다, 제시하다, 제안하다
come down to (=amount to)	결국 ~이 되다, ~에 이르다
come down with (=contract)	병에 걸리다
cry out for (=seriously require)	절실히 필요로 하다, 간절히 바라다
cut in on (=interrupt)	~을 방해하다
do away with (=exterminate)	죽이다, 그만두다, 처분하다, 폐지하다
face up to (=acknowledge)	인정하다, 받아들이다, 직시하다
fall back on (=rely on if necessary)	기대다, 의지하다
get along with (=coexist peacefully)	~와 잘 지내다
get away with (=escape without punishment)	교묘히 모면하다, 무사히 빠져나가다
get out of (=avoid doing something, escape)	회피하다, 떠나다, 나가다
go along with (=accept, cooperate)	동의하다, 찬성하다, 동조하다
go out for (=become engaged in an activity)	얻으려고 애쓰다, ~을 하러 나가다
go through with (=carry out, execute, e.g., a plan)	탐색하다, 수행하다, 거치다
hold on to (=retain)	유지하다, 고수하다, 지키다
look down on(=hold in lesser esteem)	낮춰 보다, 얕보다, 경시하다
look forward to (=anticipate)	기대하다, 고대하다
look in on (=visit, call on)	방문하다
look up to (=admire)	우러러보다, 존경하다
measure up to (=meet a standard)	~대로 되다
own up to (=admit)	~을 인정하다
pick up on (=comprehend)	이해하다, 알아차리다
play along with (=cooperate)	협조하다, 협력하다, 동의하다, 동의하는 척하다
put up with (=tolerate)	참다, 참고 견디다
put (someone) up to (=induce someone to do something)	~을 부추기다, 설득하다
put (something) down to (=ascribe something to)	~을 ~의 탓으로 보다
play (someone) off against (=create strife between two people)	남을 누구와 반목시켜 어부지리를 얻다
run up against (=encounter)	~에 맞부딪치다, ~와 충돌하다
stand up to (=withstand pressure or scrutiny)	잘 견디다, 오래 가다
take (something) out on (=direct anger, frustration at someone)	~에게 화풀이하다, 분풀이하다

DATIVE VERBS

❶ To dative verbs that optionally take the dative movement rule

allot	hand	play	slip
assign	hand back	preach	supply
award	issue	quote	take
bring	leave	read	teach
cable	lend	rent	tell
cede	loan	sell	throw
feed	mail	send	toss
forward	offer	serve	type
give	owe	ship	wire
give back	pass	show	write
grant	pay	sing	

❷ To dative verbs that are restricted to the prepositional pattern

administer	display	propose	roll
admit	donate	push	say
announce	explain	recite	slide
confess	extend	recommend	state
contribute	float	recount	submit
convey	haul	relay	suggest
communicate	illustrate	repeat	transfer
declare	indicate	report	transport
describe	introduce	restore	
deliver	mention	return	
demonstrate	narrate	reveal	

❸ For dative verbs that optionally take the dative movement rule

bake	dig	hire	plow
boil	donate	leave	prepare
build	draw	make	print
buy	draw up	mix	quote
call	fetch	order	reserve
catch	find	pack	roast
choose	fix	paint	save
cook	fry	peel	sing
cut	get	pick out	spare
design	guarantee	play	

❹ For dative verbs that are restricted to the prepositional word order

acquire	copy	kill	select
answer	correct	look over	sew
capture	create	obtain	take down
carry	dance	plain	take over
cash	eat	recite	unload
clean up	examine	remove	whistle
collate	finish	repeat	
complete	fix	retrieve	
compose	guard	sacrifice	

중요 숙어

a factor of two

2배

a train of

일련의, 따라오는

(e.g.) His death set in motion a train of events that led to the outbreak of war.

acute effect

단기 효과(=short-term effect)

age out of

나이가 들어 ~로부터 벗어나다(=mature out of)

aid in

~을 돕다

all over the place

엉망인

(e.g.) The government is all over the place on this.

ask A for loan

A에게 대출(차용)을 부탁하다

(e.g.) He ask a bank for a loan.

at long intervals

간혹, 오랜 시간을 두고

(e.g.) Above all, let him eat regularly and not at too long intervals.

| **barge in** | 불쑥 끼어들다 |

(e.g.) I'm sorry to barge in like this, but I have a problem I hope you can solve.

| **be attributable to** | ~에 기인하다 |

(e.g.) Part of their popularity and success must be attributable to their denominational status.

| **be committed to** | ~에 헌신(전념)하다 |

(e.g.) Government will continue to be committed to this problem.

| **be dotted with** | 여기저기 흩어 놓다(흩어져 있다), 산재하다 |

(e.g.) Campsites used to be dotted with tents arranged in a circle.

| **be entitled to** | ~에 대한 자격이 되다; ~가 주어지다 |

(e.g.) I understand I could be entitled to more of a discount.

| **be meant to** | ~하기로 되어 있다 |

(e.g.) I guess it wasn't meant to be.

| **be saddled with** | ~을 짊어지다, 싫어하다 |

(e.g.) He's unlikely to be saddled with the public's hatred by proxy.

| **be subject to** | ~에 종속되다, ~의 대상이다 |

(e.g.) Any changes proposed would be subject to consultation.

be up to par

기대에 부응하다, 수준에 달하다

(e.g.) The classroom computers were not quite up to par with today's needs.

be worse off

더욱더 궁색한

(e.g.) The increase in taxes means that we'll be £40 a month worse off than before.

belong in

~에 속하다(알맞다)

(e.g.) Police officers do not belong in schools.

bluff one's way through

(곤란한 상황을) 허세를 부려 성공적으로 넘기다

(e.g.) How to bluff your way through the world of art - an idiot's guide by Steve Smith.

burn to

~에 사로잡혀 있다, ~에 안달 나 있다

(e.g.) People who burn to win fame, will be ruined some day.

by virtue of

~덕택에, ~위하여

(syn) via, by dint of
(e.g.) By virtue of the 2001 and 2005 general election results, Conservatives have remained in Opposition.

carry around

들고 다니다

(e.g.) It's compact enough to carry around in your pocket.

cash a bond

채권을 현금화하다

(e.g.) He said he cashed a bond.

catch on	유행하다(인기를 얻다), 이해하다
	(e.g.) This design will surely catch on splendidly with young people.

cost a fortune	엄청나게 비싸다
	(e.g.) The first is that flashy cars cost a fortune to run.

count sheep	(잠이 오지 않을 때 잠들기 위해) 머릿속으로 양을 세다
	(e.g.) I was counting sheep.

deal with	~과 거래하다; 상대하다; 다루다
	(e.g.) Nobody wanted to deal with that client.

deceive A into B	A를 속여 B하게 하다
	(e.g.) In previous years, the regime tried to deceive the US into increasing pressures on the residents of Ashraf.

delve into	탐구(조사)하다(=probe)
	(e.g.) Bomb the System is the first feature in over 20 years to delve into the world of graffiti art.

depart from	~에서 벗어나다
	(e.g.) The greater the lines depart from being parallel, the greater the strength of the interaction.

desperate to	~하려고 필사적인
	(e.g.) It's a friendly game but both teams will be desperate to win.

doctor-issued

의사가 발행한

(e.g.) The doctor issued an ultimatum: start stop-smoking or die.

easy call

쉬운 선택

(e.g.) I'd booked well in advance it was equivalent, and hence an easy call.

edge out

서서히 몰아내다

(e.g.) France edged out the British team by less than a second.

feel flattered

아첨당하고 있다고 느끼다

(e.g.) I feel greatly flattered by your compliment.

feel obliged (to)

~할 의무감이 들다

(e.g.) I feel obliged to introduce a new stuff.

fill (in) time

시간을 보내다

(e.g.) The operation performed, the leg in plaster, the question now is what to do to fill in the time.

fly in the face of

~에 위배되다

(e.g.) Ann made it a practice to fly in the face of standard procedures.

fold over

접다

(e.g.) Place filling across middle and fold over.

foot the bill	비용을 부담하다
	ⓔ.ⓖ. BBC News should foot the bill and downsize if necessary.

for anything else	다른 것들에 대해서는
	ⓔ.ⓖ. I think he could see I didn't have a lot of aptitude for anything else.

for that matter	그 점에 있어서
	ⓔ.ⓖ. I am partly responsible for that matter.

get A out of the way	A를 제거하다, 피하다
	ⓔ.ⓖ. Let's schedule a meeting on it for later this week and get it out of the way.

give away	폭로하다, 누설하다, 나누어 주다
	ⓔ.ⓖ. I won't give away the ending—you have to go see it!

given (that)	~을 고려하면; ~을 고려할 때
	ⓔ.ⓖ. Given his political connections, he thought he was untouchable.

given to	~하는 버릇이 있는
	ⓔ.ⓖ. He's given to going for long walks on his own.

gnaw at	~를 오랫동안 괴롭히다
	ⓔ.ⓖ. The doubts continued to gnaw at me.

go out of one's way

굳이(일부러) ~하다

(syn) make a special effort
(e.g.) I went out of my way to please my mom.

gorge on

~을 게걸스럽게 먹다(=binge on)

(e.g.) But once home I'd have dinner then gorge on bread and cheese.

hang out

걸려 있다

(e.g.) hang out [hoist] a flag half-mast high

have the stomach to

~하려고 하다; ~할 배포가 있다

hold one's breath

숨을 죽이다

(e.g.) Second, hold your breath for three seconds.

hold one's ground

입장을 고수하다, 공격에 견디다

(syn) stand one's ground, stick to one's guns
(e.g.) He hold tenaciously to his ground.

impute A to B

A를 B에게 전가하다(씌우다)

(e.g.) It is grossly unfair to impute blame to the United Nations.

in relation(ship) to

~와 결부해서, ~에 관해서

(e.g.) He is the sixth person to be arrested in relation to the coup plot.

in the first place

애(시당)초, 우선

(e.g.) This is why we're here in the first place.

in the service of	~에 이용되어, ~에 복무하여
	(e.g.) His father was a court official in the service of the Holy Roman Emperor, and so was his grandfather.

in the throes	극심한 고통을 겪는
	(e.g.) Despite being in the throes of school exams, Tamsin made the long trek from Liverpool.

just about	거의
	(syn) almost, to all intents and purposes
	(e.g.) The company just about broke even last year.

keep A at bay	A를 저지하다
	(syn) hold off
	(e.g.) Dogs will keep them at bay for a while.

keep A clear for B	B를 위해 A를 정리해두다, B가 A를 피하도록 하다
	(e.g.) keep the ring clear for boxers.

keep one's eyes peeled on	눈을 똑바로 뜨고 지켜보다, 계속 경계를 하고 있다
	(e.g.) Keep your eyes peeled on the road.

keep pace with	~와 보조를 맞추다, ~에 따라가다
	(e.g.) Our systems have to keep pace with those changes.

kiss off	~을 거절하다; 무시하다; 피하다
	(e.g.) I sent them a complain but they just kissed it off.

kneel down

무릎 꿇다

(e.g.) There was a moment when he knelt down and saluted.

loom large

(걱정·위기 등이) 크게 다가오다

(e.g.) Issues such as immigration and asylum loom large in our consciousness.

make a case

논거의 정당함을 입증하다, ~에 대한 의견을 진술하다

(e.g.) You could make a case for a rise in taxes in order to reduce public borrowing.

make a face

얼굴을 찌푸리다

(e.g.) Why'd you make a face?

make a splash

세상을 깜짝 놀라게 하다, 평판이 자자해지다

(e.g.) Lastly, you don't have to do anything fancy to make a splash.

make a stand

일정한 입장을 견지하다, 저항하다

(e.g.) We need to make a stand on these issues.

make room for

~에 양보하다

(e.g.) Would you please move along and make room for this old man?

make way for

~에 길을 열어주다, (사람이 지나가도록) 자리를 내주다

(e.g.) The crowd parted right and left to make way for the party.

no shortage

많은

(syn) many
(e.g.) There is no shortage of wars in this world.

on net

요컨대(in sum)

out of place

제자리에 있지 않은, (특정한 상황에) 맞지 않는(부적절한)

(syn) muddled, ill at ease
(e.g.) There's not a thing out of place.

out of thin air

난데없이

phase out

단계적 철수하다, 폐지하다

(e.g.) The UK Government had hoped for a 2010 phase out.

play a part in

일익을 담당하다

(syn) contribute
(e.g.) Behavior, Environment and Genetics also play a part in obesity.

plump for

~을 (신중히) 선택하다, ~에게 표를 던지다(=support)

(e.g.) Mr King is plumping for "quantitative easing", or printing money.

propensity for

~하는 성향(버릇)

(e.g.) Europe has a propensity for ostrich-ism.

put A on full blast

A를 가장 세게 틀다

(e.g.) I put my stereo on full blast and enjoy music.

| **put forth an effort** | 노력하다 |

(syn) make an effort
(e.g.) You know, we all put forth a great effort.

| **put forward** | (사람들 앞에) 나서다; 나타나다; 제안하다 |

| **put out of existence** | ~을 죽이다, 소멸시키다 |

| **relative to** | ~에 비례해서, ~에 관하여 |

(syn) in proportion to
(e.g.) Singapore has the world's highest execution rate relative to its population.

| **resort to** | ~을 일으키다, ~에 의지하다 |

(e.g.) They resorted to bribery to get what they wanted.

| **round the clock** | 계속해서 쭉, 밤낮으로 |

(e.g.) Chanel Ten was the only station not playing round the clock 9/11 stories.

| **run out of** | ~이 떨어지다, 다 써버리다 |

(syn) be used up
(e.g.) We just happened to run out of that product.

| **select against** | 도태시키다 |

| **settle on** | ~을 결정하다 |

(e.g.) We all settled on plan A.

shed light on	(문제 등에 대해) 해결의 실마리를 던져 주다, 보다 분명하게 하다
	(syn) cast/throw light on (e.g.) We will shed light on the truth.

sit around	빈둥거리다; 빈둥거리며 세월을 보내다; 둘러앉다
	(e.g.) And I don't sit around all day.

skim through	~을 대충 읽다(=read quickly)
	(e.g.) It was terrible to even skim through it.

slip by	~을 (슬쩍) 통과하다(get by unnoticed)
	(e.g.) Don't let this opportunity slip by.

take A into consideration	A를 고려하다
	(e.g.) The ranking is based on a points system that takes the chart success of each group into consideration.

take out a mortgage on	~을 저당 잡히다
	(e.g.) I could take out a mortgage on my house.

to a degree	어느 정도; 꽤
	(e.g.) The data are subject to a degree of statistical error.

to date	지금까지
	(e.g.) We have fifteen people enrolled to date.

to one's surprise

놀랍게도

(e.g.) To my surprise, he was my brother.

to some extent

얼마간, 어느 정도까지, 다소

(e.g.) To some extent it is true.

track down

~을 찾아내다

(syn) trace, detect
(e.g.) I don't know where that old story came from, I've never been able to track it down.

tune into

~로 채널을 맞추다

(e.g.) Tune into 104.4 FM.

turn out

만들어내다, 생산하다(produce)

(e.g.) The factory turns out thousands of cars a week.

upwards of

~이상

(e.g.) In some Chicago districts, Kennedy got upwards of 95% of the vote with upwards of 95% turnout.

walk abroad

활보하다; 만연하다

walk away from

~로부터 걸어 나오다; 벗어나다; 이탈하다

(e.g.) Don't walk away from the right path.

weigh down

~을 짓누르다

(e.g.) It is the accumulation of all the above evidence types that weigh down the case at hand.

with a view to	~할 생각(목적)으로

(e.g.) They came to this island with a view to digging up the ruins.

with that said	그렇긴 하지만

(e.g.) With that said, however, the hatred I feel for politicians is incredible.

writing-off	탕감, 감가상각, 평가인하

(e.g.) Their banks are still writing off bad debts.

MEMO

INDEX

A

abandonment	386
aberrant	363
aberration	352
abject	359
abnormal	381
abnormality	191
abrogate	338
abstain	304
abstract	290
abstraction	148
abstruse	363
abundance	38
abyss	54
acceptable behavior	50
acclaim	228
accompany	178
accretion	363
acculturation	394
accurate	15
acquire	144
acquisition	74
acrimonious	352
activate	353
acumen	191
adamant	179
addiction	51
adequate	123
adhere	121
adherent	363
adjacent	292
adjective of degree	262
adjoined	276
adjunct	175

adjutant	380
administrator	107
adolescent	65
adorn	204
adversary	364
adverse	115
aesthetic	88
affiliate	241
affix	165
agent	146
aggregate	240
agitation	330
agony	49
ailment	151
algorithm	92
alienation	200
allege	330
allegorical	395
allegory	322
alleviate	133
allocate	124
allomorph	393
allude	160
almshouse	362
aloof	307
alter	91
alteration	206
alternation	227
altruistic	364
alveolar	278
ambiguity	79
ambiguous	120
ameliorate	364
ammunition	231
amplify	200

amuck/amok	8
amusement	251
anachronism	364
analog	92
analogy	54
analytic	287
analyze	148
anaphor	313
anatomy	291
ancillary	200
annotate	166
annuity	386
anomalous	81
anomaly	194
anomaly	354
antecedent	302
anthropology	85
antibacterial	257
apparent	95
appeal to authority	275
applicability	208
appointment	266
apportion	364
appraise	208
appreciable	253
appreciate	97
apprehension	250
appropriate	108
approximant	170
approximation	242
arbitrary	364
arbitration	198
arcane	192
archaic	119
ardent	245

arduous	129	attenuated	218	benevolent	134
argument	146	attest	244	benign	245
aristocratic	61	attribute	36	beseech	284
arms	46	attributive	261	beyond doubt	8
aroma-free	64	attune	237	biased	149
arrangement	107	attuned	365	bicultural	239
article	239	audacious	214	bilabial	278
articulate	123	audiovisual	94	biome	38
articulatory	241	augment	379	blur	355
artifact	326	augmentation	365	bogus	161
artificialize	16	aural	193	bolster	344
artisan	88	austere	294	bound	16
artistry	327	authentic	214	bounded	67
ascend	284	authenticity	88	brace	12
ascertain	299	automation bias	144	brainstorm	46
ascetic	340	automatization	394	braised	20
aspirated	171	autonomous	104	breakdown	228
aspiring	104	autonomy	260	breeze	263
assault	162	auxiliary	53	brevity	365
assert	105	avoid	41	bring about	237
assertive	365	avoidance	274	bulge	382
assess	230	awaken	98	bulky	356
assessment	83	awareness	55	bully	272
assiduous	152	awkward	253	buoyant	365
assign	331	axiom	192	burgeoning	345
assimilation	145			bustle	329
associate	263			by-product	107
associative adjective	263	**B**		
assume	13			
astound	181	babble	203	**C**	
astute	69	balsa	318		
atelic	15	bare	16	cadence	77
atmospheric	394	barren	130	calamity	51
atomistic	251	base adjective	68	calibration	212
atrophy	345	beat (policeman's)	268	callous	179
attain	250	belittle	365	candid	179
		bellicose	334	candor	284

capricious	339	coalesce	366	competence	240
cardinal	215	co-construct	160	complacency	152
Case-less	81	coda	145	complacent	367
castaway	48	code switching	274	complement	175
catalyst	366	coerce	215	complementizer	174
cataphoric	224	coercion	130	complex onset	177
categorical	204	cognates	107	complexity	95
category	188	cognition	366	compliment	107
cater to	83	cognitive	260	component	97
causation	12	coherence	147	comprehension	74
c-command	314	coherent	172	compress	163
cellar	11	cohesion	171	compulsive	41
censored	303	coinage	255	compunction	319
ceremonial	302	coincidence	277	conceal	256
chalked	7	collaborative	386	conceive	46
challenging	286	collaboratively	32	conceptualized	39
change the goal set earlier		collar	268	concession	20
	285	collate	366	conciliate	203
charade	248	collocation	214	concise	239
chatbot	55	colloquy	249	concord	359
chide	340	come up with	236	concordancer	130
chisel	157	commemorate	6	concrete	123
chump	161	commence	122	concur	367
circumlocution	386	commendable	85	concurrently	194
circumspect	366	commensurate	366	condition	36
circumvent	343	commentary	306	conditional	49
citation	185	committed	281	condone	367
clandestine	346	commodification	392	conducive	301
clash	68	communal	367	confer	245
clausal modifier	276	communication strategy	308	configuration	207
clear their throat	317	communicative competence		configure	369
climax	321		275	confine	190
close-up shot	25	communicative	76	conflate	367
closure	300	comparative	53	conflict	279
clout	231	compendium	111	confluence	220
club	268	compensate	255	conform to	301

confound	115	contradiction	35	cryptic	344
confrontation	341	contrary	204	culminate	368
conjectural	120	contrast	187	cultivation	191
conjecture	137	contrite	341	cultural capsule	144
conjoin	303	contrived	227	cunning	255
conjunction	82	controversy	94	cursory	150
conjure	20	conundrum	333	curtail	383
connective device	88	convergence	158	cuttlefish	48
consciousness	386	conversion	318	cynical	134
consecutive	328	convert	49		
consensus	107	convey	26		
consequence	123	convince	12		
consistency	83	convoluted	151	**D**	
consolidation	300	coordinating	82		
consonant	77	coordination	175	damp	8
conspicuity	367	coordinative	82	dearly	229
conspicuous	292	coronal	15	dearth	346
conspiracy	380	corpulent	350	debunk	368
constant flux	114	corpus	214	decease	10
constantly	238	correlation	176	decent	108
constituent	304	correspond	97	deceptively	328
constitutive	220	corroborate	128	decimeter	315
constrain	293	corrosion	156	decipher	383
constraint	175	countable	146	declarative	301
construct	142	counter	260	decode	176
consult	205	counterfeit	160	decontextualize	180
contemplate	290	counterintuitive	231	decorum	152
contemporary	136	court	8	decoy	164
contend	368	covet	362	decry	359
contention	261	craving	89	deduce	95
context	108	credence	355	defaced	280
contextual cue	322	crisp	263	defeat	276
contiguous	77	criterion	249	deferential	368
contingency	115	criterion-referenced	142	deft	150
continuous	281	critic	28	defy	277
contraction	38	cross	253	degeneration of culture	7
				degenerative	189

degraded	94	diagnostic test	62	disregard	34
delete	265	dialectical	243	disseminate	335
deleterious	338	diaspora	200	dissent	370
deletion	206	dichotomization	393	dissimilation	78
delicacy	21	dichotomy	190	dissonance	189
delicate	119	differentiate	192	dissuade	215
delineate	368	diffident	369	distaste	9
demarcate	368	digital	92	distinct	144
demands	96	dignity	8	distinctive	227
demarcate	368	dilute	369	distinguish	46
demur	338	diminish	124	distort	149
denizen	38	dimple	205	distractor	143
denotational	150	diphthong	187	distributionally	279
denote	369	disassociated	91	disyllabic	53
depict	178	discern	180	ditransitive	50
deprivation	14	discontinuous	226	diversity	39
deride	353	discount	130	divine	220
derivation	165	discourse	184	divulge	116
derivational suffix	12	discrepancy	121	dogmatic	340
derivative	202	discrepant	184	domesticated	299
descriptive	243	discrete	281	dominating	162
desist	369	discretion	115	dormant	292
destined	229	discrimination	84	dorsal	20
destitute	381	discursive	108	double blind	306
detection	97	disdain	118	doublespeak	159
deter	122	disenfranchised	61	doubtfully	269
deteriorate	293	dishonest	355	dowsing	313
determinant	203	disloyal	356	doze off	332
detract	326	dismal	280	drag	14
detrimental	134	dismantle	128	draggled	185
deviate from	301	dismiss	162	drastic	122
deviation	54	disparate	369	dreadnought	362
devious	382	dispel	326	drifting	39
devise	237	displace	216	dummy	53
devout	284	display	219	durability	198
dew	230	dispute	36	duration	250
diachronic	395				

E

ease	151
ebb and flow	254
ebullient	338
eccentric	204
eclectic	370
efficacy	83
efficient	65
effusive	340
elaborate	10
elaboration	123
elicit	143
elicitation	322
eliminate	201
ellipsis	165
eloquent	130
elucidate	124
elude	245
elusive	152
emanate	314
embed	76
embedded	147
embodiment	393
emerge	205
eminent	116
emission	14
empathetic	331
empathy	134
empirical	95
empiricism	333
emulate	370
enact	193
encapsulation	208
encoded	92
encourage	47
endemic	370
endorsement	56
endow	362
end-weight principle	23
engagement	137
engrave	40
enhance	47
enigmatic	181
enlist	290
entail	177
entailment	390
enterprise	95
entirely	238
entity	263
enumerate	326
enunciation	212
environment	266
ephemeral	332
epiphany	161
epistemic	389
epistemology	219
equanimity	386
equate	190
equilibrium	90
equitable	326
equivalent	35
erosion	93
erratic	370
error-prone behavior	171
esoteric	334
espouse	370
essence	106
ethical	94
ethnicity	240
ethnography	394
ethos	193
euphemism	303
evaluation	387
evangelist	49
eventuate	381
evince	193
evolutionary	90
exacerbate	371
excerpt	156
excessive	34
exclaim	254
exclude	204
excursion	109
executive	387
exemplified	328
exemplify	371
exhaustive	123
exigent	355
existential	137
expansion	387
expected outcomes	273
expedite	95
expeditious	330
expertise	233
expletive	81
explicate	219
exposure	96
expression	387
exquisite	185
extension activity	27
extent	84
extol	346
extraneous	220
extraordinary	159
extraposition	276
extrinsic	115

F

fabricate	245
fabulous	12
facetiously	203
facework	162
facilitate	96
facility	84
failing	34
faith	114
fall victim to	134
fallacious	371
falsity	35
falter	284
fanciful	332
farmhand	105
fastidious	334
fatalism	320
fathom	350
fatigue	346
fault	229
feasible	67
feature	170
feedback	37
feign	8
felicity	391
fervently	34
fervid	345
fiasco	130
figurative	299
finite	92
fishmonger	64
flaunting	6
flawed	304
fling onto	10
flourish	102
fluctuate	371
focalization	391
foot	78
footstep	281
foreboding	186
foreground	69
foresee	327
forgo	46
forlorn	185
formative	199
formidable	371
formulate	158
formulated problem	135
forthright	152
fortify	371
fortuitous	338
foster	42
fragile	381
framed	109
framework	207
fraudulent	314
frequency	262
fret	251
frigid	293
frivolous	292
fronted	27
frugal	219
function	262
futile	293

G

gait	52
galvanize	353
garner	228
garrulous	341
gaze upon	272
generalization	187
Generals	318
generate	239
generative	138
genre	172
genuine	159
germane	346
get through	236
giggle	308
glare	272
global error	308
global rating	288
glottal	387
go over	238
gossamer	316
gouge	156
gradience	390
grandiose	102
grasp	298
grasping	269
gratuitous	374
gravitate	341
gregarious	371
grieve	251
groveling	302
grumpy	63
guarantee	35
guideline	143
guile	350
gustatory	213

H

haggling	33
hallowed hall	307
hamper	161
haphazard	220
haptics	357
harbinger	344
hardly	265
hardware store	266
haughty	356
haul	105
hawk	305
hazard	131
hazardous	314
head noun	261
heed	232
hegemony	392
heritage	241
heterogeneous	135
heuristic	242
hiatus	353
hierarchical	109
highlight	128
hinder	128
hindrance	374
hollow	103
homophone	212
hoodwink	382
hornet	10
hospitable	131
host society	145
hostile	256
hue	213
hum	312
humid	263
humidity	264
humiliation	118
hurry	269
hybrid	239
hybridity	393
hypocritical	28
hypothesize	149

I

idiolect	395
idiosyncrasy	353
ill-formed expression	288
illicit	374
illocutionary	224
illumination	256
illusionism	319
imbibe	304
imitation	332
immerse	284
imminent	292
immutable	341
impairment	260
impart	316
impartial	131
impassive	356
impecunious	334
impediment	374
imperative	374
impervious	350
implausible	326
implement	37
implicate	374
implication	148
implicature	64
imply	329
imprint	41
improperly	189
improvisation	66
improvised	375
impunity	355
impute	357
in contrast	262
in existence	269
inadequate	194
inadvertent	375
inanimate	255
inattentive	150
inborn	294
incessant	375
inchoate	333
incipient	375
incisive	215
incongruous	70
inconsiderate	178
inconsistency	119
incriminate	375
incumbent	375
indelible	150
in-depth analysis	13
indexicality	391
indicate	11
indice	188
indigenous	376
indiscriminately	249
indispensable	135
individualized	111
indoctrination	189
indolent	376
inductive	75
indulgence	63

inept	376	interlocutor	389	**J**	
inevitably	60	interplay	102	jargon	160
inferencing	96	interrelated	63	jockey for place	317
inferential	376	intertextual	392	jocular	341
infiniteness	76	intervention	213	jostling	316
inflated	159	interwoven	198	jot down	300
inflection	176	intestine	163	judicious	379
inflectional	201	intimacy	11	judiciously	328
ingenious	89	intimate	27	juncture	377
ingenuity	218	intonation	20	juxtapose	131
inherent	149	intrapersonal	116		
inhibition	329	intrepid	377		
initial course goal	285	intricate	377	**K**	
initiate	200	intriguing	226	keel	318
innate	137	intrinsic	115	keen	254
inquiry	50	intrusion	89	keep up with	237
inscription	291	intuition	131	kindle	350
insertion	298	inundated	328	kinetics	202
insidious	376	invariably	256	kowtow	204
insightful	327	inversion	206	kudos	342
instigate	376	investigate	148		
instinct	231	investigated	106		
institutionalize	242	invigorate	377	**L**	
insulate	225	invoke	233	labial	25
intangible	88	irony	321	laconic	334
integrate	147	irrefutable	232	lag	103
integrity	185	irremediably	104	lament	131
intend	308	irreplaceable	105	landmark	21
intensive	62	irrevocable	218	landscape	14
intentionally	106	irritability	256	language community	241
interaction	387	irritation	21	languid	342
interactive	144	isolated	21	languish	353
intercourse	109	isomorphic	166	last	269
intercultural	90			latent	377
interference	252				
interlanguage	53				

lateral	228
lay out	237
lean	266
leash	21
legitimate	290
legitimize	178
lenient	377
lethargy	350
lexical	172
lexicalization	241
liberate	305
liberty	251
liminality	392
limited command	274
lineage	244
linking word	132
literally	298
literary	61
loaf around	279
loathsome	329
locating	96
locative	206
locus	178
logic gate	11
logically	35
loophole	161
lucid	66
lucidity	199
lucrative	203
lullaby	161
luminescent	164
luring	186

M

macroeconomic	108
magnanimous	340
magnitude	327
make certain	267
makeweight	186
malevolent	378
malleable	66
mandate	226
manicured	21
manifest	217
manifestation	6
manipulate	148
manipulator	91
manufacture	39
manuscript	291
marginality	225
marine avian	48
mass destruction	225
materialism	320
matrix	313
maturation	253
mature	180
maverick	354
maxim	67
maxim of quantity	36
maxim of relation	67
maximize	248
meaning-focused feedback	289
medial	206
mediate	292
medium	238
melancholy	157
melatonin	257

mellifluous	342
mellow	230
merely	238
messiness	64
metacognitive	55
metalanguage	173
metalinguistic	389
metamorphosis	344
metaphor	205
methodology	96
meticulous	338
meticulously	106
metrical	205
midway	266
milieu	172
minutia	157
misanthrope	359
mishap	22
miskeying	85
mislabelling	332
mismatch	257
mitigate	135
mixed-ability	22
mnemonic	142
mobilize	191
modal	80
modality	240
moderate	228
modify	261
mollusc	164
momentum	198
monitor	188
monologue	103
monophthong	187
monopoly	217
morbid	294

morpheme boundary	277
morpheme	78
mortgage	229
mortised	156
motif	322
mountain mold	22
movement	147
multi-layered	110
multimodal	76
multimodality	394
multitasking	330
mundane	378
muscular effort	278
musing	230
mutation	388
mute play	26
myopia	229
myriad	351

N

nadir	339
narrative	63
narrativity	392
nascent	335
navigate	33
nefarious	378
negative transfer	287
neglect	156
negligible	135
negotiation	110
nervously	186
netiquette	184
neurological	33
neutral	306

neutralize	170
nihilism	320
noise pollution	25
nominal	178
nominalization	390
nonchalant	357
non-permissible	298
norm	172
norm-referenced	142
nostalgia	132
nothingness	388
noticeable	97
notoriety	362
notwithstanding	359
novice	110
noxious	342
nuance	347
nudge	308
numbness	215
numerical	93
nutmeg	317

O

obdurate	340
objective	286
obligation	37
obligatory	249
oblige	128
obliged	186
obliterate	347
oblivion	289
obnoxious	257
obscene	380
obscure	157

observant	9
observer	132
obsess	124
obsolete	68
obstinate	351
obstruent	170
occasion	280
offensive	231
offset	260
olfactory	213
omnipresent	56
one-on-one assistance	288
onerous	378
one-shot assessment	285
ongoing	175
onset	145
opaque	157
open syllable	279
opposite (of what's expected)	274
opposite	269
optimization	207
ordeal	52
ordinance	198
organism	281
ornate	233
oscillate	335
ostensible	232
ostracize	342
outcome	110
outdated	302
outlive	39
output	330
outskirt	225
outstrip	185
outward	98

overcoat 268
overemphasize 89
over-generalization 287
overhear 7
overt 245
overtly 26
overwhelmed 327
owe 10

P

pace 302
palate 213
pale 267
pallid 333
panacea 347
panorama 179
paradigm 173
paradoxical 117
paragon 383
parallelism 111
parameter 242
paraphrase 250
parasite 51
paratext 391
parity 342
parlor 230
part 27
participatory 236
particle 202
particularity 36
passive counterpart 69
pathetic 6
pathos 52
patrolman 254

paucity 354
pedagogical task 322
pedagogy 75
peer feedback 22
pejorative 319
pensive 151
perceptive 138
perennial 233
performativity 391
perfunctory 344
periodic 261
periodical 239
peripheral 378
perlocutionary 224
permeate 378
permissive 106
permit 13
pernicious 338
perpendicular 315
perpetuity 388
persevere 275
persistence 201
persistent 61
personification 103
perspire 380
persuade 40
pertinent 379
peruse 41
pervasive 122
phenomena 187
phenomenon 148
phonetic 61
phonological 145
phonotactic 177
phrasal constituent 276
phylogenetically 38

pierce 40
piercing 264
pigment 163
pilot testing 85
pineal gland 257
pinion 299
pipe dream 320
pity 118
placate 70
placeholder 81
plague 253
plain clothes man 273
plaque 9
plausible 143
pleasurable 62
plethora 339
plot 320
poignant 333
polarized 192
polysemy 393
ponder 293
portray 227
positive transfer 287
postposing 207
postulated 277
potentially 91
practical 124
practicality 54
pragmatic skill 15
pragmatic 74
precarious 136
precedence 202
precedent 122
preceding 328
precipitate 237
preclude 232

precursor	379	process loss	24	proviso	332
predator	162	process	41	proximity	111
predecessor	217	process-oriented	142	prudent	232
predetermined	165	procrastinate	379	pruning	156
predicament	117	proctor	93	pseudo-event	225
predicate	146	prodigious	335	pseudomorph	163
predicative	261	prodigy	232	pseudonym	50
prediction	299	productive	75	punctuality	162
pre-emptive	173	profane	329	pursue	147
prefabricated	255	proficiency	240	pursuit	49
preference	248	proficient	382	purveyor	52
preliminary	314	profound	136	puzzled	186
prenatal	109	profundity	160		
preoccupation	13	prohibition	55		
preoccupied	108	projection	315	**Q**	
preposing	207	proliferate	220		
prerequisite	216	prolonged	121	quadricycle	275
prescriptive	242	prominent	97	qualitative	243
pressing	330	promote	47	quandary	132
prestige	158	promoting	275	quantifying adjective	262
presumably	120	prompt	249	quantitative	243
presume	217	pronominal NP	277	quantum mechanics	13
presuppose	171	propensity	351	querulous	347
presupposition	391	proponent	216	questionnaire	248
preverbal	388	proportion	84	quiescent	343
pre-writing activity	288	proposal	12	quill	48
primary	238	proposition	80	quintessential	215
prime	206	prosaic	69	quixotic	354
primordial	64	prosodic	390		
principle	83	prospectus	75		
printable	302	protégé	346	**R**	
prioritize	63	protocol	218		
proactive	24	prototype	231	radiation	314
probity	345	prototypicality	395	radical	388
problem-solving	56	providence	388	ramification	218
procedural	301	province	303	random assignment	304
				random	315

rate of speech	22	reflexive	207	resigned	118
ratio	212	reflexively	389	resilient	67
reactive	173	reformulate	249	resolute	180
real communication	306	regression	158	resolution	321
realign	257	regulation	219	resonance	170
realistically	227	reification	392	resonate	221
realization	265	reincarnation	203	resort	121
reassuringly	254	reinforcing	90	respective	242
rebuke	285	reinterpretation	194	respite	347
recalcitrant	132	reinventing	301	restriction	37
recalibration	33	reiterate	221	result state	68
recall	111	rejoice	252	retain	74
recast	174	relational	202	reticent	343
receiver	91	release	272	retreat	279
receptive	75	relevance	149	retrieval	208
reciprocal	217	reliable	91	retrospection	179
reclusive	199	reliance	117	revelation	55
recognition	94	relic	192	revere	319
recondite	116	relief	264	reverie	278
reconfiguration	20	relinquish	289	reverse	80
reconstruction	193	rely on	151	reversion	190
recorded test	288	reminiscence	117	revert	177
recreational	22	remission	252	revulsion	213
recruit	199	reorder	76	rhetoric	219
rectify	233	repertoire	216	rhetorically	188
recursive	27	repetition	79	ridge	264
redemption	54	replete	354	ridicule	6
reduction	158	replicate	294	rifle	9
redundancy	176	repository	300	rigid	164
redundant	351	representation	93	rigor	173
reevaluated	300	reprobate	357	rigorous	157
referencing	151	resemblance	205	rite of passage	318
referential	114	resentful	355	robust	383
refine	289	reside	36	Roman (nose)	272
reflect	46	residual	389	rootless	226
reflective journal	289	residue	382	rosetree	230

rubbish	105	selectively	65	sloth	49
rubric	50	self-assessment	286	small bankers	317
rucksack	380	self-delusion	250	smallpox	68
		selflessness	52	snapped	272
		semantic contribution	11	snippet	114
S		semantically	79	social construct	307
		semiotics	214	social-skill training	288
salience	390	sensible	273	sociocultural perspective	
saloon	105	sentimentally	250		312
salutation	23	sequence	201	sociolinguistic	224
sanction	128	serendipity	358	solemn	277
sanctuary	65	serene	285	solicitous	343
sanguine	351	serial	252	solidarity	224
sardonic	356	sermon	248	soliloquy	23
satire	303	sever	129	solitude	103
saturate	233	sewer	313	somber	345
savage	7	shade	265	sonorant	170
scaffolded help	312	shed	253	sophistry	354
scanning	40	shipwreck	47	sorrow	118
scar	267	shrink	129	sparse	102
scarfpin	268	shun	42	specification	28
scatter	54	side effect	26	specimen	327
schema	174	significance	298	speck	317
schemata	38	signify	23	spectator sports	24
schematicity	390	simile	321	spectral	174
scolded	23	simulation	331	spectrum	184
scope	79	sinewy	60	spigot	24
scorch	254	sipping on the flask	9	spontaneous	150
scornful	34	situational irony	255	spot-on	382
scrutiny	65	skeptical	380	spurious	339
sea swine	25	skepticism	217	spurt	290
seclusion	79	skill-integration	138	squander	294
secrete	163	skim	212	square-jawed	267
sedentary	62	skip over	65	squirt	163
segment	78	slave's atmosphere	305	staged authenticity	77
seize	23	slender	381	staged	102

stagnant	221
stalwart	312
stammer	291
stanza	321
startle	24
static	93
steadfast	329
steadily	106
stealthy	294
stem	28
stench	6
stifle	116
stimulus	214
stipulation	51
straight forwardly	226
strain	25
strategic competence	275
stratification	395
streamline	244
stress	279
strictly following	286
strike a match	267
stroll	11
structuralist	201
structure	37
stubborn	229
subdued	189
subjacency	174
subjective	286
sublime	383
subordinating	82
subscription	48
subsequent	287
subsidiary	62
substantive	243
substitution	176

subsume	190
subtle	117
subtlety	251
suburban	60
subvert	319
successively	188
succinct	66
succumb	293
suffix	78
supercharge	226
superficial	331
superordinate	395
supervise	316
supply	225
supposition	280
suppress	120
suprasegmental feature	15
sure as fate	269
surface structure	80
surfeit	358
surge	280
surmise	221
surreptitious	335
sustain	136
sustainable	24
sycophant	132
syllabic	166
syllable	77
symptom	74
synchronous	389
syntax	165
synthetic	194

T

tacit	335
take part in	236
tally	212
tangible	89
tantamount	343
tap into	252
target language	274
tasteless	159
tavern	320
tawny	60
taxonomic	164
tear down	267
tedious	381
teetotaling	305
telegram	27
temper tantrum	33
temperance	133
temporal	379
tenacious	69
tenacity	116
tendency	180
tenet	90
tense vowel	278
tentative	383
tenuous	344
terrace	48
terrain	137
testament	32
theft	55
thematic role	146
therapy	252
thermodynamics	240
theta role	313
theta-criterion	32

Third Culture Kids 199
threshold effect 110
threshold 51
thrust 363
toil-hardened 60
tolerate 40
topical 37
torpid 345
totter 363
toxic 260
trace 26
trace 47
tractable 109
transaction 224
transcend 121
transcribe 177
transform 41
transformative 98
transient 70
transit 256
transitive 81
transitivity 393
translanguaging 394
translate 60
transmission 193
transnational 191
transparency 39
tremble 273
trenchant 334
trepidation 351
trigger 228
trivial 119
trochaic 171
truth-value 35
tunnel vision 133
turbulent 136

turpitude 52
turret 317
twirl 268

U

ubiquitous 133
ultimate 291
ultimately 63
unanimous 216
unattested 42
unbearable 298
uncanny 352
undeniable 199
under arrest 272
undergo 227
underlie 29
undermine 218
under-represented 307
underscored 299
understate 216
undertaking 104
unequivocal 120
unfathomable 215
unfold 273
uninhibited 29
unintended 149
unlighted 266
unmarked 82
unmoved 40
unprecedented 129
unremitting 358
unsettling 114
unveiling 9
unwarranted 177

unwilling 281
unyielding 331
uphold 244
urban planner 264
utilitarian 110
utterance 74

V

vacant barn 306
validate 331
validated 84
validity 143
vantage 32
variable 241
variant forms 80
varieties 264
vast majority 248
vehement 352
vehicle 29
velar 278
velum 265
vendor 64
venerable 129
venerate 356
venture out 133
veracity 350
verify 7
verisimilitude 333
vermilion 25
vernacular 307
verse 321
vertical 29
vessel 280
viability 194

vibrant 98
vicarious 358
vice-versa 10
vicinity 187
vicious 119
viewpoint 111
vigilance 244
vindicate 70
violate 221
violation 32
virtual 94
virtually 159
visceral 66
visual waveform 14
visualize 47
vitality 158
vocalization 265
vocalize 104
vociferous 358
voice recognition 104
voiced 316
voiceless 316
voicing 145
volatility 114
volitional 300
VP preposing 276
vulnerability 115

W

wane 243
wanted (by police) 273
wanton 352
warily 103
warrant 129

wavelength 29
well-formed 315
whereabouts 28
whimsical 357
wicked 61
widening gyre 305
wilderness 62
windfall 26
wistful 339
withstand 244
work on 236
workload 236
worksheet 28
worthwhile 29
wrestle with 137
wretched 7
wriggling 102
wry 358

Y

yardstick 184
yield 92
yoke 352

Z

zany 357
zealous 343
zenith 339
zephyr 133
Zone of Proximal Development 312

VOCA

유희태 일반영어
⑤ 기출 VOCA 30days

초판 1쇄	2012년 2월 20일	
2판 1쇄	2015년 2월 10일	
3판 1쇄	2018년 3월 26일	
4판 1쇄	2021년 1월 4일	
2쇄	2021년 7월 30일	
3쇄	2023년 1월 5일	
4쇄	2024년 4월 25일	
5판 1쇄	2026년 1월 15일	

저자와의
협의하에
인지생략

저자 유희태 **발행인** 박 용 **발행처** (주)박문각출판
표지디자인 박문각 디자인팀
등록 2015. 4. 29. 제2019-000137호
주소 06654 서울시 서초구 효령로 283 서경 B/D
팩스 (02)584-2927
전화 교재 문의 (02)6466-7202

정 가 27,000원
ISBN 979-11-7519-620-9